RaDiCaL SaBbATiCaL

A HILARIOUS JOURNEY FROM A STIFLING RUT TO A LIFE WITHOUT BOUNDARIES

GLEN TIBALDEO and LAURA BERGER

Berdéo LLC™

Chicago and Fort Lauderdale

Berdéo LLC ™

BERDÉO LLC
P.O. Box 2361
Fort Lauderdale, FL 33303

For information about special discounts for bulk purchases,
please contact Berdéo LLC at 1-877-233-3450 or info@berdeo.com.

Berdéo LLC can bring the authors to your live event. For more
information or to book an event, contact Berdéo LLC at
1-877-233-3450 or visit our website at www.lifeleapsprogram.com.

Editing by Christine Pride
Cover design by Kathi Dunn, www.dunn-design.com
Book interior layout by Adina Cucicov, Flamingo Designs

Manufactured in the United States of America.

ISBN 978-0-9840433-2-3
ISBN 978-0-9840433-3-0 (ebook)

Library of Congress Control Number: 2013910545

Also by Glen & Laura
Fall in Love Again Every Day:
3 Steps to True Connection for Any Couple

Meet Glen & Laura online and take your free
Life Leaps Readiness Survey. Plus get your free
Life Leaps Quick-Launch Brain Teaser at
www.lifeleapsprogram.com.

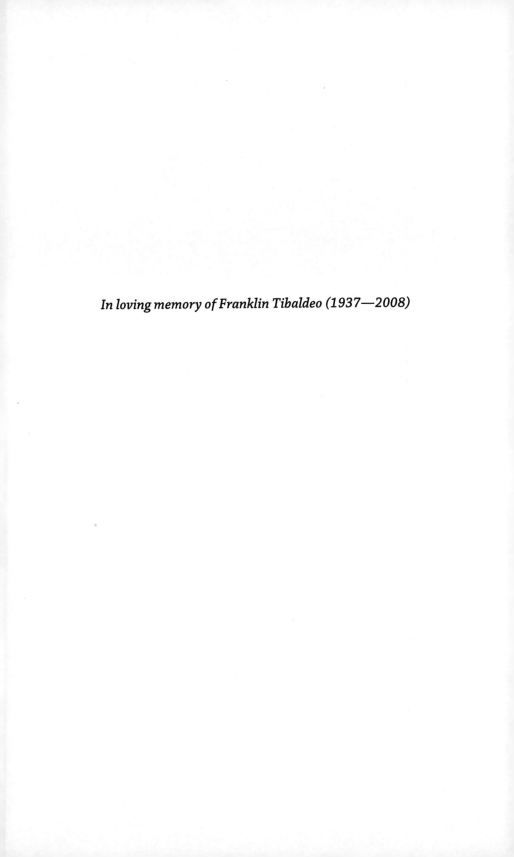

In loving memory of Franklin Tibaldeo (1937—2008)

The Comfort Zone

I used to have a comfort zone, where I knew I could not fail.
The same four walls and busy work were really more like jail.
I longed so much to do the things I'd never done before,
But I stayed inside the comfort zone and paced the same old floor.
I said "it did not matter," that I wasn't doing much.
I thought I didn't care for things, like diamonds, cars and such.
I claimed to be so busy with the things inside my zone,
But deep inside I longed for some victory of my own.
I couldn't let my life go by just watching others win.
I held my breath and stepped outside to let the change begin.
I took a step and with the strength I never felt before,
I kissed my comfort zone goodbye, and closed and locked the door.
If you are in a comfort zone afraid to venture out,
Remember that all winners at one time were filled with doubt.
A step or two and words of praise can make your dreams come true,
So greet your future with a smile, success is there for you.

Anonymous

The following took place on Costa Rica's heavenly Ballena Coast. Names of characters and locations have been altered, where necessary, to protect the privacy of the wonderful friends we encountered on our journey.

Table of Contents

Share Your Story

We are putting together a book series with real-life stories of radical sabbaticals and bold life leaps. Please submit your story, and maybe it will be published! To submit and for guidelines on how to do so, please visit www.lifeleapsprogram.com/radical-sabbatical-submissions.

We look forward to seeing your exciting stories in print!

Prologue

February 2005

"Because you're going to think I'm crazy."

"Only if what you say is crazy," Laura replied.

"It is." I adjusted my position to free myself, only sinking deeper. "So *this* is what a taco feels like!"

I had spent the preceding week of our Costa Rica vacation engrossed in finding a way to explain my new life plan to my wife. The fact that I didn't find it as outrageous as I thought I should made delivering it to her in a level-headed way feel especially awkward.

Laura giggled as I continued to squirm from the airborne macramé quick-sand device. "If we were any closer, you'd be pregnant," I said.

"You're tickling me!"

"This must be the Stephen King model. I think it's carnivorous. 'They went to Costa Rica tourists and came back hammock poo.'"

The more I fidgeted, the more I tickled her, the more she squirmed, and the more the hammock wrapped around us–like being tied in a net with a kangaroo.

"How do you like that? Took me thirty-five years to find out I'm double-jointed!" I said.

"Ow!" Laura exclaimed as our skulls collided.

"OK, eject! Abort! Abort!" *Thud!* The hammock expelled me onto the sand like half-digested lunch.

"Are you OK?" Laura asked.

1

"Yeah, I hear they replace hips." I stood up. "Here. Lie this way to even out the grill marks." I waved my hand crosswise to the hammock.

Laura adjusted. I lay next to her, now facing the monster waves of Playa Santa Theresa, Costa Rica.

"Aaaahhh. Better," I said.

"OK, so what's this crazy thing?" she asked.

I hesitated.

"Out with it! You're clearly excited about it, whatever it is."

"I sat on a Magic Rock," I replied.

"OooooKaaaay. Where?"

"At lunch on the horseback ride in Santa Elena. Remember? The group ate together, and I walked to the middle of the stream to lunch on that rock."

"Yeah. I wondered why you sat there all by yourself." If you look up "Laura Berger" in the thesaurus, the first entry is "social."

I explained to her the feeling that welled up inside me on the way down the mountain on the horse to the waterfall. I intuitively knew something momentous was about to happen, and I needed to make space for it for fear that the opportunity would pass. "So I went and sat on the Magic Rock," I explained.

"The Magic Rock," Laura repeated.

"Yeah, it only took a minute or two. The thought whacked me in the head out of the blue sky," I said, treading lightly as I approached my big reveal.

"What thought?"

I paused. "Wait. Bear with me."

Laura sighed. "OK. I'm pretty open-minded, you know?"

My excitement drove me forward in my explanation. I recited the reasons silently rehearsed over hills, ferries, potholes, dirt roads, and across rivers over the past days. Laura was freezing in Chicago and couldn't stand it. We had been talking about living in Hawaii—Laura having grown up there— but thought it would be hard to afford.

Laura loved cultures and travel—as did I—and meeting new people. She was amazing at the corporate game but wanted to do something that really helped people or animals. "Animal lover" is Laura's second thesaurus entry.

2

As far as I was concerned, my current corporate persona fit my personality like Charles Dickens playing center for the Bulls. My favorite things in the world were comedy and cooking a dish that others could enjoy. I was fluent in Spanish and Italian—and was quite advanced in stuttering in French—and I wasn't using my language skills. I also loved Hawaii about as much as Laura did.

"Yeah?" She now knew where this was going.

"On the Magic Rock, I thought, 'We could run a B&B here just like Ingrid's!'" That day, we were staying at a bed-and-breakfast we absolutely fell in love with.

I checked the Laura aura. *Not bad. No reaction. Better than "How did I marry this crazy Italian?"*

"You agreed with me back in Santa Elena that it would cost a fraction of what it would in Hawaii to run a B&B, and it's really similar," I said.

"And we'd be closer to family," Laura said.

"So you see, there was logic behind this. But from the moment I had that thought, I've just felt alive like never before. It's like falling in love but different," I said.

"Different how?" Laura asked.

"I didn't make love to the Magic Rock."

"You're a goof," she said with a smile.

I explained to Laura that after I had the thought, one of the guests shot across the stream like a skipping rock. His feet barely touched the bottom. He jumped into a squat, his nose about an inch from mine, and said, "Looks like the Pura Vida of Costa Rica just got ya!" Then he cackled like a freak coated in fire ants and ran away as fast as he arrived. And I'm thinking, "Wow, is it that obvious?"

I also reviewed the litany of signs that were presenting themselves since the thought came. "I'll just invoke some random wish like, 'If we're meant to live here, the next person I'll see will be wearing a red checkered shirt.' And what'ya know? The tico version of Larry the Cable Guy comes swaggering by. And did you notice all the rainbows over the past few days?" I asked.

"Come to think of it . . ."

"Right, and did you see *any* before the horseback ride?" I paused, knowing I was charging headlong into Freaky Town now. "Look, the signs are just the icing on the cake. This makes sense to me. You?"

Laura processed for several seconds. "I don't think you're crazy," she said. "The land in Santa Elena was charged with positive energy for me, too."

Laura recounted the encounters we had with Ingrid, the owner of the B&B where we had stayed, who had a bizarrely good talent for mind-reading. "I mean she was giving me the answers to my life problems without me telling her any of them." My wife was brimming with enthusiasm. "And then I had that dream about Mitchell."

"Yeah, any progress there?" I asked.

"No," Laura said, frustrated. "I still can't remember the dream. But I get more exhilarated every time I think of it. It's like some joyous infection. But all I have to go on is that voice that woke me up telling me 'Mitchell knows the answer.' It's killing me," she said.

This talk was out of character for Laura—no touchy-feely in her game. She methodically planned to achieve her personal and corporate goals as efficiently as possible. Seeking the meaning of life from some phantom visitor in a dream was not her thing.

"Why am I asking you if *I'm* crazy?" I asked.

She smiled. "No, I can see it. But it would require a lot of legwork and mental adjustment." She had told me long ago she had to know where her next paycheck would come from.

"I love you for even entertaining the idea," I said.

"I love you for coming up with it," she said. We kissed for what seemed like forever but not long enough.

"So we'll come back for a recon trip," I said.

"Wait. I said you weren't crazy. That's all I can do right now. We'll go back to Chicago and digest."

"Wait. I'm hearing a message from Mitchell," I said. "He said it's the best idea he ever heard."

She elbowed me. "Whatever. Let's go hang out by the pool."

We about-faced back onto hotel grounds, an elegant set of bungalows surrounding a tropical lawn surrounding the pool and an outdoor restaurant.

A thirty-something guy about our age smiled at the desk/bar where I had checked in an hour before. He poured several gallons of calmness into my demeanor with just a look. I asked him for a couple waters, and we sat at the table closest to the bar.

"So what brings you to paradise?" he asked, putting our drinks on the table. He wore a loose tank top, board shorts, and flip-flops. He had a tan, muscular, lean surfer's build. His roots were darker than the rest of his shaggy coif, but you could tell this was the sun's doing. Laura pointed out that he was obviously not from the area, which prompted him to reveal some background.

He had been a public middle school teacher outside L.A. He said he lived a simple life, so the money wasn't a problem, but he was "wound up like a top."

"You?" Laura asked in a disbelieving tone.

"Aw, this is the version of me in the middle of Pura Vida," he said. Back home, he braved the inner city every day. He loved his students with all his heart and tried everything he could to make a difference but was losing the battle. "It doesn't work like all those movies. The classroom was no match for the streets." He said he went home every day feeling he could do more to make things better for the kids but was at a loss. "I'd lose one here and there to a gun, a stabbing, or juvi. My heart broke every time."

"Sounds like you were made for it . . . kinda," I said.

"Yeah, look at me. Do I look like a teacher?" he asked.

"Maybe a surf instructor," I said.

He smiled. "I was raised tough, groomed to be a pro athlete. I turned those opportunities down to help kids. Fast forward, I had no savings to show for it. I could only be proud of my intentions."

He had come to Costa Rica to decompress three years ago and fell in love with it. He told the love of his life (so far) he wanted to come down to live for a while and try it out. She thought differently and stayed behind. "We said

5

we'd see how it turned out." He held his hands out wide with a proud smile, "and this is how it turned out!"

"Welcome to Fantasy Island," I thought.

"And you like it?" Laura asked.

"Aw, hells yeah! This is the only place for me right now." He was still "sportin' some poverty," but his only life rule was to surf twice a day. He arranged his schedule around the tides. He was comfortable that with the booming growth in Costa Rica, he'd always have work. He loved the local people. When we asked him if it was hard to pick up and leave, he said no because he just knew.

"Hey, I know we just met, but can I be honest with you?" he asked. Laura and I shrugged approval without a word.

"I recognize your spirits. I had that look three years ago when I came. You just found something. You haven't said anything, but I know."

Laura and I looked at each other, amazed. "You can tell?" Laura asked.

"Yeah, I can."

"*She* has the look?" I thought.

"Other people here probably can, too. Here's something important you can only know on the other side where I am—a place where others, and you, think you'd be completely nuts going to. Drunks wake up with headaches only to drink again. People stay in abusive relationships. People keep gambling when they've been going broke for years. We're all addicted to where we are right now. It's comfortable on some level even if it hurts. We want what we know best. You can get to know hell and heaven just the same. But where are you going to spend your time? Cuz that's what you're going to get to know and where you're going to want to stay, realize it or not. Back home turned into hell, so I came to heaven. And since then, I've found that the top of the world moves around."

"Moves where?" I asked.

He aimed a gotcha smile at me. "Wherever *I* am. Yeah, man. Happy is always just around the corner. You just have to see it and go for it."

"As simple as that?" Laura asked.

"Couldn't be simpler," he said. "Make the choice a flash in the pan and the aftermath the reward. No hesitations. No worries."

"I hear what you're saying, but it's really hard . . ." Laura tapered off. "I'm sorry. We never asked your name."

He walked from behind the counter with his hand extended. "Oh, hey. I'm Mitchell."

One

CHAPTER I
Battling the Inner Dumbass

"If you think adventure is dangerous you should
try routine . . . It's lethal!"
Paulo Coelho

WE RETURNED TO Chicago with our brains rewired. It was frightening and, at the same time, wondrous.

Despite fearing our abrupt epiphanies, we thought if we were crazy then maybe the crazies had it better than the rest. But from then on, we spent what seemed an eternity battling our inner dumbass, that ruthless voice of fear trying to delete everything we had experienced in the land of Mitchell and the Magic Rock.

March 2005

Despite agreeing with Laura that we would take it slow, my free spirit was now blown wide open. At the risk of sounding insensitive, I imagined my boredom with office work to rival solitary confinement. My conscience screamed at me incessantly—in meetings, in the car, in bed, everywhere—telling me my chosen life was alarmingly misplaced.

Laura was between jobs, easier for her to fall back to her old life of great friends, family, subways, and a million restaurants. But there was one discomfort she could never shake. Despite living in the Midwest for sixteen years, she trembled in temperatures below seventy. The cold, for her, rivaled my career discomfort. Yet, she wasn't convinced that Costa Rica was the solution. She surely honored what we had experienced, but it took two to tango. Alternatives of California, Texas, Hawaii, or Rome seemed more sane for us as a couple.

We resorted to a communication exercise called 10/10 to talk through these monumental feelings. Sometimes called "dialoguing," it was our simple "break glass in case of emergency" communication technique we used when things got tough or we needed deeper mutual understanding. We'd ask ourselves a question and write our answers for ten minutes. Then we'd read each other's responses and talk another ten minutes—twenty minutes in all. Each person absorbed the other's point of view without interruptions before we started talking, making tough conversations often a thing of the past. Through 10/10, we began working through our decision of what the future might have in store.

April—May 2005

"He was at the vet on Thursday! They said he was fine! I killed him! It was my decision! What am I going to do?" Laura wailed in despair.

Laura has a connection to animals that deserves a book unto itself. We suddenly had to euthanize Puck, her middle-aged Orange Tabby cat for a clot blocking the blood supply to his legs.

Laura was to start a new job the next day. After a couple of diplomatic maneuvers with her future boss, she kept her bridges intact and started volunteering at an animal shelter in honor of Puck, trying it out to see if we could sustain it and if she'd like it. Laura was terrified for leaving her career. I had similar trepidations, since she made considerably more than I did.

Then, Laura's uncle Doug lost a very quick several-month bout with lung cancer in his mid-fifties. With her grandmother already having passed in February, a machine gun of tragedy was firing off a rapid succession of rounds at Laura.

One

"This is it! I've left my job. My mind is free. This is the moment," she said. Laura decided it was time to go look for property in Costa Rica. Of course, buying property as an investment was counterintuitive to quitting one's career, but to me it felt closer to the life path. Most importantly, it got logical Laura closer to Costa Rica. I went along with it, spiritually enthused and financially uneasy.

October—November 2005

As we educated ourselves about Costa Rican real estate, the summer came and went. With the cold back, we ramped up our 10/10s, and the corporate strategists in us supplemented our conversations with decision-making tools contained in texts lining the walls of libraries in purgatory.

From the outside, it looked like we were playing existential Whac-A-Mole—announcing a new "decided" destination to friends and family every few weeks. Costa Rica was never one of them, despite often getting high ratings from our decision-making tools. So far removed from Central America now, it seemed like too big a pill (i.e., change) for either of us to swallow.

One day in November, my discomfort with my job got the best of me. The same night, Laura and I wrote a couple of 10/10s and talked my career over. The clarity of that exercise had me walk into my boss's office the next day and respectfully quit. He was the best boss I ever had. It was another leap of faith until, within a day of announcing my resignation, I received contracting opportunities that doubled my salary. The universe had spoken. Path confirmed.

December 2005

The pilot buzzed the grassy Golfito airstrip to scare off the cows before landing. I signed a car rental agreement against the agent's back. He had driven the car to us from San José, the capital. He chased the plane as it taxied to take off back to the capital. They dropped the ladder again, and off he went. Four kids juggling a soccer ball thankfully knew where our truck was parked.

We started our search for property farther south in Zancudo, where a B&B was for sale, an idea for which I was still pushing but we likely couldn't afford.

We concluded Zancudo wasn't for us, not because we had to put our truck on a motorized cable pontoon with a crank starter engine to cross a river to get there. Nor was it the translation of the town's name—mosquito—that deterred us. What did was seeing the same twenty people everywhere.

While on the plane to Costa Rica from the States, Laura had read a guidebook, plotting out our path of exploration. I glanced over at a paragraph that seemed to almost change color before my eyes. Without reading it, I said, "Wherever that is, I want to go. It speaks to me." Our next stop—Pair-o-Dice Village—was described as being diverse with European flair and was exactly on our intended route. We popped in only to check out what the world-class lunch the guidebook promised was all about, frankly skeptical.

We checked into and out of the same hotel for seven days until it was time to go home. The lush jungle mountains overlooking the ocean, the conversations, and smiles of the villagers made Pair-o-Dice Village its own Magic Rock.

By the end of our trip, we stood on a mountainside ocean view lot near Pair-o-Dice Village about two hours north of Zancudo. The price of such a lot was one-tenth what it would have cost back home.

"Do I need to say it?" I asked Laura.

She smiled and said nothing. It was ours by February.

April 2006

Our connection to Costa Rica now reinforced, our 10/10's and corporate models all pointed to the country as *the* place to live. Finally, one night Laura wrote in her 10/10 book, "I would regret it if we didn't at least try to live in Costa Rica."

Where'd "Life Plan" Laura go? We were married a little more than a year and in our mid-thirties. We announced to our friends and families that we were moving, who silently assumed some freak science experiment had mixed our DNA with that of Indiana Jones.

Logical Laura had a twist on my preferred plan, however. We would rent out our Chicago condo for a year while we decided whether Pair-o-Dice Village was for us. For me, it was time to cut bait and not look back. No, Mr. Bungee Jump attendant, please don't check my cord. I sat on the Magic Rock!

"Psssss."

"What's that?" she asked.

"The air coming out of my joy balloon," I said.

"Speak to any rational person, and they'll tell you I'm right."

"I'm allergic to those people," I said. Yet, I knew that in matters of risk, hers was always the right way. "All right, all right, all right! We'll do this and try not to wreck our lives in the process! Are you happy?"

"Look, I feel trapped right now between fear and desire," Laura said. There is this desire to be bold, throw caution to the wind, and go against my grain. My usual self says I am crazy. But I think about all of the signs leading us down this path. And then again, how do I know that we are making the right decision? It's like I am completely trapped in a box, and I am pounding to get out but afraid of what's outside. So I am sorry if I am popping your balloon, but the only way I am comfortable going is if we have a solid plan."

By July, we were in Pair-o-Dice Village searching for a modestly priced rental, which proved a surprising needle in a haystack despite the affordable lifestyle. The night before our scheduled return to Chicago, we finally succeeded. We toured a home in the dead of night, and it was ours.

And just as importantly, Allan, the developer who sold us our land, unexpectedly asked us to help him sell his new development after we moved. Just like that, we had a means to make a living.

With these developments and the Magic Rock-ness of Pair-o-Dice Village, the universe reaffirmed our path.

October 2006

It was time to leave. Laura was nervous beyond measure, but my excitement knew no bounds. Yet, I had one stone left unturned that was a source of unease for me. I knew my parents were swallowing our decision like a family-sized jar of Vegemite. They said little, but my father had been acting quite differently for months. I wanted to hear the reason for myself.

14

I already knew what it was. I could never do wrong in my father's eyes, like the healthy number of occasions I mentioned I had been a heavy smoker for ten years, which I had since quit. "Why do you say those things when they're not true? No son of mine smokes! It's impossible!" he'd say.

Growing up, I was never asked to go get a job. I barely made my bed. All that mattered was that I get a good education and a high-paying job after graduation and save as much as I possibly could in my lifetime. That was the path that was encourage and that I had followed until somewhat recently—until Laura and I combined our lives.

Now, I was going to live in an economically dead jungle! Surely, I couldn't have been behind such a crazy idea. Laura was influencing me in ways completely counter to "the plan," but he hadn't told me outright. It also didn't help that Laura and my father were two completely different people—in ways that would require yet another book unto itself to explain. His distant behavior was his way of voicing protest.

I initiated a line of questioning I knew would lead to the ultimate answer.

"So you're not going to visit us in Costa Rica, either, then?" I asked.

"No."

"And what? You're going to avoid us now forevermore?"

"Oh, I'm not avoiding both of you," he said.

"Dad, look. Put yourself in my shoes. I'm married. We kind of come as a package. I go where she goes. Why do you have to make it this way?" I pressed.

"Look, I'm not telling you why," he replied.

I kept attempting to get some admission. I got none.

"OK, well just know it doesn't work that way," I said. The most intuitively rotten feeling ever immediately welled up inside me.

"OK, well now that's too bad," he said.

"Just like that?"

"I guess so."

"I think we'd better hang up," I said.

"OK."

Click.

One

Dad and I were doing the dance he and I always did. He had often uttered drastic declarations and ultimatums to make his points. All of them had passed with time, usually just swept under the rug and having their intended effect. After I hung up, I realized the very act of hanging up was important. It put my signature at the bottom of my counter-ultimatum. A stalemate was set between two men in a traditional Italian family.

Those tended to stick.

And it came at the worst possible time. I would be in a far-off land with no proximity to repair the damage. I didn't even have the immediate faculties to untangle the problem. So close to departure, there was so much to do, and this was an issue requiring surgical and precise handling.

Our upcoming early morning departure was the defining moment I had thought of day-in and out for months—a wormhole to paradise. Yet, a phrase echoed in my mind after hanging up with Dad. I recalled our local South Florida weatherman's voice on the radio as Hurricane Andrew approached over a decade before.

"It's absolutely sure. No question about it. It is going to happen tonight."

Our life leap was approaching, and the effects of its outer bands were moving ashore.

CHAPTER 2
Into the Wild New Yonder

*"Twenty years from now you will be more disappointed by
the things that you didn't do than by the ones you did do.
So throw off the bowlines. Sail away from the safe harbor.
Catch the trade winds in your sails.
Explore. Dream. Discover."*
Samuel Clemens, a.k.a. Mark Twain

October 16, 2006
We exited Juan Santamaria International Airport at 12:45 p.m. into another dimension. A fairly uneventful trip behind us, we were in the arms of mother Costa Rica.

Laura forged on to meet Miguel, our driver to Pair-o-Dice Village. Meanwhile, ten baggage handlers surrounded me, lobbying that my two hippo-sized luggage carts couldn't leave the airport. Someone tugged at the shiny new camera tripod hanging from my backpack. I swung around quickly to find four guys with blank looks on their tropically tanned faces. *Paradise will be a tremendous adjustment.*

I entered the garage, baggage handlers in tow—one carrying only a water bottle I had dropped. Miguel and Laura were searching for the rental car agent who was supposed to be there and wasn't.

"He's starting to pant," Laura said, fear on her face.

Skippy and Rugby, aka the Boys, were engaged in heavy breathing like teenagers watching a neighbor undress—not that I would know.

"We've gotta go now!" I said in Spanish, more than implying to Miguel the imminent nervous breakdown afoot.

Miguel radioed to someone, and a tico—the non-offensive term foreigners and natives alike use to refer to Costa Ricans—immediately drove up. He drove a death trap jalopy Geo Tracker—purple, no less—and wore a smile a mile wide. A waft of gasoline that could have stripped the paint off a dumpster emanated from the car. Meanwhile the wrenching sound coming from under the hood was terrifying. Car rental fees in Costa Rica are outrageous, and Laura had found the absolute cheapest rates in Costa Rica for our initial rental, to last until we could buy something.

By the time we completed the car and cell phone rental contracts, the Boys had conveyed a very clear message with their emphatic panting. It was time to jam.

The back of Miguel's van opened. "This is my cousin, Enrique," Miguel said, draping his arm around a lanky tico well beyond middle age. "He will take you to Pair-o-Dice Village," Miguel said.

Our payload of animals and domestic items had necessitated the hiring of a van—a glorified moving truck—for us to follow.

Enrique looked like Jed Clampett after a morphine drip and nine Lynchburg Lemonades. *Either we go with the flow or it will take us with it.*

We hopped in the hazmat-soaked purple 4x4. I finally engaged the engine after several tries. It sounded like a Bee Gees and Edith Bunker rendition of Act 4 of *The Marriage of Figaro.*

We dodged and weaved through San José, trying to keep up with Enrique. This was imperative since we (rather idiotically) didn't bring a map to a country where the surface streets had no names. We needed to get out of the capital to open highway where chances of getting lost drastically diminished. Laura consoled the Boys. San José is bedlam to a newbie driver. The rest of Costa Rica was like Mother Nature's opium, looping in and out of varied microclimates–foliage lush as Pierce Brosnan's hair, and wildlife drip-ping from the trees. We already longed for serene Pair-o-Dice Village, where road chaos was limited to a rare mudslide or herd of cows.

"I can't believe we're actually here," I said every ten minutes. *I can't believe we actually did it! We're crazy! But why does it feel so right?*

"I can't believe it either," Laura answered each time—sounding a bit like, "I can't believe I married a guy who convinced me to do this."

By the last major town before Pair-o-Dice Village, we had been in transit fifteen hours, and the Boys had reached their limits long before. After exit-ing town, the potholes were constant and required weaving and slow driv-ing. The truck smelled like napalm and could barely do fifty-five.

"This is like driving a stinky grape Skittle—a sport futility vehicle," I said to Laura, attempting levity for the sake of the cat situation.

She wasn't laughing, distracted by Skippy who had flopped over, passed out and limp. Rugby realized something was very wrong and began comfort-ing him with licks. Laura was about to faint, but there was no way I was lick-ing her after this long trip with no A/C. Having finished the pothole stretch, we got on the main highway along the Ballena Coast and ran a straight shot to Pair-o-Dice Village. Laura punched numbers on the cell phone.

"No signal! Adèle told us to call her so that she could be there with the cat stuff and to open the house!" she said. She spoke of the property manager who had the house keys.

"Well, we can't go back. It will just have to work out," I said with no other available solutions.

We entered Pair-o-Dice Village, crossed the bridge over the river onto the main dirt road, and continued up one of the two major hillside roads.

Enrique impulsively stopped short at the mouth of our driveway and jumped out of the van ahead. He put both his hands up in the air inquisi-tively and gave me a look that said, "Enrique don't play dat."

I remembered the driveway all too well. I had even wandered onto it a year prior, mistaking it for another road. And since it was rainy season on that trip—like now—I immediately assumed I'd get stuck on it, sloshing through deep, muddy puddles as the bottom of our RAV4 slammed against the uneven ground repeatedly. Granted, it had been re-graded—the local method of resurfacing, where it was refreshed with a layer of leveled dirt—since then, but the rains had already taken their toll.

The driveway was about 150 meters long. It began with a stunningly steep left-turning incline, continued down a steep decline, a little bit of flat, and another pitched right turn into the main parking area of the house.

"It won't climb that," Enrique said, pointing to the van and shaking his head in dejection.

"Put it in four?" I suggested.

"I don't have it," he said. I looked at the van filled with luggage. *You'd have better luck on a unicycle.*

Without another word, he backed up to give me way, and I drove Laura and the Boys up to the house.

And while Laura revived the cats, I made six trips back and forth by myself, schlepping one hundred pounds of luggage at a time in the grape Skittle SFV from the base of the driveway to the house. The herniated disk in my back had already picked up the local slang, screaming, "You are one crazy-ass gringo!"

"Adèle still hasn't answered the phone," Laura notified me in a panic as she sat on the step to the back pool area and I unloaded my second shipment of goods. *What the hell? We planned this out to the nines!*

I drove back down the driveway in the empty Skittle, handed Enrique his fee, and bid him farewell.

I listened as his diesel passenger stallion descended the road and then it was so quiet—a quiet like I had never experienced. We had been in this very spot several times before, but this wasn't a tourist attraction for us now. It was our home. *I can't hear any human activity. Nothing!*

The quiet of Pair-o-Dice Village, with a population so small that no one had bothered to count, came over me with the setting sun.

I walked to the Skittle, turned the key, and got it started. But there was a new noise, like a hyena at a helium factory. I engaged first gear up the steep first left turn and realized that it suddenly had half its previous horsepower. *Damn! Not good, not good!*

Alas, the Skittle made it up the driveway and into the main parking area where Laura stood outside, rented cell phone in hand. She wore desperation on her face. "I still can't reach Adèle!"

OK, what now? We had a cat who may as well have gone twelve rounds with Jack Dempsey, it was rainy season—miraculous it wasn't already pouring—and we had no keys.

As our worry reached a fever pitch, a car pulled into the parking area. "Hallo!" the voice of an angel crossed the pristinely quiet air.

"You said you would call!" Adèle protested in her sweet French Canadian accent.

"We didn't have a signal until we got up here, and then you didn't answer," Laura said.

"Ah, yes. We don't have the phone at the new house yet." Adèle had moved out of our new house a week prior. "Sometimes the cellular does not work," she said matter-of-factly.

"OK, so I have to let you know two bad newses," she said. "I could not reach Allan to get the things for the cats. He does not answer his phone."

"We have enough food for one day. We'll try to find him tomorrow," Laura said. Under normal circumstances, the world would have stopped for Laura if the Boys were at the slightest risk. We had already raised our threshold for shock.

"That's good," Adèle said regretfully. "The other problem is that your water tank on the road broke, so you will not have water."

"How long?" I asked.

"This is difficult. We have to get someone coming to fix," she said.

"Well, of course. Someone has to come," I said. *Damn! I sound like an ass.*

She smiled. "Yes, but you are in Costa Rica. We have to *make* them come," she said with emphasis. "But for now, open the valve for the pool water to pump to the house so you can take showers." She still smiled peacefully.

OK, not so bad! But we needed drinking water—for us and for the Boys.

One

I shot a look at Laura with unspoken mutual understanding. I hopped into the Skittle, knowing that the Pair-o-Dice Village's only market would surely close shortly.

On the way to the town center—and I use that term very loosely—our purple grape confection on wheels heightened its shrieks of protest. I had lost more power during the seven-minute drive, and a thick white plume trailed behind me.

The three locals seated against the wall in front of the market stared at me as if I was a porpoise on a pogo stick. I jumped out of the Skittle, heading straight into the market without making eye contact.

I flew through the store, grabbing all the water, milk, and cereal I could carry. The cashier gave me an odd look as the Skittle wailed outside—Costa Rican markets are almost all open-air with no front door.

I approached the wailing vehicle, marveling at how such a seemingly primitive machine could have some type of emergency alarm that wailed even with the engine off. I was barely able to start it again.

Nonetheless, as I made the ten-minute drive back to the house, even my frenetic need to get home couldn't distract me from the beauty of the village. I knew no matter what was happening in the Skittle, outside there was peace and serenity.

Entering the house's parking area was a true miracle since the Skittle at that point was a hybrid, running on 10 percent gas and 90 percent my fear of getting stranded in the jungle. It stalled like clockwork as it coasted into position at the house. I walked around the house to the back deck facing the ocean. It was gorgeous. Here we finally were in Pair-o-Dice Village—the object of our hopes and dreams—for less than an hour. We had no running water and only cereal to eat until we had wheels again to get more food, with no concept of when that could be.

I surveyed the ocean, the lush valley, and the faint orange clouds streaking across the sky. My disposition was flooded by nature's morphine drip. *This is going to be awesome! I'm home.*

CHAPTER 3
The Squirminator

And those things do best please me,
that do befall preposterously.
Puck, Shakespeare's *A Midsummer Night's Dream*, 3. 2. 122-123

I HAD YET to set foot in the beautiful Spanish-style house that would be home for the next year. I entered the living room, where Adèle's furniture remained, though not for long. She was completing a new bed-and-breakfast and, as she did so, would slowly retrieve her belongings, eventually leaving us with nothing but two beds.

Suddenly, Laura flew down the stairs, dripping sweat like a wet seal.

"Glen! I was setting up their disposable litter box and cat food in some old detergent cups I found, and I saw this black thing on the ground. I thought it was a dirty cloth," she said, pointing up the stairs to our bedroom.

She was on the verge of vaporizing with panic as I admired her usual foresight to have brought temporary cat supplies.

"So I bent over to pick it up. The lighting sucks up there, but it moved right before my hand got to it. It was a bat! I kicked it right out the door and off the balcony," she said, choking on her own angst.

"OK, so you took care of it. I'll keep unpacking down here." I had mentally rehearsed nonreaction in my mind for so long in preparation for this first day of our move, it was instinctive. I went about my homemaking, pulling out the portable Bed Bath & Beyond we had packed in anticipation of our inaccessibility to stuff.

Laura exited the living area and went back upstairs. I felt guilty not outwardly sympathizing, but I knew feeding into chaos would be anything but constructive.

As I unpacked, items we previously considered tactical and ingenious seemed not so resourceful. *Did we think we were moving to an asteroid? Surely this stuff is available somewhere here.* I unpacked a full set of knives, a full set of pots and pans, and two coffee mugs.

Coffee. For months I dreamed of our first morning on the deck watching the ocean with Costa Rican coffee. It wasn't like I was addicted to coffee. It was more a symbol. Like drinking a margarita when you've moved to Cancun. *We have no coffee!* I panicked, looked up, and just like that, I looked over at a recessed cubbyhole to see an open bag of Britt coffee.

"Hey, Adèle left coffee!" I yelled upstairs.

Coffeemaker. I made it a point to remember where it was packed. *Clang, clang.*

"Laura," I called upward.

"What?" she asked.

"The coffee carafe didn't make it," I said.

And I began to feel the limitations we had expected—but earlier than I thought. *Excuse me, kind sir on the donkey with the bananas, do you know where I can get a Braun carafe around here?* We would have to have our first visitor bring a replacement from the States. My first morning would not be as I had envisioned for so long.

"Glen, Glen, Glen, get up here!" I heard Laura's yell. *Scorpion.* I calmly walked up the stairs toward the bedroom. Laura stood outside the bathroom door facing in.

"Scorpion?" I asked before she could say a word.

"How'd you know?" she asked.

"No clue," I replied. She looked at me like I was the CEO of the Psychic Friends Network.

I walked up to the sink to observe the four-inch creature with standard equipment—full-on claws and a stinger pointed at me like a Howitzer.

I surprisingly continued to be unfazed, like an action hero who casually expects every ninja just around the corner. I went over to one of the many boxes, ripped off a flap, and returned to the sink to scoop him up. He headed straight for my hand. I let go. He fell back into the sink and scurried up the smooth porcelain to no avail.

I went back into the bedroom and picked up a dress shoe. *When am I ever going to wear this?* I placed the box flap over the predator and started wailing at it with abandon.

Whack, whack, whack, whack, whack, whack . . . whack—how many times, I don't know. I put my hand on the flap to assess vitals. *Squirming! What the—? Oh, now you're messing with the Squirminator!* Whack, whack, whack, whackety whack! Hand over flap. *Squirming!* My last tirade did him in.

What in God's name is going on? The house was only unoccupied for a week and we have bats, scorpions, and no water?

But, then again, if that Skittle had stalled anywhere out there, the night would have been a whole different type of animal.

But not every day would be like this, right?

Exhausted from the battles with the welcoming committee, we went to bed rather on edge. I turned to kiss Laura goodnight. My heart still racing a bit, I was so grateful that she took this adventure with me. I was also curious what might be going through her mind but knew we were too tired to talk.

A few seconds into the kiss, she laughed.

"What?" I asked, my entire focus now redirected to my potentially inferior kissing skills.

"You should have seen yourself," she said, "hammering away at that two-clawed two-ounce beast."

"Obliged to come to your rescue m'lady," I said with a middle-English accent.

"Welcome to the jungle," Laura said.

We both began laughing like two loons.

One

"Well, we did it. We friggin' did it," I said. She turned and kissed me good-night once again.

I lay motionless, trying to wind down from our almost inexplicable experience. After a while, I could tell Laura wasn't sleeping, either. We turned at exactly the same moment and studied each other in the moonlight from the curtainless window above the bed. It was like I was looking in an emotional mirror. There was a beautiful smile there—a nervous one.

CHAPTER 4
Ow de Toilette

When you rise in the morning, give thanks for the light,
for your life, for your strength. Give thanks for your food
and for the joy of living. If you see no reason to give thanks,
the fault lies in yourself.
Tecumseh

CHIRP, SQUAWK, HOWL . . . *birds, monkey? . . . stir, toss, turn . . . wings flapping . . .*
stir, toss, turn . . . mild headache, fuzzy eyelids . . . flap, flap, flap . . . wait, those
wings sound like plastic or something . . . insect wings . . . big insect . . . inside?
No, outside. Back pain. Lots of back pain. Uh, everything aches. All that luggage!
It's hot . . . different smells . . . something's different . . . everything's different.

The early bird in Costa Rica apparently gets the worm, deposits it in the
nest on your roof, and wakes your gringo ass up at five in the morning. I immediately had flashbacks to the chaos of the prior evening and tensed up. I
had the motility of Stonehenge.

I opened one eye. *Wait! Costa Rica! We're in Costa Rica!* The pain vanished
instantly.

I threw the west balcony doors open. *The ocean! The view! A view worthy*
of kings and gods! Past the backyard was a shallow valley basin. Beyond the
valley spread a lush green hill and the continuation of our road. Behind that

hill, less than a quarter mile away, shimmered the vast Pacific with whitewater breaking onto the beach.

We had visited this house the last night of our trip in July and couldn't see these views through the darkness. *Why didn't they tell us as we haggled over the price? Thank you! Thank you!*

I hopped onto the bed, jumping up and down on my knees like a kid who got a new puppy. Laura awoke suddenly given the human sea lion flopping about her quarters.

"Get up! Get up! You've gotta see this!" I yelled.

I grabbed her hand, still limp with sleepiness and dragged her across the room.

On the balcony, I exclaimed, "My dear, I present to you," pausing for effect, I spread my arms as if to display my finest life's work, "paradise!"

Tears came to Laura's eyes. "It's so unbelievably beautiful," she said with the little breath she had. "All that work to get here. It was so worth it."

"We are going to see this every morning," I said. "There are billionaires at home who haven't woken up to a view like this."

"It's so gorgeous. It's just so gorgeous," Laura said. We were both nearly in shock.

I went across the bedroom to the east balcony. Aside from a couple of houses dotting the landscape, it was nothing but green for miles. I was facing the main town of Pair-o-Dice Village in the valley below, hidden by a tall canopy of trees. Our house was atop a ridge with valleys on both sides. The west valley stretched for miles and was bookended by a steep mountain of the deepest green hue.

The expansive rainforest breathed vapor into the air like a cold winter day in Chicago, but it was anything but cold. These sparse little clouds of mist drifting sideways across the valley and through the trees gave an air of peaceful frosting on top of the Earth's most magnificent cake.

We had arrived, but this wasn't just an arrival in the traditional sense. This was a life-altering arrival—entry to a completely new world full of possibility. It was like we had exited our lives and entered those of someone else. But these lives were still ours—with every moment of every day a new and, hopefully, fulfilling experience.

As I stood on the east balcony, I reflected on the e-mail I sent to a friend before we left. "As excited as I am, a big part of me wishes that I didn't have to do this. Life would be so much easier if I could just have kids, the yard, and the house like you. No movers, no jungles, no saying good-bye to family, no third-world countries. But something inside me knows I'd be miserable. I guess I just need to accept I am different."

Most people not super-close to us thought Laura was the one who pushed for Costa Rica. She was born in Pittsburgh with Tom, her older brother, already three years old. At age eight, her parents did the exact same thing we did, dropping everything except their house. They, too, rented it out and headed for Hawaii. Jeanne—Laura's sister—was born two years later.

Laura's father was a purchasing manager on a rather small island, meaning he worked long hours and traveled often. Her mother a school teacher, Laura was often left to her own devices and took advantage of the independence she was given. She quickly learned to self-entertain and toughen up on the streets and as a mall rat. By age fifteen, she was already working at the movie theater and had her driver's license. She became a natural athlete and leader—competing on the high school track team in junior high and becoming a star basketball player. The only thing that kept her out of any game was her natural tendency to foul out.

What's more, being a pale Caucasian in Hawaii, Laura lived as a minority. From that came her sense of justice, fearlessness, and her amazing problem-solving skills.

Laura was encouraged to go out and perform for the world whenever possible. I was always amazed at her outgoing nature. She would readily start conversations with strangers that lasted for hours. In fact, whenever I'm out with the Berger family and think, "Oh, God that looks embarrassing," a Berger is first in line to do that very thing. Thanks to their skills in auto-enrolling people in contests, I have won 1st place gold-coated plastic trophies for both chicken legs and hairy chest on two separate cruises.

One

When Laura's family came to her college graduation to bring her back to Hawaii, she made the knee-jerk reaction to send them home without her. Finding island life too limiting, she moved to Chicago with no living arrangements or money. She picked up a house-sitting gig until she could find a roommate, and with absolutely no training, she became the director of an Alzheimer's home. Two years later, she secured the type of consulting job that is typical of Ivy League MBAs and star professionals with significant business experience. She just applied for the job, learned PowerPoint in a week, and prepared a business case that she presented to three partners. She was hired on the spot.

She valued her independence. It was the topic of my wedding vows, partly for fear that she might get cold feet and bolt on me if I didn't reinforce that she'd still be her own person.

And so it seemed odd that with all the barriers she had already shattered, I had been the one so ready to parachute into the jungle at a moment's notice. Left up to me, instead of eleven suitcases, we'd have arrived with a single serving of trail mix.

The benefit of hindsight reveals why I pushed so hard for Costa Rica. I was self-caged for so long.

Laura and I are a case study of opposites attracting. I spent most of my teen years indoors and afraid of going out for fear of being picked on. For instance, I was terrified of parties, thinking I would come home with the elastics of my underwear yanked over my head. So I hung out a lot in my room, memorizing movies and playing on my computer. The one respite I got was five weeks per year visiting my grandparents in Italy. I got along so well with the Italians. Those summers were like social explosions for me.

Adding to my reserved nature, all my life choices were the ones that looked best to everyone else and not me. In my sophomore year, my introductory accounting teacher called me aside to point out that I had gotten the highest grade on the first exam. I'm sure it was a fluke, as it was all multiple choice. "You could be a great accountant if you think you'd like it," he said. I changed my major fifteen minutes later.

In the spring of 1994, I walked out of the CPA exam one semester away from graduating with a master's degree and decided that being an accountant was probably the most diametrically opposite choice I could have made for my personality.

It meant I had passed, having survived a near-nervous breakdown in the process. I could only think, "How the Hell did I get here? What a waste!"

But I was to graduate from the University of Texas at Austin, the top accounting school in the country, and the "big six" accounting firms were courting me.

That was quite a professional chip on my shoulder. My ambition gained momentum. I finished my grad program in fifteen months, heading right into a big firm. I was a magnet to a better professional image. If all of a sudden those guys following horses in parades with shovels drove BMWs, wore Armani, and were the talk at cocktail parties, I'd be the first to sign up for a Masters of Science in Equestrian Excrement Elimination. Add to that my all-or-nothing mentality and my need to be a hero for more kudos and accolades, and at my job, I always accepted responsibility that put me on the edge of failure—that is, if these firms didn't work you hard enough in the first place. If too much of a good thing is bad, then what's too much of a bad thing?

That's where the all-nighters came in, working all hours to catch up when I was near disaster. Hearing I had failed was not something in my realm of acceptable outcomes. My mind had even developed a coping mechanism for when I absolutely had to sleep. I'd teeter just on the inner boundary of slumber but would sort through all my work issues in the meantime. I'd arrive at work the next day with all my problems already solved. I would dream up solutions—literally.

Thankfully, this extreme deviation required extreme payback. Five years or so before arriving in Pair-o-Dice Village, I started fantasizing life in every vacation destination we visited. And now here I was, scanning the green landscape for sights and sounds of any stirring humans. There were none.

Taking in the view of Pair-o-Dice Village, I could think of no moment in life when I felt more validated or more at home. What I was not thinking—

maybe by choice—was this was just the beginning. Until we really answered the main question of this trip at the end of a year, "Would we live here permanently?" uncertainty would be our constant.

After several minutes of beholding bliss, I realized my forward compartment was flooded. Laura must have had the same idea because the only thing that could remove anyone from our new outdoor scenes would be the potential of making potty in one's jammies.

"Can I come in?" I asked Laura. Marriage translation: "Are you going number one or number two?"

"You can come in," she said.

Bonk! "Ow!"

"What?" I asked, peeking around the edge of the open door.

Laura, assuming her temporary throne, held her forehead. "Aw, what the heck?" she protested.

"What were you doing?" I asked, noticing she must have been in an unusual position for me to have hit her with the door the way I had.

"I was checking for scorpions," she whimpered.

I noticed the house's design defect. The hinges were on the wrong side of the door, which swung straight into the toilet.

"Let me see," I said. She moved her hand to reveal what is referred to in Miami as a *chichón*—a bump.

We caught each other's gaze and busted into laughter.

After all the showerless chaos of the prior day, I was basically a walking landfill. It was time for me to swab the funk off.

"Hey, there's a suicide shower in here now," Laura said the night before. This was a clear modification since our July house tour. The oversized plastic showerhead with a three-setting temperature switch was attached to a highly conspicuous electrical cord wrapped in tape. That cord snaked along the wall to the nearest plug socket, in this case by the mirror above the sink. Granted, it was economical as the water was heated as it ran through the device, clear from the sound of boiling water emanating from its innards.

Allan, the keeper of all our pet supplies and the developer who sold us our property, joked about the showers when we paid him our first visit.

"Yeah, they're oddly common in houses older than yours. You can tell when they're going bad when your skin tingles from the electricity in the water," he helpfully advised. "Hence the nickname—suicide shower. I like to call them widow makers."

I opened the shower curtain and was made breathless from the view. The window framed that same heavenly east valley view with the huge green mountain in the backdrop. *I could get used to this!* "Every morning, I shower to the sound of toucans and monkeys with a huge view of primary and secondary rainforest and lush mountains," I'd write home.

I was suddenly reminded our windows had no screens when a fly entered the bathroom.

We had battled about this very issue and over basic necessities with our landlords, the Richardsons—who had hired Adèle as our property manager—for several months before arriving. They called Arizona home and had admitted spending only a total of two weeks as residents since purchasing it.

Mr. Richardson said, "I don't know why you keep insisting on having screens. When we're there, we sleep with the windows open all the time. No bugs come in." This was the Costa Rican jungle. "Oh, silly me," I was tempted to say, "the next thing on my list was a couple of towels, but when you took showers there, of course you didn't get wet?"

Eh, who cares? First day in Costa Rica!

I examined the three valves on the shower wall and remembered Adèle's instructions. "Please not to touching the two side valves," she said. As water trickled from the showerhead, I wondered what would happen if I were so audacious as to turn the right or left one. Would a fire hydrant maybe fly off its base in Vatican square?

The water was nice and hot—and then it wasn't. The lights in the bathroom flipped me the tropical bird, and the water went cold.

Sure glad I turned the proper valve!

One

I threw on clothes and entered the bedroom. The ceiling fan was now still. *I must have tripped a breaker.*

I went downstairs and around the house to the exterior storage room—the *bodega*—and reset the tripped breaker. Walking back into the house, I imagined my reaction in the States to renting a place where attempting basic hygiene caused power outages. Here, I took it in stride. *The suicide shower must have a science about it. I'll learn.* I didn't even have to think about focusing on the positive. *It's coming naturally. The context has changed.*

CHAPTER 5
Housebroken

Get busy living, or get busy dying.
Andy Dufresne played by Tim Robbins,
The Shawshank Redemption

"A TOUCAN!" I said.

"Where?" Laura asked.

"Right there in that tall tree! See? Looks like a papaya tree!" I pointed.

"He's right . . ." My excitement was matched only by my frustration that Laura couldn't see it. *Our first toucan! She has to see it!* "He's got like yellow, maroon, and black in his beak that really blends in with the trees."

She still couldn't see, now on her feet and clearly frustrated.

"Wait! There! He just completely turned his head!" I said.

"I see it! I see it! Our first toucan!" Laura beamed.

This sighting completely erased all my regret that I could not have the other textbook pleasure for our first morning—a cup of coffee. I was taken aback by my disappointment when exiting the shower earlier that the carafe had broken. Visions were powerful. I had imagined and tasted that first cup of coffee for months as part of this scene. Ironically, I had also envisioned us spotting a toucan.

Then I came to my senses—or at least tried. I didn't know what our first day had in store, but I said to myself, "If you're going to live here, you're going to have to learn to let go."

Now nature had filled the void that still lingered despite my self-pep talk.

"There he goes!" I said as he flew away.

"Oh, another one is following him!" Laura noticed his friend.

"Everyone at home is doing their thing. I guess that thing's not for us." Laura inhaled the pure air with satisfaction. "It's just so gorgeous."

An engine approached on the road about seventy-five steep feet below the house—completely out of sight.

"You hear that?" I asked Laura.

"Yeah, a truck or something. Why?"

I paused. "Noticing that sound put a little chill in my spine."

"A chill? This is our first morning in paradise! What's with the chills?" Laura objected playfully.

I explained how I thought my spirit just internalized how much things are going to change. Multiple cars passed our house every minute in Chicago, and this was the first one we had heard in a half hour.

"I guess that's what you notice when you live in a village," Laura said.

"Exactly—the village. We've gone from Chicago to a friggin' village," I said.

Laura's perspective was that everything had its good and bad. We wouldn't have the conveniences we were used to or possibly even a lot in common with the village people. "But that will help us to grow—to have different points of view."

I speculated that within a few months we'd know everybody. It already seemed like we had met half the village in July. "Imagine going around town running errands and striking conversation with everyone you meet."

"Did you just say errands?" Laura asked.

Stupid me. With the nearest traffic light an hour away, errands were known to be quite difficult. *Errand* was almost a four-letter word in the village.

"Speaking of that, we really need to get that cat stuff from Allan," Laura said. "I know you probably think we have much bigger things to worry about, but you know that if the Boys aren't comfortable, I'm not either. Think about what a big change this is for them, like it's going to be for us, and they have no voice. The least we can do is get them the treats, litter, food, and toys they were used to at home."

Previous assessments of the Ballena Coast, the name of the area where we now lived, revealed it was easier to achieve eternal salvation than find a good bag of kitty litter. Laura filled four oversized suitcases with everything a feline could want and left them under beds and in closets at Allan's house since July.

I shook my head. "Dead car."

"Well, the rental car place needs to get it running," Laura said.

"I left a message last night, but they are all the way in San José!" I said.

Laura pointed out that it was not our fault the country was as big as West Virginia and it took twelve hours to drive top-to-bottom. "It's their car. They have to make it right." Laura's logical tendencies were confronting my emotional ones, leading, as usual, to heightened emotions.

I cringed at the potential imposition on the rental car company. *But she's right. There's no other way.* I had no idea where the nearest mechanic was, and even then, who would come all the way up here? And a tow truck? In the jungle? Plus, we had no phone book. 411 seemed a pipe dream. And surely there was no process for submitting repair bills to a rental outfit that conducted business from random parking spaces in the airport garage.

I thought of the half box of Bran Flakes we had already plowed through, and suddenly, things came into perspective. I went to place the call, perched on the farthest edge of the pool deck, the only part of the property where it seemed we could get a cell signal. I dialed the voice-mail number and pass code given to me by the rental car company, which also rented us the phone. "You have entered an invalid password," the cyber-Spanish voice explained. Convinced that the phone had it wrong, I brainlessly repeated the entry until "your account is blocked."

One

A solitude-induced sinking feeling occupied my stomach. I immediately chased it away, remembering all the kind and magical people we had met in July. *I could always call Adèle or Allan. I could even walk down to town and get groceries.*

Spit, spat! What was that? I scanned the pool. Was the water level that low before? *Spat!*

No, no, no! The pool jets were shooting across the surface like high-powered squirt guns. Per Adèle's instructions, I had opened the valve to replenish the pool with water from the street. But it was emptying! I went inside. *Holy crap it's hot in here!* Admittedly, we had accounted for heat in the house before we arrived, which is why we were so desperate for screens. If we opened doors or the windows without them, the cats could get out. These jungles were no place for cats, we had heard from former kitty widowers. *But we can't live in this heat!*

Laura came down the stairs. She had turned into a natural sweat spring.

"Hey, honey! Another bonus, I guess." I wiped my brow. "We rented a spa!"

"What time is it?" A hint of despair tainted her voice.

"Nine thirty."

"It's like fifteen degrees hotter inside than during breakfast! It'll be like ninety-five in here by noon!" Laura said.

"Um, I know I'm quick to judge," I said, "but I think we scored a real FlawedShack here. With the water breasts-up, the weak electricity, and the microwave climate in here, we're going to need a real FlawedShack redemption and fast!"

She cringed, embarrassed for me. "Nice! Cheesy! Why do you say that?"

I explained that the pool was a rainwater strainer. "It's leaking—fast, and I don't know why."

"No showers so soon?" Laura asked.

"Maybe so." I also informed her about the locked voice-mail password and that no one would pick up the phone at the rental agency.

"Could you please say something positive?" she asked.

"You look stunning in that shade of sweat."

She wasn't all that amused.

"A negative times a negative equals a positive?" I tried again.

Still nothing.

I rationalized with her that these were all things we could get past, even being able to wash with bottled water. But the rate that all these discoveries were hitting us was freaky-deaky.

"Well, it's beautiful outside. Remember how crappy it was in Chicago yesterday?" she said. On cue, I pulled her outside.

"Look at that, huh? Who has that?" I said, pointing to the ocean. "Breathe. Focus on the view, the trees, the sun, and the clean air." I was like a Lamaze coach for the birth of a blissful state.

She hugged me tightly. "Just call Adèle. We need your FlawedShack Redemption."

I hoped Adèle could maybe help with food and drinking water. I reassumed my perch at command central on the pool deck. "Hallo?" the sweet sound of her French accent fluttered across the line.

Fifteen minutes later, we both gave Adèle a strong hug on the patio. She had brought a crate full of fruits, vegetables, and some condiments.

"Thank you so much, Adèle." Laura said, hugging her again with intense emotion.

"No problem. Some of Jean's bread is in there, too," she said cheerily.

The fact that she didn't think context was necessary was a testimonial to how much research and circulating about town she knew we had already done. A village seemingly of no extravagances—aside from its lavish natural surroundings—Pair-o-Dice Village enjoyed the comforts of its French roots. Surely not the least of which were the amazing restaurants and the bread Adèle presented to us, baked by Jean. We had been told that bread day was a true blockbuster that everyone anticipated twice a week.

"I need to ask you some things about the house," I said.

"OoooKkkk?" she said, hesitantly. *She expected this.*

I told her I was thankful that we were able to pump pool water into the house but asked about the apparent pool leaks, wary of the potential explanations.

Frustrated, she sighed. "Yes, I told you last night that your reserve water system is broken." She explained all houses had this reserve system because "the Pair-o-Dice Village water system is no good. When everyone takes showers and use much water, there is no pressure for the village. When we lived in this house, we'd wake up at 4:30 to fill the pool and take showers sometimes."

She explained that today, the village water was out and lamented the main at the bottom of the hill that broke twice or more times per week. "There's a person that almost all he does is fix the pipes. Last month was fifteen days with no water." She explained that when there was no town water, if I opened the valve to fill the pool with no water pressure, it would all go down the hill.

"Get up at 4:30?" I confirmed.

She nodded reluctantly.

I turned to Laura. "Well, add a rooster to our shopping list."

"OK." Laura wore a surprisingly calm smile.

Then it dawned on me. *Save the water supply!* I sprinted to shut off the water main to the pool nearby.

Adèle said she would have her husband, Gerard, come to help me understand the inner-workings of the pool. "OK, and most of the plug sockets upstairs are not working," I said.

Her face twisted in what I read as regret. I felt for her. Her reactions revealed prior knowledge of all of these problems, and her task was to represent the FlawedShack to us on behalf of the Richardsons and vice versa. Finding issues with this house was proving as difficult as fishing in a barrel with a stick of dynamite. She would need to mediate a solution for each one. "Gerard was also an electrician in Canada. He can look at it," she said.

Laura jumped in. "I'm sorry. I know it's not your fault. Why are there suicide showers now?"

She explained that when they originally moved in, all the house water was hot. Everything was plumbed through the water heater. The pool and the toilet filled with hot water. "Our electricity was more than $500 each month!" I remembered people saying how cheap electricity was. Notwithstanding, they immediately disconnected the water heater and put in the shower heads.

"Wow!" Laura said.

"But your hineys must have been supple as marshmallows," I said.

Adèle was deadpan. *Note to self—language barrier.*

Our hydraulics were inferior to the paper maché aqueduct I built for the sixth-grade science fair. *But at least we won't have that water bill.*

"Is that why you told us to turn only one knob in the shower?" I asked.

"No. That's different. Just don't do it. Trust me," she said, clearly sympathetic.

"Have we found all the problems?" I asked.

"Emmm. Mostly." She sounded like the suspect when a close police officer friend of mine in Miami asked him, "Sir, have I found all the drugs?"

Laura told her that we intended to resolve the car situation quickly but asked if she would come by occasionally to check on us.

She happily agreed. "Everyone starts this way. Some can adjust and some can't."

"Well we're the ones who can," Laura said.

"Well, I don't know about you, but I could sure use some more Bran Flakes," I said.

"Pardon?" Adèle said.

"Never mind," I replied. I thought back to the Magic Rock and all our preparation. "This is all going to work out," I said to Laura.

CHAPTER 6
Gasket Case

Smile at a stranger. See what happens.
Patti LuPone

"WE'RE NOT STRANDED. There's a grocery store in town a forty-five minute walk away," I told Laura.

In this, she seemed to take comfort without a word.

And yet, in my mind, my North American expectations were secretly getting the best of me. *We give rental car agent credit card. Car agent takes money from card. Car should work.* Add to that how used we were to having transportation at the ready, and I felt stranded. Getting a functioning set of wheels became my obsession.

Am I already creating stuff to keep me busy in a tranquil setting?

This despair led to my unwavering perch upon the pool deck for the day, anticipating a ring from the cell phone.

I was absorbed in, but conflicted with my surroundings. The ambiance was one written about in travel and leisure magazines. On the other hand, I had worked an average of eighty hours a week before our departure. My new role as jungle receptionist made me feel about as useful as a ball of body lint.

"Some can adjust and some can't," Adèle said. What mental adjustments

would we need to live here? How would we deal with the inaccessibility of things, to the FlawedShack, and to the new culture out there?

By noon, the wildlife—birds, insects, and other creatures I was completely unprepared to identify—had virtually silenced their songs and were no longer visible. I took in the beauty of the grounds of the house. We had hibiscus, papaya, banana, coconut palms, and flowering bougainvillea. I spotted a few Cecropia trees, which tended to attract toucans. I searched for almond trees since Allan had told us those attracted scarlet mccaws.

I felt an interest in nature that I had never before recognized. Clearly, "know thyself" had been a mantra lost on me.

And then I scanned the house. It was modest in size but a rather magnificent sight. Spanish in design, it was mostly one story with the second floor half the size of the first, containing our bedroom and the master bath. Below our bedroom was the guest apartment, identical in design to the master with its own duplicate bathroom. The majority of the first floor was the living room and kitchen area, a relatively enormous space that could have used a few more walls to make it more practical. The stairs from the kitchen to the master bedroom ran along the wall and led to a tiled platform—outside the master bathroom—under a vaulted circular tower. This final accent was the finishing touch that made the entire house look like a miniature Spanish-style castle and house combination.

At around 4 p.m., I may have jumped out of the chair before the phone even rang.

"¡Óigo!" I said.

It was the car rental agent! I explained that if my Spanish was off when we ordered the car, I learned it in the classroom and hadn't spoken in a while. Yet, if I had somehow conveyed that I wanted a car with a perpetually declining top speed, vapor trail, and hazmat smell, I had misspoken.

He was gracious. "Don't you worry, Don Glen!" he said in Spanish. "Someone will arrive in Pair-o-Dice Village before the tomorrow morning to help you *si Dios quiere.*"

Now that last part meant "if God wants it." Since I was an alumnus of all sacraments prescribed for a man my age, if such matters required God's involvement, I was certain he would want this for me very much.

"Do you know what time?" I asked.

"Oh, around the late evening maybe. Hopefully, before sunrise," he replied.

"*¡Muchas gracias y adios!* I said, at a loss to say anything else.

I reentered the FlawedShack, where Laura had volunteered to keep unpacking. As predicted, it was at least ninety-five degrees inside, even with the sun already hinting at retiring for the evening. She actually had risked opening a window, a clear sign of her suffering. She had also stripped completely!

"I think I like it better without screens," I said.

"Ha, ha, ha."

I gave her an update.

"What time will he be here?" she asked.

"Let's not get into that," I said.

"Well, didn't he give you a time?"

"Let's kneel and pray for a time," I said.

"Huh?" she asked.

"Before noon tomorrow, OK? Let's just leave it at that. It's all I've got."

We unpacked for another hour and ate dinner.

"Wow! The darkness doesn't mess around here," Laura said. "I never realized how much we can see around us at night in the States, with all the lights. In a way, this darkness seems so peaceful, like we're the only ones in the world. Then again, I feel like if we took a walk across the lawn, we might fall off the Earth!"

There was a string of widely spaced streetlights down our road dotting the valley. Other than that, it was spooky dark—like you might be able to see every star in every galaxy—that is, if rain hadn't started to fall as if we were under attack.

"What? I can't hear you!" The rain slammed into the typical faux Spanish-style tin roof. The style of roof was as cost effective as it was practical—major fault zones basically surrounding us, even offshore to the west. At a loss for conversation, a TV, and tired of unpacking, we retired early.

A car horn blew at 11:30 p.m.

Although it had stopped raining, I was once again struck by the darkness of the front parking area as I went outside, the clouds blocking the moon.

The same rental car agent who signed our agreement in San José got out of a comparable Skittle–this time black. He shook my hand with an enthusiastic smile as if I was some Hollywood star.

"¡Buenas noches, Don Glen!" he said excitedly.

I could get used to this Don stuff!

I remembered the definition of agent from business school: "One entrusted with the business of another." *This guy's no agent. He's owner, customer service rep, driver, mechanic, and superintendent!*

I began at the bottom of our hierarchy of needs.

I handed him the phone to unlock the voice mail. He poked at it, a perfect imitation of me earlier that morning—enter pass code, listen, curse, repeat.

"Here, take mine." He handed me a different phone and piece of paper, presumably with the new number and pass code. I thanked him.

"¿Y las llaves, por fa?" he asked. I gladly exchanged keys.

He asked for a flashlight to examine the engine. I handed him mine and went in to get another.

"It's empty." He pointed at the radiator upon my return. "Do you have a hose?"

"I'm sorry, but no." *Put it on the list.*

He grabbed a bottle of antifreeze from the trunk of the new Skittle, which was basically a small auto parts store. As he fed the radiator, I realized it was water. I refilled the jug repeatedly from the pool—as he quenched the Skittle's thirst. Then it started.

The driveway was instantly blanketed in a field of the same white smoke from the day before. A few bubbles from the tailpipe, and we could have filmed *The Lawrence Welk Show*, Jungle Edition.

He exited the car long-faced. I understood Spanish mechanic speak with the alacrity of a coma victim, but I finally understood it was the head gasket.

He said he couldn't fix it and would need to take it to a mechanic the next day. "I will stay here tonight?" *Was that a question or a statement? And who is going to run the multinational rental car agency while you're gone?*

I have a rudimentary personal flaw. I can't hurt feelings or say no to people. In that regard, life tends to have its way with me.

I turned around and immediately shuddered. Laura was right behind me, clearly angry. *Oh, boy.* The only time she scared me was in cases where the forces of my affability versus her logic were at odds. Letting him stay was dodgy, but could I say no?

"He's going to stay the night," I said.

"Can I speak to you inside?" she asked.

Never once had my wife asked me to relocate for a conversation.

"Uh, sure!"

I told the rental car agent to please wait outside a moment. He nodded, visibly wise of the situation.

"Are you out of your mind?" she asked.

"Well, he can sleep in the guest apartment, and we can lock the front door," I said.

"Uh, huh. This is the perfect setting for a horror movie. The only person who knows we're up here is Adèle, and the only police are two guys on one Chinese motorcycle," she said. A police station at the village entrance serviced a forty-mile radius. Indeed, it was equipped with two guys and one dirt bike.

"But where's he going to sleep?" I asked.

"He has a car. And even though it might feel we've fallen off the edge of the Earth," she paused, "the village has hotels." Despite the village's near evacuation for rainy season, several hoteliers indeed did stay to brave it out until the sparse flow of tourists returned.

"How is he going to afford a hotel?" I asked with a deafening tone that had quickly escalated to match Laura's.

"How do you know he *can't* afford a hotel?"

I immediately realized I was painting with an elitist's broad brush.

"I mean he seems to have a fleet of cars," she said.

"Well, we've seen evidence of two, and I don't know if you can call them cars," I replied.

Her look told me that if the conversation went any further, she was going to be my greatest danger, not the rental car agent. Why I persisted, I can't explain.

"But how am I going to tell him . . .?"

"Well, how do you say, thank you for coming, but we just got here and are not comfortable with you staying? However you say that."

I realized my argument was holding water like the radiator in the driveway. I was standing in quicksand. Both of our larynges had turned inside out from yelling, and once the first drop of quicksand entered my left nostril, I yielded.

Head hung low, I went back out and gave him an encyclopedic assortment of excuses. He looked at me as if I had the word "eunuch" tattooed on my forehead. It felt that my yielding to my wife and turning him away went against cultural norms.

After transferring the auto parts store to the other trunk, he simply drove away in the crippled Skittle we had fostered for a day, a cloud of white vapor in his wake.

That squealing engine alarm from the prior day sounded again. I waited for his progress to cease, but it didn't. Apparently he had picked up enough speed on the first driveway decline to make it over the next incline and out to the road.

Now he faced the task of getting out of Pair-o-Dice Village. Having been up and down various inclines, declines, and bridges during our prior visits, this seemed a task to practice repeatedly like a video game before succeeding. I listened closely as the engine alarm drifted into the distance and then turned heel toward the FlawedShack.

That night, I was proud that we had resolved our stranded state so quickly. Yet, I lay awake as the downpour imitated a highly caffeinated drummer on the metal roof.

"Some can adjust and some can't." Adèle's record skipped in my head—the last song I wanted to hear to close out our first day.

CHAPTER 7
Pair-o-Dice Village

"A tree as big around as you can reach starts with a small seed; a thousand-mile journey starts with one small step."

Lao-tse

October 17, 2006

The next morning still felt like some sort of fantasy as I opened one eye and found myself in Pair-o-Dice Village once again. And then immediately, the word "guilt" screamed through my head. I went out to the pool deck and dialed the rental car agent.

It was six in the morning, and he had the energy of a kid who just found out he was going to Disney World for the first time.

"*Poooora Viiiida*, Don Glen," he crooned as we ended our conversation.

"*Adios amigo y gracias,*" I replied and hung up, baffled that he truly seemed to have no hard feelings and was just having another wonderful tico day.

I turned to survey the pool, with several inches left to fill. *Good progress, though.* I decided to wait to close the water supply valve until I noticed the level receding again slightly. *Every drop counts.*

I traversed through the pristine, humid, cool air hanging over the yard back to the FlawedShack.

"All right, so we'll eat breakfast, go over to Allan's for the kitty stuff, and run errands—eh, whatever you call them here," I said.

"Oh, my God!" Laura said through a mouth full of bread.

"That good?" I asked.

"The best ever," she said enthusiastically. "That's what I remember loving about this place. Everything is so fresh. The fruit is so flavorful and juicy. Remember the chicken? It's the same—moist and so delicious. And the eggs. Everything must be organic and free range."

"Well, that would be a good description of the whole country," I said. "Free range."

I told her the rental agent had already revived our formerly dead purple Skittle and was on his way to San José.

"Wow!" she said.

It should have come as no surprise to either of us, as our experience with ticos during previous trips was that they could be the most resourceful lot on Earth.

"Where did he sleep?" Laura asked.

"He wouldn't tell me. I get the impression probably in the car," I said.

"Well *that* sucks," Laura said.

"Really?" I said sarcastically. *Eeeaasy.* "Anyway, all he said the whole conversation was *Poooora Viiiida*—you know how they lean on those vowels to make it sound even happier?"

Pura Vida was the classic Costa Rican expression of pure life and happiness. Ticos used it to say hello, good-bye, and a lot in between.

"No matter what happens, they all seem happy," she said. "Speaking of happy, this is like crack frosted with crack. Here, taste." She shoved Pair-o-Dice Village bread in my mouth like wedding cake.

Ecstasy welled up inside me as I chewed. "Oh, I'm not worthy! Aw! I'm speechless!"

She told me to grab some bread to eat in the car.

I looked at her, a bit startled. "Are you going to miss a meeting?"

"No, wisenheimer. I'm jittery about the cat stuff. Maybe Allan went back to California and didn't tell us? You know how laid-back everyone is. He hasn't called, right?" she asked.

I told her that he had our old cell number, and I hadn't called him with the new one. Either way, Laura wanted to get the cat stuff behind us. "When they're comfortable, maybe I'll be comfortable."

We agreed, and we went out to our new foster car in the driveway.

I opened the door and plunged my foot into at least four inches of water resting on the floorboards. "Hey, look! It comes with a footbath!" I said. We looked at the roof for holes and at the windows to make sure they were closed. Tight as could be, it seemed.

"Just get in. As long as it runs . . .," I said.

"The seats were completely dry! How's that even possible?" Laura asked.

"No idea." I engaged the ignition and quickly realized our new footbath didn't have A/C—a regretful downgrade.

I pushed lightly against the sagging canvas roof to see if it might be easy to take off. "There's water up here, too."

As if on cue, we pushed our respective sides up. A gallon of water entered each window.

"Well, the seats are wet *now*," I said. We laughed ourselves breathless. *This is ridiculous but fun.*

"Well, they teach at the Second City funny is about creating the unexpected," Laura completed my sentence. "Well, then this is the Second Village." As an aside, the Second City Training Center may be the greatest comedy school in the world.

Water sloshed around under us as I backed up like a wave pool at a water park. I christened the truck "the wave pool footbath" as we laughed all the way down our hill to climb up the village's other major hill to Allan's house. His huge rottweiler, who Allan swore was a sweetheart, greeted us. He could have been a bronco who got into five pounds of espresso beans as far as I was concerned. I leaned on the horn without getting out of the car as Laura smiled and flirted with the dog through the window.

Allan wasn't home.

I watched Laura suppress anxiety of seismic proportions.

"Well, what do you want to do now?" I asked.

"Let's get to some of this," she said, waving the list of errands artfully created before our arrival. "And then we can check back." I about-faced the car and after a two hundred sixty-three point turn, I started down the hill. I had my own catalog of to-dos I called "the list of random crap in my head."

Our needs were truly ordinary for starting a new life in a new place—house wares, consumer goods, and some furniture.

And then there was the machete. The anatomy of a tico was, unsurprisingly, same as that of a gringo, except that the average jungle tico was adorned with this blade of about eighteen inches. They were like an appendage. Like pistols in the old West, whether on hip or in hand, the bank was the only place these jungle swords were shunned.

"You'll need one," Allan said in July. "It's like duct tape. You'll be amazed at all its uses."

I suddenly dreaded plunging into errands on our third day in paradise. "Hey, I know how hard you worked on that list, but please get it as far away from me as you can, just for today. We can use the same two mugs and plate until tomorrow. Let's drive and drool over our new village, shall we?"

Laura tossed the list into the back seat for effect—right into one of the floorboard puddles. "No!" She lunged backward to save it like a gem circling a drain.

Ink bled every which way as she held up the wet pages.

I handed her a pen. "When that dries, add finding a Kinko's to reprint it."

"Ha, ha, ha." She waved it in the air, a complete act of futility.

We drove the steep hillside dirt roads by the gringo houses—all shapes, sizes, and states of repair and most with magnificent valley or ocean views—back to the village's main road. This main artery bisected the town with a meandering river alongside. Unpaved, it was the only road in town wide enough for two oncoming cars to calmly pass without slowing. Our tires sunk into the muddy potholes, irrigated by the previous evening's downpours. We passed the absurdly thick vines hanging from equally lush trees, with colorful ginger and heliconia flowers whizzing by.

Along the coast, gringos tended to live high and ticos low. Until recently, ticos generally made their livings from livestock and agriculture. Herding on rugged, hilly terrain or walking home 300 to 500 feet uphill from a hard day's work—cars generally scarce—was generally undesirable. But recently gringos had arrived to treasure the formerly unpopulated highlands, and the ticos had gladly sold them the hills. Of course, with that money they bought the cars they previously lacked, but habit kept them primarily in the valley.

We made our way up through the hills to Catharsis, the French restaurant where we ate almost all our dinners during previous trips. We were excited to maybe have lunch, but it seemed only the day staff was there. "Well, that's a downer," Laura said. Aside from the amazing food, we really wanted to say hello to Françoise and Louis.

"We'll have every opportunity," I said to Laura. "It's less than ten minutes away now." The prospect of such good food and great people nearby comforted me. Laura's smile showed the same.

I resumed around a left-hand bend leading to the center of Pair-o-Dice Village. It was comprised of about fifteen tico homes, the town library (about the size of any of the modest houses), and the soccer field. This sporting ground was the village's primary social gathering place.

Tico children played in the street, and the usual two or three adults leaned up against the grocery store wall, socializing. "You should have seen when I drove up in that Skittle, whining away and trailing all that white smoke." I told Laura. "Their faces said, 'Find your women and children. More crazy gringos have moved in.'"

I paused in front of the one-way bridge that continued the main road across the river.

"I don't think we know *anybody* back here," Laura said.

"Not yet, at least," I replied. Having driven only five minutes since turning off Allan's road into the valley, we were already in the back half of town. These were the only blocks of residential road grid in the village. It seemed inhabited mostly by ticos, with some cabin complexes and a couple of restaurants for the tourists.

"Can you believe we moved to a town that takes less than ten minutes to drive across?" I asked.

"You're asking me? It was *your* idea," Laura said sarcastically.

We veered to our left at a fork and began a short descent. "Oh, I forgot about this," Laura said, concerned as we approached the docile rapids.

This was the point where the road led straight into the river with no bridge—as in through the water. This was the unspoken border between Pair-o-Dice Village and "the Phases." These back hillsides belonged to a French Canadian who flew in flocks of buyers who were hosted in spec houses as they were shown property. Many buyers committed to property and projects to build houses there, sight unseen. They were already up to Phase Nine.

I stopped to assess the current's flow, and three blue morpho butterflies flew along the stream ahead. These amazing creatures were three to four inches across. A daily sight in the jungle, their wings were iridescent blue on top and brown on the bottom. As they flapped along, they looked like daytime blue strobe lights communicating in Morse code.

I became comfortable with the rapids and put the wave pool footbath in first gear. "What are you doing?" Laura said.

"Crossing."

"Wait. No, the water's high," she said.

Yeah, I'm not so sure about this. The water was somewhat high, typical of this time of morning when the night's rains were still draining from the hills and mountains farther east.

We had been warned that crossing this river during rainy season was always a matter of study. Everyone who had lived in town for more than a few months had a story about friends' vehicles rafting straight down toward the coastal beaches. We had crossed once before with a much more respectable 4x4.

"OK. A float down to the ocean might not be the best way to mark day three. Let's wait and watch a few people cross," I said. Home was less than ten minutes in the direction we came from, but I was anxious to conquer this first obstacle. Veterans had told us on prior trips that there was a path across that was the safest and shallowest.

We sat and waited for other villagers to cross so that we could emulate their route. Two cars crossed as a half hour passed. "OK, here we go," I said.

"No, no, no!" Laura said. I didn't mean to be insolent, but there was something wimpy about turning back. My heart in my throat, our tires descended farther and farther into the depths as we neared the center. *Oh, crap. Start the ascent! Come on, come on.*

"Glen!" Laura said. "Water's coming in!" Water began to trickle in through the door frame, as if we needed a refill.

"I know, I know!" I said as I instinctively floored it, river rocks slamming into the underbelly of the wave pool footbath. I fully expected a deluge to pour over the front of the tiny SUV, but we reached the center and headed up to the bank where the road continued.

"OK, that's not so bad," I said.

"Excuse me?" Laura replied. "We were about to get stuck."

"Naah, if the water were any higher, we'd have had a problem, but we gauged that well," I said.

My wife's look said, "If you want to be a crazy-ass gringo, fine, but leave me out of it."

We continued through the Phases. Although the amount of land sold was legendary, there wasn't much development. In fact, with no signage and few landmarks, we spent the next hour bouncing from phase to phase—completely lost.

Where the hell's the road? I felt like a mouse looking for cheese, but I didn't even have scent to help me. Luckily, there were enough inhabitants to provide directions, which we would follow until we were lost again five minutes later.

But this was meandering of a different kind—through a lush heaven. "I saw before we left that our area is a bit above average for rain in Costa Rica. One hundred eighty inches per year here, where some regions get more than two hundred forty," I said.

"You just said *our*," Laura said, visibly chilled by the realization.

I turned to her and smiled.

"Think of how much vegetation there must be in those places. Where do they put all the people?" she asked rhetorically. "And during dry season we're going to be coughing up road dust."

"Correcto," I said. "Hey, look how cool!"

We came upon a hairpin curve with water rushing across it about six feet wide. "Think we're good to cross this one?" I asked sarcastically. This time the water was only about two inches deep.

We splashed through it with ease.

"Holy crap!" I slammed the breaks. We didn't need to skid to a stop as the incline took care of that.

"We're teetering!" Laura nearly shrieked.

Indeed, we were on two wheels. A few large trucks or tractors had likely been stuck, digging trenches into the mud to free themselves. We were now balanced on the edges of those trenches.

"I can't turn back. If I make a three-point turn on something steep, we might roll downhill." And I wasn't just a freshman gringo exaggerating. Sometimes, you just know.

I wished that I could teleport to this situation six months from now when I surely would have better understood the physics of mud, steep hills, and four-wheel drive.

"What do we do?" I asked Laura.

"Well, if we can't go back, we can only sit here until someone comes or just try to trudge forward," she said.

"It can't hurt to try," I said.

I raced the engine and released the clutch. All four tires began spinning as mud shot up over the car and through the windows. I smelled the clutch burning as I hadn't released it fully. I yielded, realizing this wasn't going to work.

"Ptu! Ptu!" I looked over at Laura as she spit a gob of mud out the window.

"Wow! And to think you got your nails and hair done two days ago," I said.

"We're just digging ourselves into the ground," she said. I couldn't deny that if we sunk another inch, the bottom of the truck would be flush with the road.

"I guess we wait for a bigger, legitimate four-wheeler to come along to tow us out," I said. Adept ticos tended to wander around town in footbaths like ours as they were born on these roads, but the average gringo commanded something more rugged. The reasons for this were now front and center.

Then my man-pride welled up inside me. I indeed wanted rapid notoriety in the village, but not as the stupid new gringo stuck in the mud on day three. I surveyed the road's contours. I instinctively pointed the wheels to the right, near impossible as they were nestled deep in the mud channels dug by our predecessors. I then released the clutch again.

"What are you doing?" More mud shot airborne as Laura shut her window.

"If I can get the tires up onto the edge of these ditches, we'll get elevation to maybe get out of here," I said. I attempted several times to gain purchase before exiting the tire channels. I braked as we teetered once more, the tires uneven. Then, turning the wheels back toward the incline, we drove as if on two elevated hardened mud rails.

"Ha! We did it!" I said, as we again reached level and tame road—relatively speaking.

Laura looked at me in amazement. "How'd you figure that out?"

"I don't know. I found the whole thing exhilarating. Getting across the river and out of that ditch really meant something. It's not like problem-solving for a corporation. Succeed or fail, the outcome is all ours," I said.

We drove along the mountain side with a clear and magnificent view of the ocean. The sun reflected on the water lapping a beach three hundred feet down bordering the vast rainforest.

We then descended a steep, long residential road clearly taking us back toward the ocean. The road eventually led to the same paved highway that passed the entrance to Pair-o-Dice Village. We recognized the gas station and hardware store.

"Am I seeing this right?"

"You are," Laura agreed.

We had just driven an hour and a half in a horseshoe. The village entrance was ninety seconds to our left.

After all that.

"Well, it sure was a nice drive," Laura said through the laughter.

"Yeah, and fun!" I replied. "You know, I'm proud," I said as we drove back into the village and up our hill.

"Of what?" Laura said.

"That we made it here. Think of everything we just explored and learned in just ninety minutes!" I said. "Back home, I'd sit in traffic for ninety minutes and not remember any of it."

"We've been missing a few things over the last few days, but monotony ain't one of them," Laura said and looked at me sweetly. "You know, there's a reason why we found each other. Our life is so unique and all our own. I love you," she said.

I got butterflies and smiled. "I love you, too."

We drove into the driveway. I immediately heard the pool jets. "Oh, God! I forgot to close the valve!" I darted to the back of the pool and shut the conduit to the village water supply.

"Never a dull moment!" I heard Laura giggle behind me.

Good. We're still laughing.

Yeah, if humor lies in the unexpected, Second City should open a school here.

Two

CHAPTER 8
It's Allan How You Look at It

"All suffering of mankind is produced by attachment to a previous condition of existence."
Buddhist saying

October 20, 2006

Despite the lower temperatures of the rainy season—broadly bookended by Easter and Thanksgiving—our house was unbearable after 11 a.m. Luckily, our research at the village Internet café revealed that felines could survive in temperatures much higher than those in the house. This was fortunate because the Richardsons seemed to have a low tolerance for our demands to screen their windows.

Laura hypothesized that it couldn't be too hard for us to get screens and do it my/ourselves. I explained these custom wood windows had been designed with no potential for screens, with no rails or framing to house them. "And part of me understands their perspective. This is pretty low rent for a view like this—the house notwithstanding," I said. "We're getting what we paid for."

"Just remember if I kill you, it will take a veeeeery long time for anyone to figure it out around here," she said.

"Hey, now. Easy."

"Renter pays rent. Renter lives *inside* house," Laura said.

I thought of the dry season, when the FlawedShack's average room temperature would be that of a steel mill. Given the circumstances, we were forced to leave the house every day. But with such beautiful surroundings, it surely didn't feel like an obligation.

We had spent several days running errands, having been warned that the elusive desire for accomplishment would be the most frustrating part of life. Would a place of business be closed for random unexplained reasons or what unexpected circumstance would there be *en route*? Would a worker appear for an appointment? It seemed we were best served transforming our hierarchy of needs to a menagerie of preferences.

But we now had most of our basic purchasable necessities and had determined which stores would service our basic needs over the coming year. Of course, what we considered "basic" shifted each day.

The only essential remaining was to secure the mother lode of cat supplies at Allan's house.

We made the stunning, but somewhat punishing drive to Allan's toward dusk, euphoric as he finally was there to greet us in his driveway, his massive rottweiler at his heels.

There are a select few people you meet in life that alter its course forever. The circumstance under which we met Allan tipped us off to him possibly being one of them. Almost a year prior, we wandered into Pair-o-Dice Village and asked a random village person sitting at the Internet café for an ecologically responsible and honest developer in the area. "Oh, you must meet Allan! He is exactly who you are looking for."

We skipped lunch, followed her crudely drawn map intended to get us up the hill and to Allan's house, and were instantly lost. Then, the skies opened up for a classic afternoon rain, robbing us of our visibility, which to be fair, was proving rather useless regardless.

Laura gestured toward a random house driveway along the road for me to pull into. Someone pulled in behind us.

A woman exited a haggard white 4x4, shielding her head from the rain. A deluge entered the car as I obliged her by opening my window. "We're look-ing for Allan, the developer," I said.

"Oh, well I'm his wife. He lives right here," she said.

Allan served as the agent for the lot we purchased near Pair-o-Dice Vil-lage. A gringo resident of long standing, he was apt to get the transaction done the Costa Rica way. But as first-time buyers in Costa Rica, we insisted on land surveys and soil samples. Allan trekked up the hill countless times to no-shows by the professionals we had hired to attest to the quality of the property.

We also insisted on using a lawyer who was far away from Pair-o-Dice Vil-lage to avoid local conflicts of interest. Allan made several two-hour drives to Jacó over rugged dirt roads before *they* ever got to meet.

Finally, our deal had fallen apart at the eleventh hour due to a rather large financial misunderstanding between the seller and us. Less than a day later, an e-mail magically arrived from Allan, "I paid the difference. Con-gratulations on your new property."

"Why are you doing this?" I wrote back.

"We like you two, and we hope someday you will come to live in Pair-o-Dice Village," he replied.

On our last visit, Allan offered us the prospect of our living in Costa Rica, helping him sell land in his new developments. He was a walking proxy of our reasons to move to Costa Rica.

"I hope your life insurance is paid up driving that thing," he said, disdain-ing our vehicle as we exited the wave pool footbath in his driveway.

I always loved a smart ass and Allan certainly was one of them. He was a teddy bear to some and a fire-breather to others. His formula was quite simple, really. Cheat someone, harm the environment, or be a high-mainte-nance whiner, and you were dead right out of the chute. But if he believed in you, he'd move heaven and Earth for you.

"It's just a little rental while we buy cars," I said, giving him a hug.

"*Cars*, plural?" he asked.

"We don't always want to be tied to one another," Laura said.

"Your choice. Be tied to two cars or each other. You seem to get along well. Choose each other," he said. "Cars are the biggest living expense here. If you came to Costa Rica to go broke, that money could plant a lot of trees. He laid down the ground rules for buying a car. Four-wheel drive was an obvious must as well as diesel because of the outrageous gas prices. Getting the most out of a gallon of gas was critical. We were only to buy Toyota or Nissan "cuz that's all anyone knows how to fix."

Laura's deliberate stare into my eyes persuaded me to take note of this important information as we walked onto the patio overlooking the vast valley bordering the ocean. We sat at the patio table. "Are you doing some two-year snack nut and Coke Light cleanse?" I asked. Containing almost exclusively dried fruits and nuts, aspartame, and club soda, his truck and kitchen cabinets had a certain convenience store *je ne sais pas.*

"What's that?" he asked, jamming a set of binoculars into his eye sockets. I could hear his fascination in the silence. "Tawny-capped Euphonia," he said excitedly.

By day, Allan lived to explore lands to purchase, develop, and reforest. By night, he poured through thick and convoluted nature books, to the point that he was able to name just about any living creature or plant.

"So where ya been?" I asked. "We've been calling."

"Sorry. Stupid antenna's out," he said, pointing to a metal rod fastened to the flashing bordering his roof.

"You have an antenna for your phone?" I asked.

He explained that the antenna grabbed his weak cell signal and amplified it so that he could actually communicate. "And we've got a brand-new development about twenty-five minutes up the highway that's sucking all my time, so I've been out a lot. Signal's iffy up there, too."

This was the new development that he asked us to help him sell several months prior. I reminded him we he had already seen it.

"Oh yeah, I forgot, but you've really gotta spend some time up there. Over one thousand acres of primary and secondary rainforest with the best views in the area. Wildlife in every direction. Hey, topic change. You never told me where you're living or I would have brought the cat stuff to you."

Laura apologized and explained that we had found the house the last night of our prior trip and became too busy with the move to let everyone know.

I gave him our typical address in Costa Rica. "You go up the first hillside road, pass the hotel, and then there's that compound with barbed wire fences and the big white roofs. Our driveway borders that compound." The Costa Rica address phenomenon was fascinating. In San José, there was a famous *higueron* (banyan) tree in a central square that had been cut down years ago. Now, a legitimate address is, "Five hundred feet northeast of where the old *higueron* tree used to be in Bolivar, San José, Costa Rica." And the amazing thing was that people found you.

Allan smirked. "Guys, you should have asked me first."

"Asked you what?" I replied, apprehensive.

"I think my look said it all," he said.

"Well, having lived in the house firsthand has proven your look accurate," I said. He was right. He knew a lot about the town and could have warned us.

"Welcome to the jungle. Look, this is paradise, but if it wasn't the house, it'd be something else. Why do you think I sit here and read books every chance I get? It's the land of extremes and the unexpected. Adjust to it or perish," he said in earnest.

"Great," Laura said.

"And hey, you probably already know this, but no matter what happens, it's the change. Don't take it out on each other. I don't know what the exact stat is because no one ever took it, but most expat relationships go home in body bags—a lot more than in the States," he said.

We had heard. I asked him why. He really couldn't say but did offer, "I'm sure you've seen the ticas are not all that hard on the eyes."

"Uh, nope, never noticed," I said sarcastically.

"Luckily not as attractive as Laura," Allan said.

"Nice save," Laura smiled.

Allan explained that couples generally came to the coastal areas with good savings because it's hard to find work. With help relatively cheap compared to North America, they hire people to help with the house. "But these gorgeous women roam around the house, one thing leads to another, and next thing you know, the guy is suddenly quite interested in housekeeping. Then you can easily start ripping each other to shreds when things don't work and everything's different in this new place. You start pointing the finger and resenting each other. One thing leads to another, and *adios!*"

He paused, examining our ungrateful looks. "Hey, look. Love or hate it, I give it to you straight," he said.

"Yeah, we love it." I was mordantly grateful. As we prepared for our move, I became fascinated to remember that we had never asked Allan how he came to Costa Rica. Now was the perfect chance to ask.

He reclined in his chair as if to say, "This is going to be a long one."

About twenty years before, he began taking several month-long nature walks and fishing trips to places from Mexico down Central America. It took him a while to discover this area, and the mountains meeting the ocean left him breathless. "Without sounding crass, the prices were a complete joke." He started buying, and luckily for him, the prices had doubled every year for ten years.

"Not bad work if you can get it," I said.

Then Allan reached a point where he had to get out of dentistry. He was a heavy drinker in his younger days. One night, he found himself in a car hurtling out of control at over one hundred miles per hour with three friends. The driver and the two others died. His back was never the same. "And after twenty years of leaning over patients, I'd spend all my nonwork time horizontal. I'd even eat dinner lying down."

"You look fine now," Laura said.

"That's what happens when you call a spade a spade and stop what's not working for you," he said. He talked to his wife and told her his work really couldn't go on. He told her he also had always had the thought of moving to the village in the back of his mind. "If I was going to do something so radical, it seemed like a good time."

She agreed, but he had a house, all its furniture, and a practice to liquidate. "I knew I was doing the right thing, but my head was swimming."

"Yeah," I snickered, "you don't have to tell us."

"Then the next day, I'm mowing the front yard with my back screaming at me, and this guy drives up. I turn off the mower, and the next words out of his mouth were, 'Ever thought of selling your house?'"

"I couldn't believe it. About an hour later, we had a deal—furniture, cars, all of it," he said.

"You're kidding!" Laura exclaimed.

"Oh, it gets better," Allan said. The problem of the dental practice remained. He had had a lunch appointment scheduled with one of his old dental school friends, and he asked Allan, out of the blue, if his practice was for sale. "I hadn't said a word to anyone! I didn't even really know how much I wanted for it!"

"Man, that is a killer story," I said.

"You know, people come here for all kinds of reasons. And the place is pretty quick to let you know if they're right or wrong. The people with the wrong reasons usually don't last more than a year. You'll find that those who stick around all had a rough go of it in the beginning but have stories like mine," he said.

"It's like a horror story in reverse," I said. "If it's meant to be, then the universe gives you positive signs."

"About right," Allan said.

"But now you're telling us we moved into the 'Amityville Horror' house," I said.

"Relax," Allan said. "Nobody died in it. A crew just almost killed themselves building it."

We told Allan we were wearing out our welcome and that we should probably get our cat supplies and move on.

"What the heck did you have in these anyway?" he asked as I loaded the suitcases into the wave pool footbath.

"Cat litter, toys, food, treats, play houses. You know, stuff you get when you have a cat," Laura said.

"You're in the jungle, not on the moon," he said with a devilish smile. "All that's available about forty-five minutes away."

"OK, Allan. Not now," Laura said.

I felt like a complete moron, back-calculating all the wasted baggage fees.

I asked when we could go up and start taking a good look around the development. Laura had allotted herself a couple months for us to get our footing before starting to sell property, but we were both already anxious to see if we could pull in some cash in Costa Rica.

"I'm there every day as long as the sun's up. We've got a nursery and are planting all kinds of stuff. We're also hiking around every day to see where we're going to cut lots and roads," he said.

As eager as we were to get started, we made no commitments, given our life might be more of a start-up than we had anticipated. We bid him farewell and hit the road.

The drive through the dark jungle was exhilarating. Allan's road had no streetlights. The adrenaline rush came from knowing that if you got stuck, it would be blacker than tar outside. What also made the juices flow was the feeling of desolation on some of these patches of road. The only visible sign of life were these seemingly idiotic birds the same color as the road. They lay fully camouflaged and flew away right before being squashed by our tires. Every sight and emotion was so different. It was awesome.

"Don't you feel kind of legitimized by Allan's story about how he got here?" Laura asked.

"You mean because we kind of have a story like his?" I asked. I felt a nod I couldn't see in the dark. "Yeah, sort of. But then there's the whole relationship stat that has got me thinking."

"OK, now stop thinking like that," Laura said. "The worse thing that can happen is for us to lose sight of the fact that no matter what, we're not trapped—thanks to me, by the way." I could hear her proud grin in her voice.

"Yeah, it's like you're reading my mind. I just realized I'm approaching everything like this is it. Do or die. Make or break," I replied.

"Nope. No houses or dental practices sold," she said.

I looked at Laura's face in the reflective glow of the headlights. This raw jungle road in this moment gave the feeling that all we had was each other.

I heard Allan's voice echoing in my head. *Most expat relationships go home in body bags.*

"Well, we came here to fulfill our dreams, and I'm having fun so far like I never thought possible," I said.

But it seemed only a year could tell us whether we would sink or swim.

CHAPTER 9
Turds of Paradise

*"Discovery consists of looking at the same thing as
everyone else and thinking something different."*
Albert Szent-Gyorgyi

October 26, 2006

Our reasons for landing in Pair-o-Dice Village remained—sometimes to
our dismay—elusive. Yet, we did know that coming to such a place would
certainly give us a new outlook on everyday issues and problem-solving. It
didn't take long for nature to swoop in and confirm just that.

One night, I lay awake around 2 a.m. I was getting less and less sleep,
mostly for good reasons. My brain was like an inquisitive action movie each
night. I was enthralled with our new world. Yet I knew the fullness and new-
ness of this thrill couldn't last. After all, we lived in the jungle. Surely, certain realities—already possibly foreshadowed by the FlawedShack—would
soon settle in. Each night, a catalog of questions, rhetorical in that all I could
do was ask them over and over in my head, grew.

*How lucky could we possibly be? Is it luck, though, or are we just a couple that
had the guts to make a decision? Will we be able to take advantage and sit in silence to gain outstanding wisdom, coming out of this experience gurus of our own
existence? Will the unexpected be too much for us? Will we go crazy? Are we crazy*

for coming here in the first place? Does it really matter since most people at home think we're crazy regardless? And what about the people here? Are they crazy, and will we blend in? Surely, we'll need good friends and companionship.

As I pondered, I cursed the sounds of debauchery emanating from our pool. Having gone to grad school in Texas, I had heard of horned frogs. Here, we had horny frogs that became particularly randy on certain nights. The piercing rumpus of *amphibiporn* was shameless, croaking climaxes carrying through the night air.

Whoosh! A wisp of wind suddenly breezed by my face. *Fluttering noise.* Was it an errant gust from the ceiling fan?

Another gust. *What the hell?*

We hadn't yet caved in to open the windows. Had we, our bed would have surely been a scene from *Jumanji*. *Was it something that got in during the day?* We had seen roaches larger than a pack of cigarettes, but this was bigger than an insect.

Adrenaline coursed through my veins. *What could it be?*

Aahh! It touched me! Something grazed my nose. I had no desire to walk through the dark toward a light switch. I strained my eyes to focus as the clouds partially shrouded the moonlight showing through the window above the bed. *Movement! Oh, it's big!* I faintly identified something of impressive velocity the width of a salad plate.

A bird? A big moth? An owl? There it is again! Although I truly couldn't predict her reaction, I was careful not to wake Laura.

Squeak, squeak! Aha! Case solved? Bat?

I had already come to learn this sound during our brief stay in Pair-o-Dice Village. With the sun's first glow each morning, squadrons of bats would squeal and scratch faintly along the narrow space between the timber ceiling and the tin roof, returning from their overnight sortie.

Oddly enough, once I knew it was a bat, I was completely comforted and completely undaunted. What's more, identifying the intruder had solved another riddle. Each morning, there was a wet, lumpy liquid eating varnish from the interior stairs. We'd clean it up every day only to find more the next.

That morning, I looked straight up from the small puddle on the step. *Bingo!* I spotted a missing triangle of ceiling wood directly above. *That's how he got in.*

The simple life in Pair-o-Dice Village made everyone's struggles equal, familiar, and understood. Sharing our curiosities and struggles proved a fantastic way to strike up new acquaintances, as it seemed like we were following scripted rites of passage they had already experienced. I knew from teaching martial arts and being a trainer in corporations that people loved to have people to learn from their prior struggles.

A smile would spread across a new acquaintance's face like crawling ivy when I lamented, "We have no running water."

"Ah, yes. I remember when we first got here we had no water or electricity," they would say with an air of, "You think you have it bad."

On the other hand the, "Oh, well have I got one for you," retorts from those who arrived just five years before made us feel like complete dopes. Despite our occasional shock at its antiquity, the area had, indeed, developed remarkably over the past decade, sprouting quite a few conveniences relative to its primitive history.

What's more, given my dealing with stress by poking fun at it, the locals came to know my sense of humor rather quickly. They seemed to enjoy hearing someone poke fun at their past struggles with a fresh set of eyes, making them receptive to us as newcomers.

We also had our own share of laughter and awe at the creative solutions they had devised to prevail over our parallel circumstances.

"The only people anywhere near Ballena Coast with a long ladder to plug the bat hole are the two DirecTV men," Adèle said. "You will see their truck in the village. Ask them to bring the ladder by one day when they are working on a house."

How did all these houses get built with no ladders? "And they'll just bring it?" I asked.

"Oh, yes," Adèle said, almost surprised I would ask.

"For free?" I asked.

"Yes?" Her inflection questioned my skepticism.

"Why?" I asked.

"Why not?" she countered. "People help people here. That is how it is." I was relieved that there might be a great support structure for those days when paradise might not be enough to conquer our adversity.

Then there was the random lady at the hardware store. "You need a boa constrictor!" she said nonchalantly.

I uttered a hesitant giggle, wary of offending her.

"You're serious, aren't you?" Laura said.

"Oh, yes. Those bats are just a nuisance, and that guano really starts to smell after a while. I had the same problem for months until someone recommended I get a boa, and there was no turning back. No more bats. It's wonderful."

Child, you be in denial! You need yo-self a reptile!

"I don't understand," I said.

"In the roof. You put the boa in the roof." She acted like I was the village idiot.

"OK, you just literally snake a boa into the roof, and it stays up there, feasting at will?" I asked incredulously.

"Yep! In fact, a tree boa lives in the ceiling where we do yoga in the village. Every morning right before final mediation, it slithers down the ceiling fan and watches us. He's so cute," she said, crinkling her nose as if speaking of a tiny, precious kitten. I wondered if they had another ceiling fan and if it would support my weight as I watched the village females contorting their spandex-laden bodies each morning.

I then pondered the boa constrictor adoption process. *Are there local shelters for neglected and beaten boas? What is the adoption fee? Will the shelter do a home suitability visit? Do boas need shots?*

"OK, yes. The boa is a fantastic idea. I'll look into it," I said, lying as fervently as possible.

And then we met Georgia, possibly the town's most active socialite. A delightful, perky fifty-something, we spotted her regularly cruising at scandalous speeds on her ATV between social calls at people's houses.

"Oh, my dogs take care of those," she said about the bats as we shared beverages while facing the beautiful hilly view on her back deck.

Georgia had five street dogs that she had adopted, which attracted Laura immediately. That said, Laura was clearly horrified that she allowed the dogs to handle these winged carriers of disease.

"Oh, everyone has the bats here," she assured Laura. "After a while, you just learn to live with them. They're not hurting anyone.

"Just last night, they woke me up three times," she said, a madly excited look on her face. "They just lay them at my feet and nudge me. And so Georgia has to get up and throw them away," she said with a playful smile.

This clearly was barely a nuisance for her—like the occasional trip to the potty.

We drove from Georgia's house to a local restaurant for dinner. "The people are getting more and more interesting by the second," Laura said.

"I'm fascinated by their approaches to everything," I said. "And it makes sense. We're in a new place, and even our reactions are changing. I mean a bat flies over my face, and do I go to the computer to look up an exterminator? No. It didn't even cross my mind because it's out of the question. I immediately started to think of ways I would solve the problem myself because, like everything else, it's really the only way," I said.

"I like how the problems make us go out and socialize with people for answers," Laura said. Laura was always the one to pick up the phone and call a friend with a problem while I went straight to Google.

"Well, I gotta tell you. I have no idea when we're going to see that ladder around town," I said. "We might have bats for a while."

"I really don't care, personally, except for the cats getting sick. That can't happen." She sighed. "But there's only so much we can control, and it seems like that's not much," she said.

And how appropriate that really might have been. After all, everyone told us we were bat shit for coming to the village. It was only appropriate we wade in some for a while.

CHAPTER 10
Pair of Aces

Walking with a friend in the dark is better than walking
alone in the light.
Hellen Keller

November 3, 2006

"How do you know all these people already?" was a question we heard often.

Laura thrived on community. "The deal-breaker for me will be not finding meaningful relationships," Laura wrote in one of our 10/10s before we arrived.

Of course, she didn't need to tell me this. In fact, I completely transformed my somewhat reclusive tendencies rather spontaneously in deference for our relationship from the day we started dating.

As we met people, we found it difficult to hit it off and make a connection. We may have had an overly aggressive expectation of doing so.

Yet, during these visits, we came to know the characteristics of the best candidate for living on the Ballena Coast. The most important trait was the ability to self-entertain.

Reading between the lines, we knew this meant that solitude was a common state in the village. Life during rainy season deadened after 4 p.m., when the water dumped from the skies with abandon and the power was often intermittent. DirecTV was a true blessing for us in the morning, with the unexpected surprise of access to all the major cable channels we were so used to. But in the evening, the water slammed into the aluminum roof with such force, Laura and I could have used megaphones to communicate. Music, a true passion of mine, was similarly inaudible, as was our beloved DirecTV. The pool was unswimmable since it doubled as a frog brothel after hours, and the storms often brought savage lightning.

Going outside onto the covered porch was also a nonstarter, with battalions of bugs arriving as soon as we turned lights on and the bats went out. I surely enjoyed examining the bugs that remained during the day, with huge rhinoceros beetles, beautifully patterned moths with the diameter of tea saucers, and praying mantis commonly present.

I did have one nemesis, however—the giant queen grasshopper. This intercontinental ballistic menace hurtled itself through the air with the size, girth, and mass of a Chicago hot dog—including bun and toppings. Sometimes five in number on the porch, they'd initiate maneuvers whenever I opened the door, with a rapid wing beat sounding like baseball cards in bike spokes. Word had it that once one landed on you, it anchored its barbed legs with such tenacity that you'd rip flesh by pulling it off. Prying it off with a beer bottle was apparently your only solution.

Every time the suicide shower tripped the breaker or a load of laundry was done, it was like I was throwing out the trash as a kid again. I would duck to avoid the ninjas in the trees and a colony of mummies and zombies ready to take me as their underground hostage. Now, I was running even faster through the back porch, punching myself in the head and flailing my arms about as if I had some neurological disorder. In elementary school I always finished dead last in the Presidential Physical Fitness sprints. Had I had a great queen grasshopper chasing me, I would have been invited to the White House for Fiddle Faddle and Coke with Ronald Reagan.

Insects aside, also fueling the boredom was a lack of reading material. The only bookstore carrying English titles within an hour's radius had five paperbacks—*Shogun* and four Crichton. And so there was little to do at night but retire at eight or nine or brave the rains to go out to dinner.

75

With all of these factors at play, avid fishermen, readers who had found a system to get material from the States or village friends, meditators, hikers, and artists seemed happiest in the jungle. And unfortunately, others who could not self-entertain turned to drugs and alcohol.

Beer was a buck or so. Most people had their fridges stocked with Pilsen, Imperial, and Bavaria, and these beers flowed freely during visits.

While never to the point of dysfunction, I had already had a history with drinking. My grad school roommate, who killed a half bottle of Jack Daniels daily, told me, "I have never seen an American drink as much as you do." I was shocked. Since then I had gone through a process of pulling back, but I still enjoyed having a drink in my hand quite a little bit.

Now, in Pair-o-Dice Village, life was laid-back, consequences were few, and I, in turn, wanted more and more to drink after only a few weeks.

We had already met amazingly happy village people with amazing stories. But we knew we needed deep friendships with people our age and weren't having much success. The Ballena Coast drew people who had finished out their retirement plans and wanted to exist sanely on a fixed income. That meant that the average age of Pair-o-Dice Village's gringo inhabitants was at least twenty years greater than ours.

The isolation and tranquility started to grate on us rather quickly. It seemed that out of frustration, we might turn to behaviors destructive to ourselves and each other in short order. Despite all the other abrupt life changes we were experiencing, we realized this lack of relationship was the single biggest risk to Pair-o-Dice Village being our long-term home.

And then one morning, "I met somebody!" Laura barged into the living room, a cloud of glee in tow. I had stayed home that morning in deliberate isolated study of our pool and plumbing, which was presenting itself the way I remembered calculus. It confused me more and more the more I looked at it.

Laura's morning excursion to the Internet café was the first time either of us had left the FlawedShack alone since my excursion for water on day one.

Laura said her name was Indira, and she was about our age. "She's into fitness, and she and her husband love to travel. She sounds like us. She laughs like us. She seems to have a good ambitious head on her shoulders." We were invited to their house for lunch.

I recognized full-well this was the time to drop everything. Without a word, I ran inside to put on decent clothes. Minutes later, we turned onto the same road on which we had completed our "U" tour of Pair-o-Dice Village a few days prior. This time, we headed the opposite direction toward Indira's house.

After a few minutes of incredibly steep, verdant ups and downs and sharp turns, we came upon residential gates. Another flat was lined with thick jungle wildflowers, then more gates, a few more brutal inclines, and after fifteen minutes of driving . . . .

"Oh, my God!!" Laura exclaimed.

"Whoa!" I exclaimed reflexively.

The wall of vegetation opened up as if we had crossed a gateway into a painting.

We marveled at the scenery to our right—one of the most breathtaking views ever. We were elevated about 500 feet with a straight view of Panama, the famed Caño Island scuba paradise, and the Corcovado National Park wildlife reserve. The white breaking surf gave the shore an awe-inspiring massage as far as the eye could see.

"How did we miss this view the other day?" I asked.

"Easy. We were facing the opposite direction," Laura replied.

Duh.

We came upon a small house. "This is it!"

"Here? This is their view? My God, they're the only ones on this ridge!" I said.

I immediately found myself soaked in envy of two people to whom I had never said a word.

An attractive Asian woman maybe five to ten years our elder came out of the only house on this ridge that could have easily held ten—beaming from ear to ear.

She greeted Laura with the enthusiasm of a long-lost sister and thanked us for coming.

"Oh, it's our pleasure! What a gorgeous view!" Laura said.

She clearly heard the comment but didn't acknowledge it—maybe out of modesty.

"You must be Glen! I'm Indira," she said with a big hug. "Hal!" she called over to a building site next door.

"Yeah!" a male voice called back.

"They're here!" she said. A tall German-looking fellow approached us along the steep slope below the ridge side road.

"Look! People like us!" Indira said excitedly, extending both hands toward us like she was presenting him with a Land Rover for Christmas.

"Howdy! I'm Hal." He shook my hand, and I could immediately tell this guy was as smooth and calm as eighty-year-old cognac.

Since they were building the house they would soon be living in, Indira proposed we sit outside their neighboring *casita,* which they lived in now but would soon be a guesthouse. "So that's your property too?" I asked.

They had found that it was more convenient to be on-site to monitor construction themselves. I'm sure they were right, with all the horror stories I had already heard. Once building was complete, they'd move out of the guesthouse and rent it out.

We sat around a primitive table on the patio and chatted. The atmosphere at Hal and Indira's was visibly chaotic. They had jammed a family of three into the small *casita.* There were building materials and personal effects strewn everywhere. But there was something about this place on which I couldn't put my finger. Was it the environment? Was it our new acquaintances? Whatever the reason and despite the chaos of being on a construction site, I was experiencing a calmness not yet felt since our arrival.

Our ears were focused on every engrossing word they used to recount their life experiences while our eyes were trained unwaveringly on that view. At times, I left my seat while talking to walk off the terrace onto the grass to get a better perspective.

"This is just amazing. As a photographer, they taught me to use my feet instead of zoom lenses to get the best angle for a shot. You happened to score the best permanent angle of the coast with this view," I said.

"Aaaaa!" I jumped back as if an elephant had just relieved itself on my sandal.

With a better vantage point, Laura and our new friends burst into hysterics.

"Hey, Chicago!" Hal exclaimed. "Better watch it. We call that one Bruiser!"

I watched as the chicken that had just stepped on my toe put some spring in its step, jarred from my reaction.

Nako, their adorable three-year-old daughter with equal traces of Indira's Japanese and Hal's German features, rode by on the dog, Sake. All muscle, this Rhodesian ridgeback was like a four-legged Pepsi machine. Nako smacked its hindquarters like a jockey as she uttered an innocent juvenile laugh. Sake obliged but was less than thrilled to play her steed.

I watched as Nako chased chickens, fiddled with a burlap sack lying on the ground, and arranged rocks on the edge of the patio. She seemed to have the time of her life with little around to amuse her.

And living in these surroundings, she was clearly intrepid and fearless. Indira and Hal had clearly nurtured this attitude. My heart sat in my throat as she oscillated along the edge of the steep slope over the rainforest over a hundred feet below. Indira and Hal continued to chat, nonchalantly vigilant.

The four of us interrupted our conversation to strip clothes from the line as the monsoons began their early afternoon maneuvers. "I can't wait to put a washer/dryer in the new house," Indira said. "It takes three days to dry a towel in the jungle humidity—that is if I can keep the clothes out of the rain."

"So how did you find this land?" I had to ask.

Hal leaned back gently with a proud smile. He seemed so cool and comfortable with himself and his surroundings, a piano could have fallen on his head, but he'd have felt sorry for the piano.

Fourteen years prior, they hiked north from Panama eighty miles, not knowing at all where they were going to stop. "It was kind of an open-ended trip. This place was really primitive back then," he said.

"As opposed to . . .?" I asked as he cut me off knowingly.

"Aw, man. You're in Vegas compared to then! It was just horse trails and cow pastures. There was no *Costanera* highway *or* pavement—period."

Today, Pair-o-Dice Village was blessed to sit along the *Costanera*, Highway 34. One stretch of it north of us to Puntarenas was the most dreaded major dirt road in Costa Rica. Luckily for us, the section in the Ballena Coast was the nicest and newest paved highway in Costa Rica.

Word in the village was that the *Costanera* was built to afford access to the site of a major eco-friendly electrical project that had been planned. The Costa Rican government cut a deal with the Indians who lived on the site and intended to relocate them. And then the moment the beautiful *Costanera* had been nearly built, the Indians renegotiated to preserve ownership of their land. There was no electrical farm to show for it all, but we had this precious rarity on which to drive daily.

Hal explained that real estate really wasn't the reason for their trip at all. But when they got to the Ballena Coast and saw the mountains towering over the sea, they just had to take a look. "We grabbed a couple donkeys and machetes, and hacked our way."

I thought about making the steep fifteen-minute uphill drive we had just made without a road being cleared, much less without a car to drive it.

When they came upon the land they were sitting on, they just had to have it, and it was sold to them on the spot by a tico farmer. They hiked a bit farther and were presented with another piece that had a waterfall. "Again, that land just had to be ours as well, but we didn't have all the savings to buy both, so this was the time to call home for some financing. It seemed like the opportunity of a lifetime at the time, and that turned out to be so true."

If only I could have been here then.

"And then you came to live on it . . . ."

Eighteen months prior, they had put everything in the back of their pickup truck, and Hal and his father drove while Indira and Nako flew from Silver Springs, Nevada.

I was quickly frightened by the thought. "You must have had a heck of a time getting down here. Any trouble with border guards or people trying to take your stuff?" I asked.

Hal leaned back again and looked at me with a friendly smile that said "aw, newbies."

"Naaah. Look, people think stuff is gonna happen to them anywhere they go that's new to them. I mean, people in the roughest parts of New York and Chicago are afraid of driving through Mexico and Central America. Truth is they probably are at way higher statistical risk right at home. And why are they scared? Because of the media up there spoon-feeding them the truth"—he made quote signs in the air around truth— "about places they've never seen. Life happens and is all a gift, not a curse. The world is for all of us to explore. Danger is usually perception, not reality."

Laura expressed her marvel at the life philosophy and asked how they could have come to the Ballena Coast with such a young daughter. We were both on the edge of our seats.

He graced her with another look that said, "Oh, that's another good story."

"We've been nomads in strange lands for a long time. It began in my second year of college. I got dumped by this girl, and my head came unscrewed. I suddenly realized I didn't know who I was or what I wanted to be. I dropped out and went home to my parents—just showed up on the doorstep. I remember sitting in my dad's office. He's a preacher. I told him I needed some time to figure out what I wanted out of life. He leaned back in his chair," *so that's where he gets it from,* "and said, 'Well, that's fine son, but one thing is for sure—you're not going to figure it out sitting around here.'"

"He gave me a plane ticket to London and just enough traveler's checks to live for a few days. And off I went, terrified but knowing full well that when my dad said stuff like that, that was it."

Hal had his wallet and passport stolen at a hostel his first night in London. He didn't have the traveler's check numbers and no ID.

"I was broke and stranded. I called my dad and asked him what I should do. He said, 'Well, I know one thing that I told you before. You're not hanging around here. So you'll figure it out, right? Good-bye, son.' Click."

"So what did you do?" I asked, almost whimpering in sympathy.

"Well, my only big decision was whether I would hitchhike with my left thumb or my right. I just hooked up with random bands of travelers," he said with calm pride. "In Western and Eastern Europe, through the Middle East and North Africa. I camped in tents and did odd jobs."

"My travel groups were always in flux. People joined and left all the time," he reminisced fondly.

"Oh, those friendships never go away," Laura said. "You must have so many people you're close with all over the world. What a dream!"

Hal leaned back again with another *Gotcha. You don't know me yet* smile. "You'd think, wouldn't you? That's the thing with me."

Yes, I'm sure there's only one thing with you.

"I love people. I enjoy the hell out of good quality conversations and friendships, and when I'm with you and like you, I engage with you fully without reservation."

"And if he doesn't like you, you'll know that too," Indira said with a wily smirk.

"Aw, I'm not *that* bad. I've always given people more than enough rope to hang themselves. I don't take crap, but I think if I end up knocking you on your ass, you'll look back and see I gave you more than enough warning, and you deserved it."

"Well, I sure do look forward to that, then," I said, faking unease.

Hal giggled, smiling and clearly proud of his honest revelations. "And once you're out of sight, you're out of mind. And I don't mean anything by it. It's just who I am. I'm just experiencing too much right now to worry about what happened then. To force myself to be something I'm not is an injustice to everyone. So, in truth," he said focusing on Laura, "I don't really know where many of those people are now.

"So I've had an interesting life. I was fired on by warlords in a camp in Kenya and saw the town leaders swinging dead from posts that same morning. I was sentenced to lashings by a puppet court on a cargo ship on the Nile."

"Holy crap!" Laura said.

"Oh, relax. I got out of it by citing some made-up international law and fictitious diplomatic consequences to the ship's judge. Thank God I had studied some law. I became a night court judge in Nevada after answering a classified ad. That's usually how I got my jobs. None of them ever were related to the last one. I'd just open the paper and say, 'What do I want to do this year?' I won't work at anything unless I can learn from it. I learn pretty quickly, so I'll never do the same thing for more than a year or so. I owe a lot to my dad. Throw a kid in the fire, and some pretty amazing stuff comes out."

"You're making me want to go home and burn our passports and money," I said.

Indira made an impromptu lunch of rice mixed with peas and olive oil that was simpler than the salt of the Earth. *Rice and peas. At home, I'd be wondering how the heck someone could serve us rice and peas.* But there was something about eating simple food in the middle of the jungle—like simplicity was the jungle's magic seasoning. It tasted amazing.

"Well, I guess we should be going," I said after four hours flew by with gale force.

"You got a busy day?" Hal said sarcastically.

"Well, you have a house to build," I said.

"I do unless awesome people show up. That's what tomorrow's for," he said.

"Awesome people being you, in case you're wondering," Indira said.

We almost blushed.

Laura asked when they planned to move in.

"When it's done," Hal said. "But I don't want to be sitting here in three years blaming your awesomeness for never having finished. *Then,* I'd have to knock you on your ass."

According to Hal it was too hard to accomplish anything on the Ballena Coast to hold other people accountable for your own lack of progress. "I guarantee you, if you weren't here, I wouldn't get half the things done I had planned. So don't tell people you have to leave. It's going to annoy them because they know you're going out there to likely accomplish nothing. They'd rather have your company."

So we settled in to hear more about Indira and how she and Hal met. Indira told us they met at the embassy in Cairo over a decade prior. They were both waiting in line to get visas. Their travel groups united, and they started backpacking all over North Africa and the Middle East together.

I didn't want the afternoon to end, but my inner convictions still were looking to free them of the burden. "You want to stay for dinner?" Indira asked.

Jeez! Don't these people have lives? I pondered this for a moment. Of course, the irony was that they did. It was the very reason they were able to commit an entire afternoon and evening to two strangers.

Despite our relative confidence that all parties involved would have enjoyed themselves, our North American reservations got the best of us, and we excused ourselves.

"What the hell is that?" Hal asked, pointing to the jalopy in the driveway.

"We call it the wave pool footbath," I said. "See?" I pointed to the floorboards replenished from the fresh rains. I also explained it was a one-month rental.

Hal and Indira shook their heads and laughed. "Hey! We have a relatively new Mitsubishi Montero. You're free to borrow it as long as you want."

Did I get hit in the head by a coconut and forget these two were our best friends for years?

"That is so generous. I'm sure you know we'll be considering your offer," Laura said as she jokingly kicked some water out of the Geo Tracker.

We drove back down the steep, dark dirt road toward the highway.

"Wahooo! Yes! Yes! Yes!" Laura said, her hands smacking raindrops outside the window. We agreed they were perfect, and all we wanted to do was turn back.

"And it really feels like they want us to. Like every day," I said. "You know, I always wanted a friendship that had an open-door policy. If you show up, and it's time for a meal, I put a spatula in your hand, and we cook together. If I have some yard work to do, I give you a rake, and we finish it twice as fast—together. This feels like that, and it's only been one day!"

"But unfortunately, Indira really discouraged me a bit at the same time," Laura said. Indira had met everyone up and down the coast, and there was only one other woman she felt she could really be friends with. "They have a lot of social interactions, but she warned me that on a deep friendship level, she and I might be all we've got. But, I love her. This is a great start!"

Laura and I were two stiff corporate types compared to them—or at least we had been. Meanwhile, Hal and Indira had backpacked and hitchhiked third-world countries for who knows how long. They had built a forest cabin in Japan, basically on their own, from trees felled by their own hands. And yet, we got along screamingly.

"If someone said they had the perfect person for you to meet in the States and then gave you the description of those two back there, you'd check their temperature," I told Laura.

"No kidding," Laura said faintly.

I heard a sniffle and turned to see tears. "I feel like a big weight has been taken off me," she said. "I know you don't understand it. You can sit and watch two or three movies in a row or analyze stocks on your computer all day." She paused. A few years into a marriage and 10/10s, and I was learning the value of keeping quiet. "It's just suffocating," she said.

"What is?" I asked.

"Friends are like the air I breathe." She paused again. "You know those Gatorade commercials where the athletes sweat and sweat and, then they drink the Gatorade. Then the colored stuff seeps out of their pores? Well, the before scene is me without friends, and the after scene is me after a good, close conversation."

"Well, if that's what it feels like, I can relate," I said.

"Thank God we met them. I was so scared. Still am a bit. I mean there's hardly anyone around," she said.

"I once saw a documentary that said that howler monkeys are great listeners," I replied.

"Shut up," she said with a smirk and grabbed my hand.

As usual, the rains wreaked havoc on the roof that evening as we went to

Two

bed early out of boredom. But we no longer feared solitude. Our most critical uncertainty seemed to have been removed in one day's time. Tonight, we knew we had a pair of aces only twenty minutes away.

CHAPTER 11
West Coast Choppers

Life has meaning only if one barters it day by day for
something other than itself.
Antoine de Saint-Exupery

November 6, 2006

Aside from a little interior decorating courtesy of the bats, we had arrived from the States to a fairly well-kempt home. Unfortunately, a thick layer of dust accumulated on everything every four days or so. The villagers told us it was from the bats up above. I wanted no further information, given I regularly slept with my mouth open. Despite our need to continuously clean, the thought of hiring a housekeeper—a common theme among gringos—for the FlawedShack seemed like a sumo wrestler hiring a weight-loss coach.

We did, however, turn our attention to the garden. The locals would say, "Neglect things, especially during rainy season, and the jungle will win."

I pictured a vine two feet in girth snatching Laura from a deep sleep in the second-story bedroom. It would juggle her playfully as a Venus flytrap the size of a helipad waited below flapping its fuzzy lips hungrily.

Flora gone wild also meant more critters, snakes, and other such craziness.

Allan's wife referred us to a gardening duo of brothers called Los Desemparados. They arrived for their first *chapea* at 6 a.m. on a dirt bike with two weed whackers and an astonishing amount of gear.

I knew at first sight from their outward zeal that I'd be quite fond of them. Nonetheless, I was apprehensive to forge our first work relationship with locals. We were guests in their country and had to leave a positive impression of North Americans. Although we didn't regularly slurp our soup, we weren't confident in our abilities to ingratiate ourselves into this particular culture.

As we had been told ticos would, Los Desemparados sat with us for an hour or so to initiate a personal relationship before beginning work. Their first dumbfounding factoid was that until recently, they had traveled between jobs on foot, braving the steepness from the bottom of the hill.

They got their nickname from their home province of Desemparados. They told us they lived in public housing outside town. They were thrilled to have all this *chapea* work—sometimes driving their two-wheel shed between ten jobs per day.

After these entertaining introductions were complete, they joked with us through the windows like the Chaplin brothers as they worked. They seemed almost psychotic with happiness and had more early morning energy than two whirling dervishes in a centrifuge. One of them even chased the other around the lawn with a weed whacker for having spilled the last of the water Laura delivered to them regularly. The brother being pursued acted out his fear of death for our benefit.

They finished the *chapea* in less than two hours, including trees and everything else that could be bludgeoned with their yard swords. As they dripped with sweat as if they had just finished a good swim, they explained that the average Costa Rican could chop a large tree to bits with just the machete.

Their fee was extremely reasonable relative to North America. Allan's wife had already warned of a fifty percent increase since July. We already knew this was the pace of inflation along the coast.

The impact of the recent influx of expat investment on the affordability of basic necessities, including food, was palpable. But it also financed new houses, cars, and machinery to clean, build, and fix.

I handed them their compensation, and one of them said, "We have so much opportunity that we never had. Luck has brought us you gringos, *gracias a Dios*." The other nodded in enthusiastic agreement. We had noticed that ticos ended most sentences dealing with food, weather, and topics of survival by thanking God.

As they prepared to leave, we also were making our daily escape from the heat of the FlawedShack. On the porch, we came upon a mighty tropical arrangement of fruits and flowers poking from of a vase they had found on the property.

We ran to the driveway to thank them only to find an enormous stalk of bananas they had cut from one of our trees and hung at the front of the FlawedShack.

"*Bananos* grow like weeds here," one brother said. "No one can possibly eat it all. So we ticos hang them so everyone can eat, *gracias Dios*."

Of course, this fruit distribution method worked well in the tico villages where tiny houses lined the populated streets, and the public traveled on foot. Up here in these secluded gringo hills, I knew they'd be a fruit fly buffet in a handful of days.

Still, the few we were able to eat may have been the best we ever tasted, and we were touched by the gesture, thrilled with our first extended encounter with the tico culture.

CHAPTER 12
Placid Rain

*For in the true nature of things, if we rightly consider, every green
tree is far more glorious than if it were made of gold and silver.*
Martin Luther

November 11, 2006

Every experience still felt brand new—for better and occasionally for worse.
But I *was* astonished to notice that like everything else of repeated exposure, the sights of Pair-o-Dice Village, while still glorious, were becoming
more commonplace.

Adèle had mentioned a rainforest preserve close on the *Costanera*. "I can't
believe you did not go yet!" she said.

We made the thirty-minute drive north.

"Hey, it looks like a dog today!" Laura said, referring to a tree that over
the past few weeks had morphed from the shape of a bird to a camel to a
dog. We had a little game to predict what it would look like next.

As we arrived at the reception area of the preserve, I realized how much I
enjoyed living in the middle of a tourist attraction as a newcomer. "You live
in a paradise and don't take things for granted," I said.

Because Laura had grown up in Hawaii and I in South Florida, we were
aware of people's tendencies to neglect their local tourist attractions. Of

course, these tendencies were shameful because tourists were attracted to attractions because they were attractive.

On this day, we were giddy tourists, buying our tickets and waiting eagerly for our tour to commence. After several minutes, a heavy-set twenty-something tico rattled off various work-related statements to his colleagues in perfect tico Spanish as he approached us. Then he turned to our group and said in pristine English, "Hi, my name is DavEED, but you can call me David."

I pointed out in Spanish that he had no accent, sounding like he could be my brother. David was born in North Carolina, but his parents had moved to the States from just down the road. He pointed south. He always thought that this region of Costa Rica was the most beautiful, and after having visited several times, he decided to move. His parents didn't come with him, "which is unusual. Most ticos who go to the U.S. make money for a while and come back. They all go to North Carolina and New Jersey."

"What's in North Carolina and New Jersey?" someone in our group asked.

"Ticos," he said. "I don't know why."

A couple of his helpers—these with accents—came out of a shed with harnesses and helmets, which they fastened to our persons in short order. He introduced them as co-guides. All of them spoke English at various levels.

He asked who had been zip-lining before. Laura and I raised our hands along with a couple next to us. He took us through the instructions and safety lecture under an open-air gazebo. Once finished with introductions, we hiked a trail through secondary rainforest and then east across the highway to the primary rainforest.

Once someone understood the difference between primary and secondary rainforest, they were fairly easy to tell apart. *Primary* refers to untouched, pristine forest in its original condition. Basically, it's forest that humans haven't messed with or cleared in any way. It has a full ceiling canopy of leaves overhead and several layers of understory. Because of the thickness of the vegetation above, the ground floor is generally bear of vines, grass, or shrubs because of the lack of light.

As we stood in front of a large and wide mound that was basically an underground city, David explained the average leafcutter ant could carry a leaf fifty times its body weight. It looked like someone had buried something the shape of, but longer than, a coffin between two trees. I marveled that had I been on my own, I surely would have passed it unknowingly.

David asked us if we saw green around the mound, clearly a leading question. Once satisfied that we had failed to find any, he explained that the ants had carried all the green leaves, grass, and other vegetation underground where it would ferment and turn into their food source. "If you look around," he pointed to the earth more than several feet away from the mound, "you'll see where they journeyed to get more greenery." Minipaths spread out from the periphery of the mound like muddy veins.

"Here's a soldier." He carefully picked up an ant much larger than the few others we had spotted entering and exiting the mound between his fingers. "Now I don't know how many times his body weight *he* can carry, but," he put a stick at least a foot long up to its mouth and let go, "it's a lot." The stick hung from its claw-like jaws for at least a minute.

We proceeded to climb a number of switchbacks skyward toward the canopy of the rainforest. On the way, we encountered another trail of ants—this time black—climbing over one another in a nervous frenzy. They had big heads and, like the soldier leaf cutter, claws for jaws.

"How many of you think there are too many bugs in Costa Rica?" David asked. Everyone's hands went up. "Well, we do too, sometimes. We ticos look forward to these ants coming through our houses every once in a while. It's hard to predict when they come, but when they do, they invade for a few hours and turn everything in their path to skeletons. After they leave, your house will be completely insect-free. Of course you'll want to leave because they will run the place over."

"What about cats?" Laura asked me under her breath nervously.

"We can ask in the village," I said.

"Woohooo. Yeah!" Laura exclaimed several minutes later as she shot across the rainforest seventy-five yards on a steel cable. She was suspended from her harness and hooked onto a wheel.

My heart pounded as I did the same, spying the dense leafy forest floor and whitewater of brooks trickling one hundred feet below. Laura had been deathly afraid of heights until we had zip-lined on a previous trip to Costa Rica. "I don't know what happened. The jungle was just so magnificent, and I was concentrating so much on the trees to see the next animal that I completely forgot!" she said.

When we got to the next zip line, our guide went first and hung inverted in his harness, over one hundred feet above the jungle floor, smiling. *I guess he's not afraid of heights.*

Laura then hooked in, smiled at me, and lifted her feet off the ground which propelled her across the rainforest canyon. And then she inverted. I jumped up and down and cheered. *This is amazing. What could have gotten into her head?*

And then it began to pour, which was exactly the appropriate addition to our rainforest experience. It literally felt right as rain. We travelled fourteen lines for three hours, spying three sloths, packs of white-faced capuchin monkeys, and several *cusingas*. These were toucans we had not yet seen with greenish yellow beaks and thick bright red and yellow stripes across their chests.

"I so needed that," Laura said as we advanced down the *Costanera* toward home, completely soaked. "Being one with nature like that creates an overwhelming sense of freedom. I felt like a bird. There was so much energy in me, as usual here, but it was the right type."

"Why? When do you have the wrong type?" I said.

"I don't know what it is, but we're in this tranquil setting that people would die to escape and relax in, and I've always got this nervous feeling. I can't calm myself."

I had my struggles with the FlawedShack and getting all our logistics in order, but I didn't feel the same. "What's bothering you?" I asked. This was news to me.

"I have all these thoughts going through my head like, "Will people respect me here because I really don't do anything? Will the cats be safe, and will I get stranded in the jungle with a blowout if I go out by myself?" The last thing I want is to be this helpless woman without an identity. Plus this stomach thing is getting to me," she said.

Since our third day in Pair-o-Dice Village, Laura had contracted a stomach bug that a doctor had already been unsuccessful at diagnosing. It seemed to be getting worse, and she was beginning to lose weight noticeably. I detected pain on her face several times during our zip-lining experience.

I wanted to say something about what I saw, but I kept my mouth shut. I had a penchant for tragic thinking at times. I also seemed to take in information about the body over the course of my life like a sponge. These two factors combined often resulted in my scaring the living crap out of her with the potential scenarios that I might vocalize—not so much like a husband, but rather the Grim Reaper. "Well, if it's nature that calms you, I guess you came to the right place, huh? We just have to get out and explore it more."

"Yeah, I guess," she said.

That didn't sound good. Laura wasn't a complainer. She shrugged things off and moved forward until things got to an untenable level.

As the whirlpool footbath climbed our hill, I truly hoped I had just experienced a rare moment of weakness. If not, we might be in for a tough period to come.

CHAPTER 13
The Lunch That Wouldn't Die

"There is one fault that I must find
With the twentieth century,
And I'll put it in a couple of words:
Too adventury.
What I'd like would be some nice dull monotony,
If anyone's gotony."
Ogden Nash, American Poet

November 13, 2006

"OK, OK, wait," Hal said, almost falling from his chair—catching his breath and wiping the tears from his eyes. "Start over. Take it slow. I'll understand this time."

"All right. I led large corporate projects," I said.

"What do you mean projects?" he asked.

Dammit! These words mean nothing here and have no friggin' synonyms! "Software development and implementation, restructurings, behavioral change management, large-scale learning and development . . . ."

Ugh, he's laughing again. But I had to admit to myself it was pretty hilarious that Hal could not comprehend one word of the language I used with people at home every day.

"You're never going to get it," I said.

He waited for an elusive break in laughter. "You could repeat that every day for the rest of my life, and I wouldn't understand or be able to repeat a word of it. From what I'm hearing, it sounds like you B.S.'ed for a living," he said.

"If we had about a half hour, I'm sure I could make you understand. I've been sparing you, but if you want . . . ."

"And my family and I are eternally grateful. I've got a machete here. Wouldn't want me to take my own life now, would you?" he said, smiling at Indira.

Indira gave a smirk that said, "I love you, smartass."

"And do I dare ask what *you* did?" He turned his attention to Laura.

"I was global head of operations for a large advertising agency, and before that I worked in a mergers and acquisitions department. Before that I was global sales director for a multi-national brand consultancy. I started as a manager in change management at one of the big five consulting firms . . . You're impossible," Laura said, laughing.

"Oh, God, people. You two must have the kinkiest pillow talk!" Hal said, eyes welling up anew.

As funny as it was, I thought back to Laura's comment about wanting people to respect her. Our work achievements and stature had always been something that people honored and related to. These guys couldn't even begin to cobble together what it was! *How will we impress anybody if they can't understand?* I found myself experiencing Laura's same insecurities.

"How about this? Another beer anyone?" Hal asked.

We gladly grabbed another libation to complement our post-lunch conversation, now four hours old. Beer in Costa Rica tasted so darned good, and it was just plain blond beer.

As the rainy season sun was setting over the ocean, a calamitous storm ambushed us from over the mountaintop behind us. Heavy rain was a daily way of life, but this storm was special—water hammering down almost as if the gods were inverting a swimming pool from on high.

We all jolted periodically in our seats as lightning bolts exploded on the terrain around us.

"Frig, man! I swear to you I haven't seen water like this since Hurricane Andrew," I said. But the wind was oddly still. After twenty minutes of rain, the lights flickered. *One more flicker. OK, a third. That's it. There they go.* For reasons no one could explain, if the lights flickered three times, the electricity in Pair-o-Dice Village *always* went out. We were now in complete blackness, especially since Hal preferred to knock out the street light in front of their house.

"The Boys have got to be so scared," Laura said.

We excused ourselves and made a run for the wave pool footbath to tend to the cats who were home alone. The car had taken a fresh three inches of water, aggressively steaming its interior still hot from the afternoon sun. "Full service! It's a footbath *and* a sauna," I said.

Nearly blinded, we drove the steep mountain to the little cement bridge from which we would turn out onto the *Costanera*. I stopped suddenly, sliding sideways in the mud. Several feet of water were raging over the river's banks, around both sides of the bridge, and across the road at frightening speed.

"Oh, boy," I said.

We were stuck. As the sky continued its aquatic assault, we sat with headlights on, monitoring the raging water.

My eyes drifted haphazardly across the gas gauge. We had only enough to get home, and with the power out, the gas pumps would be out on the other side of the bridge.

I immediately cut the engine, emptying the air of all activity except the hammering rain. The blackness of night was filled with the sterile smell of the humid jungle. Now *this* was desolate.

Laura and I assessed the situation. "We probably can't make it back up the hill to Indira and Hal's," I said. With the hills so steep, I estimated we might be averaging eight miles to the gallon. I flashed the headlights every five minutes to check the intense water flow. It wasn't letting up.

"OK, let's start mentally adjusting to being here for a while. A romantic evening in the Rainy Seasons Spa and Resort wave pool footbath, now with sauna service," I said.

Laura's face was invisible, but her laugh conveyed her appreciation for my humor in this intense moment. Admittedly, we were both a bit freaked out. I flashed the headlights more and more frequently as our anxiety levels rose. "Hey, what's that?" Laura asked, peering through the reflective rain curtain.

"It's some big animal," I hypothesized openly, taking in an indistinct full silhouette.

"Somebody's there!" Laura exclaimed.

I squinted. He was thin and young—on the bridge, the water raging around him.

"I don't like this," Laura said with concern. "I can't see a centimeter in front of my face, and the nearest house is a four-minute drive back there." I couldn't see her finger but knew it was pointed in the opposite direction.

She was right. If we left the lights on, we might not be able to start the car again. Without them, I'd have no idea if he were standing right outside my door.

After another five minutes, I turned the lights on. He stood on one of the bridge sides, examining the rushing current now starting to encroach upon his space. He looked toward the car.

"A normal person would have looked over right away. This feels psycho," I said. Then I caught myself. "Sorry, I'm not helping."

"No, you're right," Laura said with eyes trained on the subject.

He evaluated his situation for a few more minutes. Then he decisively removed his boots, put them in his backpack, and leapt off the bridge.

"Oh, my God! Oh, my God! Where did he go?" I asked.

"I don't know!" Laura shot back anxiously.

"I think he went in the drink!" I exclaimed uneasily.

"Why would he do that?" Laura asked.

"I don't know, but that water's really booking," I said. Had we come to such a strange place that someone could jump off a mere four-foot bridge and decisively end his life? If so, he surely did it in a place where he wouldn't make a spectacle of it.

"Whoa! Wait! What's that?" Laura pointed.

Through the rain curtain, *movement!* With poor visibility, we didn't see he had leapt toward us into the roadside gutter. Another raging torrent was washing over him with great force back toward the bottom of the road.

"That's going to push him right into the river!" I said.

He managed to roll out of the rapids and walk uphill toward us, a machete visible across his back, unexceptional in the jungle, but a sight I was not yet used to.

He exited the glow of the headlights as he passed our bumper on my side of the car. He suddenly pressed his face against the window, pointing downward for me to open it. I reluctantly complied.

Jungle. Pitch-black. Complete seclusion. Hadn't seen a soul in forty-five minutes. It didn't matter if I opened the door or not. If he wanted to do something, it was game on. I hoped the machete had been sharpened. A mauling with the elongated butter knife variety would have been lengthy and painful.

"*Buenas, Señor! Soy Luìz!*" he greeted me cheerfully. "I am going to a construction site," he said, pointing uphill behind us. The little dome light of the mobile spa showed affirmation in Laura's eyes as I turned to her for an opinion. *So a rental car agent is a threat, but now this dude with the two-foot scalpel wins the level-headed stranger of the year award?*

"OK, get in," I said, actually feeling suddenly excited to help a citizen of our host country. Nonetheless, my logical side, of which I was famous for not having, was cautioning me.

I pointed the footbath up the hill, and off we went just as the not so negligible detail of an empty fuel tank suddenly came back to mind. And so now, after watching an impassable river for some time, we were transporting a total stranger with the little fuel we had left. The fact that we had decided not to bear children suddenly seemed a great service to our fellow man.

OK, any day now, Luiz. It's not like I have a fuel truck following me.

"*Ya llegamos*," Luiz indicated after a ten-minute climb. He waved us thank you and walked away into the darkness.

I stared at the gas gauge, hoping I could move it upward through telekinesis.

"Which way?" I asked Laura.

"How far to Indira and Hal's?"

"Eh, about five minutes," I said. Truthfully, given the nondescript landmarks of "bunch of green" everywhere, I wasn't sure. "We're pointing toward their house."

"Good enough for me," Laura said.

I reserved prayer for bedtime—that is, except in that moment. The prospect of wandering the jungle roads in what we'd classify as a downpour—except downpours are lighter—without a flashlight was completely unnerving.

"You think we're going to make it?" Laura asked.

"I'll tell you when we get there," I said, squeezing the wheel with both hands like I was hanging from it over a cliff.

"Hey!" Hal came out as we approached the *casita*.

"If you came back to explain your jobs again, I have a round of golf with Bill Gates tomorrow and need my rest," he said.

"Ha, ha," I said.

"So what? Forget something?" he asked.

"Yeah, a raft and some oars. The bridge down there is drowned in the rapids. We have no gas," I said.

"So why'd you come back up here?" he asked.

"Explaining our jobs might take less time," I said.

"I'm going to chalk this up as newbie bad luck, but you were closer to your house," he said.

Thank you Major Moot!

The speed at which I had become close to this couple in a few weeks notwithstanding, I wasn't quite ready to show Hal how stupid I felt. "Next topic, please," I said.

"Take the Montero," he said. "I was going to recommend you buy it anyway. Notice I have yet to call this thing you drive a car."

We thanked him and headed to the bottom of the hill in the swapped vehicle, which felt like a sleigh over hills of marshmallow compared with the wave pool footbath. Trickle, trickle, drip, drip. A perfectly good bridge, and there wasn't even a tico committing aerial hari-kari into the rapids below.

"You've gotta be . . .," I said.

"Where'd all the water go?" Laura asked.

It was amazing. The rain had lightened for only fifteen minutes, and already the river had gone back to normal. We crossed the bridge and headed for the FlawedShack, where the cats looked like a pack of pit bulls had chased them around the house while we were away. Laura brought them into the bed. I couldn't tell if she did it to quell their anxiety or hers.

"Well, that was the perfect beginning to some axe-murderer scene," I said. "In the middle of the pitch-black jungle with no one around but a stranger with a big blade."

Laura laughed. "Thanks. I really hadn't looked at it that way," she said.

"But if you look at it objectively, it's just the darkness with no one around that makes us *feel* scared, but we were probably safer on that road with Luíz and his machete than anywhere in Chicago."

"Just like Hal said," Laura said. "And there we are, pretty friggin' scared, and it was just like when we would come on vacation here. Something goes totally wrong, and everything just fixes itself like magic."

But to me it felt a little different now. As tourists, we could always go home. These odd occurrences were all elements of our permanent—at least for a year—environment.

The other thing that made me really realize how far from our zone we had wandered was Hal being so baffled into hysterics by our corporate lives. He couldn't even begin to relate to what I was describing, but he was a master of the environment in the village because he's been around for a while. "You want to relate to people and have them respect you, and talking about the corporate stuff is one of the ways I know how," I said to Laura.

"Funny you should say that. I told myself today that I should stop trying to impress people with my own life and learn about theirs," Laura said.

Two

"Yeah, my knee-jerk reaction is that it's so stupid that we care what they say. And then I find myself caring," I replied.

"Seems like we're going to have to start to learn to value what the people around here do." Laura sighed in the dark as a bat fluttered by.

CHAPTER 14
This Will Be an Awesome Chapter, If God Wants It

"I am so clever that sometimes I don't understand a single word of what I am saying."
Oscar Wilde

November 25, 2006

Our dear friend Jack would be visiting from the States in less than two weeks, and there was no way we could fit his girlfriend Dora and him in a whirlpool footbath or something similar. We also were dealing with trying to get a cheaper working cell phone because the phone we currently were renting was for tourists—at tourist prices. A cell phone was was our only way to communicate with anyone but each other. It was time to go back to San José and acquire our own phones and vehicle.

"It's better if you get a driver while in the capital," a local army veteran suggested. "The streets are just too confusing, and going there for the first time, you don't know the names of any of the stores and where to go to get what. Plus, there's a way of doing things here that you're going to have to learn. But I know a guy."

Everyone else in the village knew Ricardo too. When uncovered, news of a hot commodity hit the village like a biological weapon. "I think Ricardo is basically making his living driving our neighbors around the capital," another woman told us.

Ricardo had the typical late-model, tiny, red Hyundai taxi, which—along with their orange brethren—swarmed San José like ladybugs. He was a dynamo—always on the phone and eager to help cross an errand off your list. Yet the juxtaposition of his energy and the visual wear and tear of his fifteen-hour workdays made his age difficult to estimate.

Laura and I showed him our errand list—including many on behalf of fellow villagers back on the Pacific Coast. "Oh, you need phones first," Ricardo said.

He took us to the huge Multiplaza mall in Escazú. Like any other suburban mall in North America, it was bi-level, indoor, and air conditioned. It had a movie theater and anchor stores at its corners and retailers from Gucci to KFC between them.

Upon entrance to the mall, I sprung to action, leaving Laura with Ricardo. Over the past month, Laura's hope for verbal self-sufficiency had waned. She had taken several years of Spanish and was even a teaching assistant in college. She had also studied aggressively for four months before our arrival in Costa Rica. However, she had also lived in Rome for a year in college, and this was posing the unexpected problem of the two languages getting mixed up. "What's your name?" is "*¿Como te llamas?*" But Laura's version was "*Como ti chiami?*" I jokingly called this Italo-Spanish mix tortilla minestrone. She was frustrated and embarrassed, even though, with all the expats in the coastal areas, knowledge of Spanish was not a true necessity, it did make life much easier. What's more, Allan's Pacific-view lots would likely be sold to English-speaking foreigners, so she could work without it as well.

Nonetheless, the last thing Laura ever wanted was to be reliant on me. My wedding vows were primarily about her independence. But having also established that my Italian cultural background blended better with the predispositions of the locals, things seemed to be going in the opposite direction.

"Hi. I'd like to buy two cell phones," I said to a clerk in an electronics store. "Something really simple. All we want to do is talk on it." The kind fellow in his early twenties presented exactly what I needed.

"¿*Cuánto sale?*" I asked.

They cost 150,000 *colones* each—about three hundred dollars. Basic staples were often less than half the price we were used to in North America, but any manufactured import was more than double. As such, setting up our lives—the purpose of the months of October and November—was to be the expensive part. I agreed for lack of any choice.

He pulled one phone out of its box and asked for my GSM card, holding out his palm expectantly. I regretfully informed him I didn't have one. He regretfully informed me that my phone number was in the GSM card, and he didn't sell them. I asked where I could buy one.

"*No hay,*" he said. There are none—pronounced "no I."

"There are none where?" I asked. "In the mall?"

"No, I'm sorry. In all of Costa Rica," he said in an aggrieved tone. "Maybe they'll be available *en ocho dias si dios quiere.*" In eight days if God wants it.

There's that "God wants it" thing again! I eyed the crucifix on his necklace.

I told him I'd return November 22, dreading the commitment I just made but trying to courteously mirror his enthusiasm.

There were two routes to San José from Pair-o-Dice Village. Both took six to ten hours, depending on traffic, mud slides, or road work. The way we had come was the two-lane Pan American Highway. It was a series of hairpin switchbacks, at one point ascending into the freezing cold clouds, and affording access to every vehicle from bicycle to semi. It was aptly named Cerro de la Muerte, The Mountain of Death. The other was via the all-dirt section of Highway 34, the *Costanera*, up the coast through Jacó and Manuel Antonio to Puntarenas. I was not eager to make the difficult trip again so soon.

My new friend at the cell phone counter told me GSM cards were only available at ICE. The Instituto Costarricense de Electricidad was the government-run phone and electric company.

"I should check there in eight days?"

"Well, actually no one knows when they will be available," he reaffirmed.

This isn't working. Time to go to the next store. Two storefronts down, I now knew to ask about the cards before phones. "GSM cards will be available *en quince dias si dios quiere*," my new acquaintance said.

Now fifteen days? And the God thing again?

I now cautiously committed to return November 29.

He confirmed that only ICE would have them and that I should call first. "No one knows when they will be available."

Given the inconsistent information, I decided to opinion shop. *Maybe there really are cards here.* But, it got worse. The consensus, while difficult to estimate, was January.

"Ricardo, I've got a problem here." Laura stood next to Ricardo as I walked up, anticipating the outcome.

"I know," Ricardo said. "No cards, right?"

"You knew that?" I asked, angered.

Ricardo grinned, angering me more. "Yes, my friend."

"Why didn't you tell me? I just spent a half hour doing donuts with these guys," I said, deliberately trying to maintain a humorous air to mask my frustration.

"You were eating at the store?" he asked.

"Never mind. Just an expression," I said.

"OK. I'm sorry Don Glen, but gringos always want a phone. I would tell them there are no lines, but they don't believe me. They get upset and think I'm dumb or lazy, but it's the reality. Now, I let you find out on your own. It's better. You're in a new place. I lived in New Jersey for years. This is not New Jersey," Ricardo said. "You will need to get used to it."

"OK, Ricardo, but I'm different from your other gringo clients," I said, tapping into my inner Engine that Could. "I am leaving in five days with a cell phone. So what do we do?"

"I'll call some friends," he said. "You go eat."

"No, can we invite you to lunch?" I asked. Selfishly, I really wanted to clear up these eight days vs. fifteen days and "if God wants it" curiosities before I choked on my own foot in another interaction.

"No, my friend. It's OK. I'll try to find you a phone. You eat."

"OK," I said reluctantly.

As she murdered a slice of Papa John's and I tore through a Burger King Whopper, Laura resolved not to come back to San José just for cell phones. We would need a list of reasons to brave the distance and danger of the drive.

This was quite a statement from her. Laura's primary life source was interpersonal communication, and the only possibility of that at the Flawed-Shack was via cell phone on the edge of the pool deck.

After lunch, we found Ricardo standing against a railing, looking like we had asked him to walk our dog, and he had lost it.

"So?" I asked, genuinely optimistic despite his dejected look. Ricardo struck us as a guy who got stuff done. He was eager and capable and would surely help us navigate this new maze.

"I call all my friends. The lines always run out, so they buy many cards and sell them for profit," he said.

"Ah, capitalism. And?" I asked.

"So sorry. There's nothing," he said.

"Can you call others?" Laura asked.

He looked down pensively. "Yes. I let you know."

I used our trip to the pool supply store—the location of our next errands—to settle the curiosities created at the MultiPlaza. "Ricardo, they told me at the mall that I could get a phone line in eight days and fifteen days, but the same people said they might not be available for months or at all."

"What do you mean?" Ricardo asked. *What do you mean what do I mean?*

"Eight days and two months are not the same," I said.

"Oh, oh!" he said. "Eight days is not eight days, my friend!" he chuckled. *Oh, of course not!* "It's almost impossible to know when things like this will happen in Costa Rica. If we say a week, you would come back in a week, and we wouldn't have your card. That would disappoint you," Ricardo said.

"But if you say eight days, I'll come back in eight days," I said.

"You can't. If someone tells you one or two weeks, you can come back. But we use the expressions eight days, fifteen days, and twenty-two to tell you we don't know for sure," Ricardo said. "And I'll tell you this truth because I see gringos have a difficult time—*mañana* is maybe tomorrow, but maybe later," he said.

"Good to know," I said, rubbing my forehead.

"Eight days is maybe a week, probably longer, but less than two weeks," he said.

He continued. "*Quince dias* means fifteen days, but we think maybe two weeks—"

"But probably longer," Laura interjected.

"Aha! Yes Miss Laura!" he said happily.

"Let me guess," I said. "One of them said *veintidos dias,* and that is three weeks, maybe longer."

Ricardo belly laughed.

"Oh, no. Someone said that? You are too logical, my friend," he said in a cautionary tone. "No, twenty-two days means you will never get it."

"*Never* get it?" I asked.

"Yes. Twenty-two is for a special purpose," he said.

"What purpose?" I asked.

"I will tell you twenty-two when you have offended me, and I don't want to help you," he said. "You will not hear it much because you are nice people."

"Well, I did once at the mall," I said.

"Ah, that guy was probably stupid," he replied.

"Thank you, Ricardo," Laura said. In an odd way I understood how it worked but not why it was so complicated or how I had offended the guy at the mall.

"Why don't they just tell me no?" I asked.

"Why would they do that?" he asked, obviously shocked at the question. "Then they'd offend you. They can't offend you."

Laura, the queen of straight shooting, looked like a skunk had just aimed its spray directly up her right nostril, and then she broke down laughing.

"OK, one last thing," I said. "You say *si dios quiere,* because you . . ."

". . . don't want to offend you [me]," he and I said in stereo.

"*Poora Viiiida, mae,*" Ricardo continued. "We live in a beautiful country with beautiful people. There is no place for anger and fighting."

"What did you just say? *Pura Vida* who?" I asked.

He smiled in the rearview mirror. "*Mae,*" he said. "It's like the word 'dude' in your country. I like you two very much, and your Spanish is very good. I don't usually use that word with gringo customers."

"Thank you, Ricardo," Laura said. We looked at each other, very proud to have made a friend.

We proceeded with our errands throughout the day. Laura and I proudly reminisced about our productivity—minus cell phones—over dinner.

"I feel like I need to get a book on the culture," I said.

"No," Laura said. "Ricardo was right to throw us in the deep end of the pool."

"Us or me?" I asked.

"Right." She pulled the rice and beans off her fork with her teeth with a devilish grin.

"I did a lot of thinking today," I said, "and I think I understand it all a little. Did you see Ricardo's face when I asked him about eight days versus two months? It was like telling him I had just discovered wind."

"Of course, because the eight days and two months are what he knows," Laura said.

"So you're with me on this." Laura and I exchanged our understanding. In the States, when we were not sure when something would happen, we'd say, "Could be a week, could be two months. I don't know." When someone was a complete mope, and you didn't want to help them, you'd say, "You're a jerk, and go pound sand." Eight days or twenty-two days and *si dios quiere* were just the way Costa Ricans knew to say the exact same thing.

We weren't hung up on what the people really meant. We were really stuck on what the words themselves meant to *us*. "And frankly, my initial reaction was that these people were trying to screw me," I said.

"Me too. But they're being as honest as we'd be, but we perceive it as dishonest because we're taking what they're saying literally, for what it would mean back home," Laura said. I agreed.

"So if what you're saying is true, then we have no problem," she continued. "We know the lingo now and what they mean instead of focusing on what it sounds like to us."

We both seemed to feel better, having hopefully figured out a key cultural nuance.

"Now one thing. No sex until I talk to Ricardo again," I said.

"Why?" Laura said with a smile.

"Well, I know both our mothers probably pray every night that you'll get pregnant, so God wants it. And who knows if babies are born in nine, fifteen, or twenty-two months here?"

CHAPTER 15
Driving Miss Crazy

*"To know how to free oneself is nothing; the arduous thing
is to know what to do with one's freedom."*
Andre Gide

November 26, 2006

While Ricardo attempted to solve our phone issue, we turned our sights to our other urgency—cars. We had known for a very long time this was to be our largest source of stress. Our mission was to find a workable solution that wouldn't kill us financially and psychologically.

The astronomical import taxes made every vehicle leaps and bounds more expensive than in the States. What's more, the roads around Pair-o-Dice Village were legendary for reducing every suspension to peanut brittle. "I buy four sets of parts at the beginning of each year and get my suspension rebuilt, every quarter," an acquaintance with a rather new Toyota pickup said. "That way, I'm fairly comfortable everything will work, and I won't get stranded."

Getting a car fixed was also tricky. "Find a good mechanic, ask him what he knows how to fix, and buy that," some friends in San José advised.

Despite the adversity, our commitment to buying two vehicles continued. Laura valued her independence dearly. Neither of us wanted to be tied to the other all the time. We wanted to preserve our independent daily lives.

A significant portion of our financial picture in Costa Rica would hopefully be from my continued successes with investments in the stock market. That said, Laura shouldn't have to sit at an intermittentnet café—at this point a legitimate pun—while she could be selling property or doing something with friends.

Nonetheless, the reality was that getting ourselves off the ground professionally was going to take longer than we originally thought. Laura's stomach upsets were getting worse, and our entire life change was more monumental than we had assumed. Regardless, this year had to be a trial as close to reality as we could muster, and that required two cars.

We experienced sticker shock everywhere we looked around Pair-o-Dice Village for a bucket of bolts. It seemed that we had an almost unsolvable puzzle. Everything new was budget-prohibitive and would plummet in value on the local roads. Anything old would be a permanent fixture at the mechanic's.

Ricardo had put me on the phone with his recommended mechanic friend, Carlos. "Toyotas and Nissans are best," which we knew, "but they're too expensive because everyone wants them," he said. I had seen several classified ads for Mitsubishi Monteros. "Oh, those are *buen carros*," he said.

On day four, after much milling and hand-wringing, we found the rotten crabapple of our eye, a 1989 large black Mitsubishi Montero.

It had more of an intimidating look than either of us fancied—big and black with dark tinted windows and grey leather interior. But, despite its age, it did seem to be in amazing shape.

"This first one will be yours," I said. I just wanted Laura to be secure that her side of the equation was solved.

From the moment price was settled, the buying process was terrifying. Ricardo called the mechanic, Carlos, who showed up immediately and took us on a test drive once around the block—flooring it once and braking abruptly.

Pulling back into the lot, he said, *"Es un muy buen carro."*

I asked the Truck Whisperer to give a quick look underneath. After no more than a thirty-second examination, he said it needed new tires but reassured me it was *"un buen carro."* A lawyer appeared and signed papers with Laura while the car-lot owner and I went to the bank and transferred a rather horrifying sum into his account.

In the meantime, I had no idea if the transaction with the lawyer back at the lot went through. I marveled and retched internally at the speed of the transaction. Our money was gone with nothing for me to show for it but a yellow bank receipt as long as a hippo's cummerbund.

"I didn't understand much," Laura said upon my return. "Please read it over." I understood precious little of the two-page contract she handed me.

Carlos said he'd change the tires and have the Montero back to our hotel for our return to Pair-o-Dice Village the next day.

"What proof do we have that we own that car?" I asked the lawyer as Carlos drove off.

"That," he said, pointing to the contract in my hand. "You will get title in the national registry in two months."

I looked at Ricardo in distress. *"Pooora Viiiida, mae!"* he said.

"Wow!" Laura said, obviously understanding.

"I hope we're not Pura Screweda. OK, so cell phone status," I said as we drove away in the red ladybug taxi. He had told me he made a few calls while I was at the bank.

"My niece has a line," he said. "We'll go to her school now. My sister is a teacher there. We can talk to them and get it for you."

"Go Ricardo!" Laura exclaimed as I realized we had just resigned ourselves to getting only one phone for now.

We pulled up to the school with the usual wrought iron bars on the windows and around it. Uniformed students—all students wore uniforms in Costa Rica—trickled out of it as the day apparently ended.

"Shorts," Ricardo said, pointing toward my mid-section. "Not allowed in Costa Rican schools."

The principal kindly bounced me from the premises. I didn't mind since I was breaking the rules.

Ricardo's niece then exited the school. *"Hola tio."* She greeted her uncle.

"This is Glen and Laura. They want to buy your cell phone line," Ricardo said in Spanish.

She looked uneasy and in no way excited. "I thought he said she was OK with this," I said to Laura under my breath.

"We have to talk to Mom." I wasn't sure if she thought I spoke Spanish and didn't care what I heard.

Ricardo put his arm around her. "Oh, don't get Mom. Let's talk," he said. He scooted her away.

They spoke feverishly off to the side, with arms waving and scornful sneers.

Ricardo returned to us clearly forlorn. "She thought you wanted to buy the phone, not the line. There are no lines, so they are getting more valuable to her," Ricardo continued.

Ricardo made one more plea as his niece walked back into the school. "You're thirteen years old! Why do you need a phone line? Sell it, and get a new one in two months for a quarter of what they paid for it!"

"Um, ehem! We're standing right here!" I thought as he yelled across the street.

"I'm going to get Mom," she yelled back with a nervous look.

She reappeared shortly thereafter, flanked by Mom, who was visibly none too happy with Ricardo or us. In short, the mom said no, Ricardo started strong-arming Mom, Mom said no, more strong-arming, and Mom gave him a glare that could have permanently changed the boiling point of water on Earth.

"It's no problem," I intervened in Spanish. "We have other options. Don't worry." I think all she heard was the "no problem" part.

We headed toward the car defeated but clearly understanding the seller's position. Ricardo walked over to a school security guard. Returning, he said, "He knows where they have lines. Let's go."

After ten blocks of thick traffic, we arrived at Gollo, the Costa Rican version of Best Buy. The company's mascot was a Foghorn Leghorn knockoff declaring the company slogan *"El gallo mas gallo,"* meaning "The most rooster rooster." Apparently, in Costa Rica poultry conjured up thoughts of home theater in Rorschach tests.

Lines would be available in fifteen days or April, and we had to go to ICE—not much new.

We had the primitive but so tasty *olla de carne* at a restaurant where we were the only foreigners, which we preferred. It was a large bowl of soup, much like Vietnamese *pho,* but instead of noodles, it had every root vegetable we had ever seen—and some we hadn't—plus corn.

I was beside myself. "We came all the way here to get two cars and a cell phone!" I told Laura. "We *probably* have one car and a bunch of crap in our hotel room, most of which is not ours, and the rest I'm not exactly sure we need."

In four days, we had collected stacks of canned and dry goods, beer and wine, plastic shelving, furniture, and pool supplies, just to name a few. It was absurd, but we—and half of Pair-o-Dice Village—were equipped, by God!

"We can't keep making random trips here every week in the off chance that a GSM card shows up. We need progress—and fast!" I said.

"Glen, at some point we have to face certain realities. We never realized how hard this car and phone thing would be," she said. "Maybe we just re-rent a phone. And of course, after what we've learned, one car is our reality."

"OK, for one thing, did you know Ricardo told me that it costs only twenty dollars a month to have a phone here? We're paying six hundred percent the going rate! And we said having two cars was going to be a pain, but we needed to simulate our true life to really make an educated decision about living here!" I said.

"Well, I think real life is going to be one car," Laura said.

"We talked about how we couldn't live the rest of our lives together full-time!" I said. "You'd dread that!"

"We are not buying a second car!" Her volume increased with every syllable as she winced and grabbed her stomach.

"But . . . ."

"And being together all the time would be hell? Well I'm sorry you feel that way!" she said.

"It was your idea, not mine! And remember how Allan and all the others warned about this place tearing relationships apart?" I said.

"Whatever! You want to own two cars in this country? That's surely hell! Or do you want to be in my presence—apparently hell as well! Why don't you save tens of thousands of dollars and choose me? I'm hell free of charge!"

I chalked Laura's outburst up to stress and discomfort and cruised the classifieds for another Montero in the hotel room that night. The next day, we bought a twin, this one green and nineteen years of age.

"For the record, I don't like this," Laura said once the price was established.

Then, repeat prior day's transaction—lawyer and Carlos show up, Carlos opines *"buen carro"* after a three-minute evaluation, money goes bye-bye as Laura handles the paperwork at the seller's house, and Carlos drives off. He said this truck needed more work than the first, and he would drive it back to Pair-o-Dice Village in a week's time.

Ricardo shook his head. "I never saw anything like that before."

"Like what?" I asked.

"You bought two cars in two days!" he said. "No one does that! You are the two craziest gringos I have ever seen!" Laura's sneer burned into the side of my face like a torch.

"But *Poora Viida, mae!* I took care of you, my friends!" He handed me a cellular phone box.

"When did this happen?" I asked.

"I get it for you while you being crazy gringos," he said.

"Whose is it?" I asked.

"My niece," he said.

"Oh, your sister wouldn't be happy if she knew," I said.

"She does, and she's not," Ricardo admitted.

"How much does your niece want?" I asked.

"She's not going to let you buy it," he said. *What?* "You have to rent it."

"How much?" I asked.

"What you think is reasonable?" he countered.

Unprepared. Think fast! A third of what we're paying now should be fine.

"One hundred per month," I said. *Wait! What am I, friggin' stupid?*

116

People attribute the acceleration of global warming since 2006 to higher production of greenhouse gasses. In reality, it's residual heating from the glare Laura gave me when I made that offer that day. Clearly, the mounting anxiety of this new world was turning me into a bumbling idiot.

"OK, my friend. You have a phone," Ricardo said excitedly, having called and hung up before I could propose a modification.

Ricardo's phone immediately rang. *"Sí!"* It's for you *mae*. He handed me his phone. It was Carlos. My heart sunk as I hung up and passed the phone back.

"What?" Laura asked in a concerned tone.

I wished I had found out about a love child from some secret affair. Instead, Carlos said the truck had compression problems. The repair estimate doubled.

Laura redirected her stare out her passenger window, and it instantly melted. "Bad idea," she said calmly.

CHAPTER 16
Violent Lucidity

"Almost anything is easier to get into than out of."
Agnes Allen, American Epigrammist

November 30, 2006

Well past checkout time upon our return, we created a sculpture of a Wal-Mart from our items in the hotel lobby as we awaited delivery of Laura's Montero. We were nervous about driving home in the dark, something we were warned not to do. Carlos arrived three hours late, so nighttime driving was a certainty.

Laura suppressed her anger with what I was sure was forced grace as she drove us home. To avoid traversing San José during rush hour, we took the truck through the coastal dirt, simulating an American pickup truck commercial.

Without the usual visibility of the splendid scenery, I had had few distractions. As I sat in just enough space for my body, with purchases piled floor-to-ceiling, it didn't take long for deep, concerned contemplation to come over me.

How is it possible that a good car is supposed to be so hard to find, and we stumbled upon two beauties? Would a vehicle twenty years old run in the States? I pray that Carlos knows what a buen carro *is.* I mulled the likelihood, and my stomach started turning. *What have I done?*

I grasped for a cause of this anxiety attack, and it didn't take long for me to make sense of it all. I had never admitted to anyone that money was the most important thing in my life, at the exclusion of absolutely all else. Money was happiness. Money was power.

I remembered double-coupon day at the grocery store as a kid. My father would dispense assignments to my sister and me based on a plan he had methodically formulated throughout the week. We had mastered extreme couponing before anyone knew what it was.

We ate out no more than once a month at Burger King, and always with coupons. "OK, so Glen, you take this coupon. Sandy, here's yours," and then my dad would hand my mother hers. Because offers were limited to one per party, we became pros at staggering ourselves in line. Eye contact was forbidden. The erudite BK employees could not know that we were a party! And then three strangers crossing three generations sat together and ate their Whoppers as if they were blood relatives.

"Hey, Dad. My bike lock is jammed," I'd say.

"Put some WD-40 on it."

"Hey, Dad. My Frisbee cracked in half."

"Put a little glue on it."

"Hey, Dad. My bike seat has no more stuffing in it."

"Stuff it with these old sponges and wrap it with duct tape."

"Hey, Dad. I can't get this duct tape off the bike seat."

"WD-40 removes duct tape."

My father could have solved the Middle Eastern crisis with a case each of duct tape, glue, and WD-40.

He was a piano tuner and musician who devoted every second to maximizing his savings toward his kids' education and a comfortable life, and he managed just that.

And he looked at money as a panacea, the same way I did. Whenever other people had problems, he'd say, "Look at John and Judy," who were experiencing some random plight, financial or not, "but we're OK. You have your studies, and we have money."

I carried the baton, measuring life satisfaction via net worth. If accounts were growing, we were happy. Of course, it didn't always work that way, but this was my day-to-day philosophy.

So why was I throwing money overboard to my wife's dismay if it was so important to me to have it? As the miles passed, my thoughts continued to evolve. We were in a beautiful new place, but with new puzzles we had no experience solving.

But these weren't professional puzzles that we used to solve in the business world. These were life puzzles. Could I be trying to solve them without logic or information or creativity, but with the only power I knew?

That's it! Money was the quickest solution I knew, and with so many things coming at us at once, I was reacting reflexively by grabbing my wallet—our wallet. *But in this country, was money valid currency for problem solving? Or was throwing money at problems like blowing on a forest fire?*

Surely it would become painfully evident that we had made a mistake buying two cars, since veterans of our experience told us so. And based on their advice, having two cars wasn't simulating the way we would live life here long-term.

Laura is sick and weakened. She doesn't speak the language. I'm in charge. I don't want to be in charge. No choice. I'm in charge. I'd better develop a strong logical and analytical side—quickly—or we're going to leave this country dead broke! And how do I tell Laura that I realized the mistake I made so soon after buying the cars?

"You're quiet. What are you thinking about?" Laura asked.

"You know, being in a whole new place sure does peel back the layers of the onion and show you your true essence," I said.

"I didn't think of the onion, but I know exactly what you're talking about. What made you think of that?" she asked.

"Well, it's actually kind of embarrassing. Is it OK if I tell you eventually?"

"Sure, but remember to tell me," she said.

I hoped like hell that I'd never have to tell her.

CHAPTER 17
Jack Attack

Don't walk behind me; I may not lead. Don't walk in front of me; I may not follow. Just walk beside me and be my friend.
Albert Camus

December 1, 2006

Jack was already in the country, touring the north before coming to see us. We could barely contain ourselves. We knew he'd have a great time. That was one of the motivators of our life leap—to be able to show our family and friends the magic we had experienced in the country. We hoped they would find their own magic as well.

We also couldn't wait to get an impression of the place through the eyes of someone who knew our world.

"Imagine when they see this view," I said to Laura.

"They're going to flip. I just can't wait for them to get here. I'm going through withdrawals for our really close friendships," Laura said. "Hal and Indira are so wonderful, but I can't reminisce with someone when we have no history."

Jack was our downstairs neighbor in Chicago. A police officer in a precinct which recently had more murders per capita than any other in the States, he was shorter than me at five feet eight inches or so. But Jack played the tough cop role perfectly—a Thai warrior with true teddy-bear tendencies.

Jack was always going to see his "ma," taking care of her above all else. With his father deceased, Jack felt himself a *de facto* head of his immediate and extended family. Whenever someone was in a fix of any sort, Jack dropped everything to save the day at any cost.

He also took care of his friends, showing us the best time in Chicago anyone could have. Always outgoing and cruising around Chicago, he never was short of fun things to do. But knowing how to be tough, he wouldn't be taken advantage of. What lay in the middle of his personas presented to the street and everyone else was a ruthless, goofy joker with a penchant for flowery language—the kind with thorns. In fact, when we first met, he repeatedly turned down my dinner invitations. Finally, he came clean. "Look dude. You're a corporate guy. I'm a copper. I'll come in and gas your guests out of the house with F-bombs before you serve the chateaubriand, OK? Jack's got a mouth on him. Jack can't control it." Jack liked to talk about himself in the third person.

We didn't know Dora, his girlfriend, all that well, but she seemed nice. They'd been together over a year. Jack liked that she had a level head. She seemed a happy person and a joy to be around.

We had talked about the relatively early timing of Jack's visit back in Chicago. We didn't know what state of preparation he'd find us in when he arrived. Nonetheless, we figured this distraction would be therapeutic, regardless of our life situation.

We decided that we would keep it simple and try to accomplish two things before Jack arrived. First, the Richardsons had maintained their stance of Costa Rica being a screen-optional country. As such, I went to get screening at the *Ferreteria No Hay*—pronounced "no I" and translated We Don't Have it Hardware. All the villagers called it this after visiting it daily for a desired item only to hear them say *no hay*. I thought it could have been called the *Ferreteria Mañana* as the item in question would always be available tomorrow.

I apparently got lucky and got screening. After two days huddled in the sills of twelve windows and sweating like a fountain, a gringo with the home improvement skills of Mr. Belvedere had the problem solved. Yet an unforeseen byproduct of the new screens was that they created humming-bird traps.

During the prior week, I had constructed some three-foot gates to wedge into our patio doors so that we could leave them open without the cats getting out. What we found in short order was that the hummingbirds would come in through the open doors and try to exit through the windows. They would plow their slender beaks through the screen and get stuck there. Saving them was as simple as grabbing them with a towel and chucking them into the air off the balcony once again. As bad as I felt for the traumatized birds, it was amazing to see the birds' wonderful iridescent blues, greens, purples, and reds.

The other order of business was to get a *chapea* (chop) of our land. This was a large portion of what we had to show for our crazy adventure, and it had grown out of control.

Los Desemparados doted over the Montero as we drove up the hill so that they could give us a quote for the chop. "This is the nicest car we've ever been in."

I'm sure their beliefs changed when they detected a boiling sound coming from the hood. I was astounded when the local mechanic confirmed the two machete men on a motorbike's diagnosis. Some temporary patching on holes in our radiator had dissolved and broken free.

And then all the air came out of my already limp balloon of hope. "The parts for this car are very expensive if you can find them," he said. "I will have to call a welder to build a radiator." The quote was twice the cost of a brand new one, which was already twice what I would have expected in the States. It also wouldn't be ready until Jack had already left Costa Rica. How would we fulfill our heartfelt promises to show him our new paradise?

For unexplainable reasons, Laura was congenial about the whole matter as we were driven back to the FlawedShack by someone who saw us in front of the mechanic's shop.

We would have been stranded for two days until Jack's arrival were it not for a lift to the grocery store from Adèle. We caught up on our world news, sports, and swimming and hammock time. Those two days were a mental

battleground between gratitude for being able to relax in a jungle resort setting and our inability to relax due to our type A fidgety predispositions.

Then Jack called. He was at the hot springs of Tabacón in north central
Costa Rica, which were nestled under the famous Arenal volcano. "Dude,
Jack's in Paradise! I can't believe it! I'm never going to leave!"

"Glad to hear it, man." A feeling of extreme satisfaction welled up inside me.

"I've been in these hot springs for two hours. Jack's skin is as supple as
a monkey's butt. He, he, he." Jack prided himself on his arsenal of six dis-
tinctive laughs he had developed and incorporated into his life, each one
reserved for a clearly defined meaning.

"All right, but that's quite a statement. If you knew how many monkeys'
butts I've felt over the past month. I'm an expert," I said.

"Hey, don't knock it. It's right here in my Lonely Planet book as one of the
top five things not to miss in Costa Rica," he said.

"That's maybe why the book's called *Lonely Planet*," I said.

"Anyway, tell all the ladies in your town over there that Jack's comin'," he
said.

"Um, Dora's still with you, right?" I asked.

"Oh, yeah. She's right here next to me. But she's here to carry Jack's luggage. He, he, he." Jack always fancied himself a womanizing animal when
the truth was he fawned over and was as loyal to his girlfriends as anyone.

"Hey, if you don't mind, I think we're going to have to need your truck
while you're here," I said.

"You said you had wheels!"

""Quite literally, we may end up having just that," I responded.

"Shit, dude. Doesn't matter. We're going to have a killer time. When
should I leave tomorrow to get to you?" he asked.

He was to take the rough *Costanera* down from the north that we had
taken only a couple of days before. I warned him against nighttime driving
and told him to leave no later than noon.

"All right, kid. Jack's makin' it by tomorrow night. I'm really excited to
see you guys. And I can't wait to drive and see more of the country!"

After hanging up, Laura and I were so satisfied to hear his excitement. Luckily, and for reasons unexplained, this cell phone actually had reception in the house, a monumental victory for us. It rang the next day at five. "OK, dude. We're leaving," Jack said.

"OK, you're going to have to drive at night."

"Yeah, I got carried away, dude. They told me that these springs are heated from the big volcano above. They told me about the minerals in the water. I had to spend some more time here. Jack's skin is like velvet!"

"All right, Mary Kay. You have the e-mail I sent you with the directions a few weeks ago?" I asked.

"Ten-four."

"Follow that, and call us when the dirt road ends and you hit pavement. We'll have dinner ready."

Jack called at ten.

"Kid, you told me to call you when I hit pavement," he said.

"Yep."

"I'm there," he said.

"No, you're not!" He was an hour and a half ahead of schedule.

"Yeah, I am. Once I saw that crazy-ass road, Jack was on a mission to brave that bonsai shit. All right, asshole. How do I get to you?" he said.

"We'll walk down the hill now and get to the village entrance when you do. Just keep driving another twenty-five miles," I said.

Off we went down the jungle road with a couple of flashlights.

With all its sounds and vast blackness, the jungle imposed its dominance and superiority. And yet the same sounds of all the creatures reminded us that we were just a speck in an almost countless list of species.

We made it to the town entrance right as Jack arrived. "Aw, man! I'm so happy to see you guys!" He gave us a big hug.

Laura teared up. "What's wrong? You live in this awesome place!" Jack asked.

"I'm just glad to see a good friend," she said.

I took the wheel and drove us to the FlawedShack.

"Dude, you guys really went backwoods on us!" Jack said as he got out of the Montero he had coincidentally rented. "Ooh, ooh, ooh, ooh, ooh!" He crouched down and scurried around with his knuckles almost dragging, imitating a chimpanzee. Dora looked at us and shook her head in what seemed like a perfect balance of embarrassment for Jack and love for the way he made everyone laugh.

We settled them into the guest apartment and made coffee and drinks in the dining room.

"Here, kid. I brought you a bottle of whiskey. Ever since you went bat shit and told me you were moving here, I knew you'd need it," Jack said.

Laura and I smiled at each other with the bat-shit comment.

He began recounting the drive. "We're driving along, OK, and it starts to get dark like at 4:30! And I'm thinking, 'Shit. I thought we had more daylight!'"

"Yeah, I told you that yesterday, and it's right here in the e-mail," I said.

"Shut up, asshole. I'm telling my story!"

"And the sky opened up and dumped on us. I could barely see. We got to that dirt road, and I told Dora, 'This is the part Glen said is the worst.' And you were right. That road sucks, dude. But I told her, 'Just as sure as I'm irresistible, we're seeing Glen and Laura tonight,' so I nearly floored it.

"And then the first bridge was one lane!" *Oh, yeah, forgot to tell him about that.* "So no big deal, you know? I've been to Thailand, and we have that shit. Then as I'm waiting, I hear all this clanging and see pieces are swinging from it as the cars are going by. Jack got worried. Then I saw this dump truck crossing it so full, all this shit's hanging off the top, and he crossed just fine! So we crossed, but that bridge was one rickety-ass iron son of a bitch, kid."

He spilled whiskey on himself. "Aw, shit, dude. Sorry. You got a napkin? That drive has got Jack all amped up. Jack's got his Crocodile Dundee on, you know?"

I handed him a rag. "Sorry Jack, we don't have any napkins."

"What is this? Land of the Lost? Three words. Back ... woods ... dude. So we get to the next one-lane bridge, and that one's one lane too," he continued.

"They all are, Jack," I said.

"No shit, kid, you're not the one who just drove it, OK?" he said.

"So we waited again, and this tour bus full of people crossed. And Dora said maybe we should stop, and I said, 'Nuh-aw bullshit! We're getting there tonight!' And as we're crossing, water is raging like less than a foot below us. And I was wondering if there was going to be a bridge farther up overrun with water. I gotta tell you, I started to freak, dude. I'd take some crack head who can't shoot straight back home any day of the week, but Jack doesn't drive class-five rapids," he said.

Jack's reaction to the drive and the village took us both by surprise. It took us back to our first visits to Costa Rica. I had never driven in four-wheel drive before, and Laura was white-knuckled as we braved the dirt roads. Now, our last drive from San José wasn't much to write home about. We didn't think twice about the rickety bridges. We crossed rivers like they were nothing.

Here was a cop from the worst precinct in Chicago aghast over things that to us were now commonplace. Our adaptability seemed extraordinary. But maybe this was just how fast humans can adapt when they had the guts to change their lives.

It was also clear that although he had had an adventurous drive, Jack was in love with Costa Rica. As we all turned in for the night, Laura and I gloated in secret.

We were proud.

CHAPTER 18
Anty Inflammatory

It is one of the blessings of old friends
that you can afford to be stupid with them.
Ralph Waldo Emerson

December 4, 2006

"I want their days to be a blend of experiencing our everyday lives and the tourist stuff," Laura said the night before.

"Totally," I said. "We're so close to them that I think they'd really appreciate getting a good impression of what our lives would be like here long-term."

"How ironic that we're trying to do the same thing," I said. "Well, then our priorities should be to take them to meet Hal and Indira, go see Allan's new development, and have a meal at Catharsis."

Laura agreed. All these things had become a centerpiece of our daily existence.

"Damn, kid. This is something!" Jack fixed his gaze out the glass kitchen doors toward the ocean as I made breakfast the next morning, and we waited for the women to awaken. "You really found a spot!"

Music to my ears.

"Like your tourist legs." I pointed to all his red no-see-um bites from the knees down and could sympathize from my own experience. We had mentally prepared ourselves for the bugs that would inflict such itchy, red, unattractive damage to our legs, without us ever seeing one of them—hence the name "no-see-um." We had also brought a case of various repellants from Skin so Soft to Off, but nothing really worked.

"I know. I was scratching all night! But you have them, too, and you're not a tourist!"

"I've kind of gotten used to the itch. Can't believe I did. And I won't have the blotches in a few months. The locals don't have them. Your body becomes resistant to the toxins after a while."

"Hey, don't bullshit the king."

"Swear, man."

"No shit. Well, Jack would take a sting or two for this view."

"Hey, you're going to meet our best friends here today. You'll dig them. Completely out of the ordinary." I fried eggs that had an almost fluorescent orange yolk and equally vibrant taste in Costa Rica.

"Well, they'd have to be to live here," Jack said.

"So you think we're crazy?" I was admittedly a bit insecure about the topic.

"Look, kid. I call 'em like I see 'em. I'll visit whenever you want, but I'm a creature of comfort," he said. "I can't live like a savage." Jack scratched at his legs with a wince.

"Come on! It's not like we moved to Saturn."

"Naw, they don't have views like this on Saturn."

The ladies woke, and we headed up Hal and Indira's hill in the rented Montero. "Wow!" Dora said.

"Hoooolllly shit, dude! You gotta warn me about these things. I'm in stallion shape, but I could have a heart attack," he said as Hal and Indira's view opened up on the ridge.

We were happy to see our friends bonded immediately. I always thought Jack's concerns about scaring our friends off were unfounded. As soon as he met new folks, he seemed to sterilize his conversation topics and word choice.

"Hey, we haven't hiked down to our waterfall yet. Let's take your friends," Hal said as we rinsed glasses in the kitchen.

I looked down at my flip-flops. We hadn't anticipated a hike that day.

Hal was wise to my concern. "Aw come on, man! It's just ants or a spider! You ate corporate sharks for lunch, right?" Hal was the king of exaggerated understatements. He'd overdo his nonchalance at anything that might scare someone else, even if he was unsettled himself.

"It's not just me. I've got three others with me."

"And they're how old?"

"Jack's like five years older than me—"

"That was rhetorical. Point is they're grownups. C'mon man! It's an awesome private waterfall on our own property. Total privacy."

"Well, grownups need to make their own decisions, and they should be informed." I paused and gave in.

"Naah. If they're going to get bitten up, at least let them have a good time until then."

Laura looked down at her flip-flops when told about the hike but didn't utter a word of concern, implicitly agreeing with Hal that the potential benefits outweighed the cost.

After about a hundred yards down the slope of their backyard, we crossed Hal and Indira's property line. We were immediately in secondary rainforest. The hike had officially begun.

Hal and Nako were the only ones in snake boots. This was the local term for galoshes. Their primary function was to protect the ankles and calves from snakes and other creatures rather than a shield from mud and water. Every tico and seasoned gringo who dared hike or do yard work wore snake boots to complement their machetes, especially in the jungle and tall grass. Possibly due to the angst of being in a new life situation—and because we still had big-city fashion predispositions—we still didn't have galoshes. On this hike, I was more concerned about the ants because we were on a somewhat groomed trail. Any snakes should be visible. *But what do I know?*

Hal, machete in hand, Nako, and Sake led the way. Trails of leaf-cutter ants bisected our path. They were clearly visible and not a concern, brandishing their green leafy cargo as if in a miniature Saint Patrick's Day parade. We casually hiked uneventfully for twenty minutes. And then suddenly, I felt like someone had injected my lower legs with forty syringes loaded with habañero pepper juice all at once. I looked down at the perpetrators marching upward toward my midsection.

I bit my lower lip and didn't utter a sound. I knew if Hal knew of my predicament, he'd laugh out loud, making a huge spectacle until I'd have to reveal the reason.

Jesus H. Christ this hurts! I stopped and stood rigid to focus on deep breathing to fend off the pain.

"You OK, Glen?" Laura asked.

"Aw, crap!" Indira wailed—completely out of the blue to everyone but me. I was baffled as we left the house that she wore a pair of Keen sandals, but I didn't comment to maintain my cover. She whacked at her legs with brute force.

"Shit, shit, shit!" Jack replicated Indira's dance.

Nako uttered a faint whimper to my right. Her tiny three-year-old hands picked calmly at ants that had made significant progress up her short legs. *Damn, that kid's tough!*

I looked down at these bulbous-bellied red ants all over the trail. I moved out of eyeshot as my six-legged passengers continued to mutilate my person.

And then Indira yanked her pants right off, darted past me, and sat directly in the shallow running brook ahead of us in nothing but her underwear.

"Jack's droppin' trou!" He followed Indira's lead and sat in front of her in the stream in his underwear.

I took advantage of the distraction to prune the intruders nearing my nether lands, so to speak. Luckily the pain tapered off slightly as the others seemed to be running out of venom. Indira and Jack must have had a fresher batch, however.

Two

"These sons of bitches are still going at me underwater!" Jack said as the rest of us watched.

Another minute or so passed before the chaos subsided. Indira stood up in the translucence of her thin, white, water-soaked panties. Much more was visible than probably should have been. But the look on her face showed first that she was completely aware of her exposure and second, that she would have been comfortable walking down Park Avenue regardless. Jack looked up, turned away immediately, and blushed. Then he turned to Indira and said, "Jesus, put some clothes on! You're embarrassing me."

"Welcome to the jungle, Jack," Indira said standing proudly in front of him.

We all erupted in amusement. Nako strolled by me in her little white snake boots with ants scurrying about her entire body. She casually sat in the stream and folded her arms in her lap, hunching her back as if she just wished we could all finish with our spectacle and move on. She looked up at Indira with her big, charming eyes, and lamented for the first time softly in Japanese.

Dora looked at me. "That's one tough kid."

"We marvel at it every day." It was still hard for me to get the words out as I endured my own lingering but subsiding pain.

Dora detected my irregular manner and scanned me. "They're all over you."

"Ssshhh!" She complied dutifully, shaking her head.

The other victims put their clothes back on, and we completed the outbound portion of our hike. Hal and Indira's property was a nature documentary and pristine primary rainforest. It had creepy vines and a thick green canopy of foliage high above. The temperature was at least ten degrees less, and it was rocky and rugged. Although still a novice, this seemed to me exactly the terrain for snakes, but I kept my thoughts to myself.

The waterfall was maybe only twelve feet tall. It was directly perpendicular to a rocky gorge several yards wide. We all took turns dunking ourselves in the periphery of this refreshing torrent emptying into the gorge. It had such force that I thought if I put myself directly in its center, it would have thrown me up against the opposite rock wall behind me. Hal proved us wrong by driving his body straight into its center, and we all followed suit.

I heard a truck from above. "There's a road up there?"

"Yeah, not far away. Go take a look if you want." Hal pointed up the steep and rocky grade.

I climbed for five minutes—a completely idiotic maneuver in my footwear. I was finding recently that my desire for exploration often trumped my sensibilities. I exited the rainforest and stood exactly where Laura and I had gotten stuck in the wave pool footbath during our first couple of days in Pair-o-Dice Village. Although I couldn't see my friends below, the stream that crossed the curve in the road was falling right on top of them down below.

Having felt it on my own skin, I developed a very tangible appreciation for the velocity of the streams that we were now crossing in our cars with hardly a second thought.

I went back down the hill and told Jack about my discovery up above. "Backwoods, dude. You went back friggin' woods."

"Hey, dude." Jack scratched his legs as he looked at mine. "Something went all-you-can eat on your legs," he said.

You don't know the half of it.

After our hike, we returned to the FlawedShack to prepare for dinner at Catharsis. "Thanks for taking us on that hike. I'm a little bitten up, but I'll never forget that. It was like I was on Survivor!"

In addition to simulating our typical lives, we wanted Jack and Dora to have a good time. We wanted them to experience the same surprises we did as tourists. One was the caliber of the restaurants in a village with such a small population.

Living in Pair-o-Dice Village, we had come to learn the general limited supply of tasty foods outside the restaurants. Beef was too lean and tough. With all the rains, vegetables generally were waterlogged. Fruit grew everywhere, even on our own papaya and banana trees, but they were on our steep backyard, basically inaccessible. The supermarket fruits and vegetables seemed to spend much time in transit, arriving in a suboptimal state. The roadside stands had fresher wares but were often out of the way and out of mind.

Two

We began to have to schedule our conquests for good-tasting groceries. Baker Jean's bread was complete ecstasy and available twice per week. A Mennonite family parked their station wagon at the village entrance each Friday morning and sold sweets out of the trunk. Their cinnamon rolls—*sinammon* rolls, rather—were gooey, nutty, homemade clusters of climax in an aluminum tray. When at anyone's house around the weekend, it was a near certainty these would be served as dessert.

And finally, a truck arrived in front of Catharsis each Thursday to distribute truly flavorful organic vegetables out its back door. Vegetable Pablo would take your written order on a form to be delivered the following week.

In strong contrast to the scarceness of culinary delights were Catharsis and its other formidable competitors. Louis and Françoise, the husband and wife owners, were, like Allan, a positive factor in our move to Costa Rica. We wanted to live in a place where someone could develop as positive a spirit as Françoise. She was jovial like Maria in *The Sound of Music* and emulated her personality in many ways with her sweet French accent. She fluttered about the restaurant like a butterfly, always complimenting people, smiling, and commenting on what a wonderful day it was.

"Oh, the two joys of our town!" Françoise hugged us both tightly as we entered with Jack and Dora. "I'm sorry your usual table will not fit four people."

Aside from Françoise herself, Catharsis was a truly unique experience for a North American. It had once clearly been a typical Costa Rican *soda*. These roadside restaurants often looked like gas stations in their architecture—except with lower roofs. They were basically an enclosed kitchen with an outdoor cement-floored dining area under a flat roof that stood on four columns.

But Catharsis had added mood lighting, decorative wine and liquor bottles, and solid wood tables. It also played a mix of flamenco and classical music to complete a decorative ensemble that filled the air with sophistication not generally available in these desolate areas. And the prices were a steal for a North American.

Laura and I ordered our usual. Each of us would have a mixed green salad with the tenderest organic lettuce you could get in Costa Rica. We'd then each get filet mignon, Laura's with Bourguignon sauce and mine with a spicy mustard cream sauce I could have licked off the underside of a garbage truck.

"This is like velvet!" Jack's big bowl of Vietnamese chicken soup vanished in a flash. "How the hell do they do this in this place? This is better than Chicago!"

"I once asked her what she has to go through to get all the ingredients and to run a place like this. You just have to be obsessed with it," I said. "She spends every blessed morning making all the desserts. She's traveled all over Costa Rica tasting the best meats that she has express-shipped from outside the country. It's really amazing."

As usual, Laura had a decadent brownie à la mode, and Françoise sat with us to talk, pumping me full of Armagnac in the process. Jack told her he was a police officer. Françoise asked him to describe the streets of Chicago, which reminded her of a story. "About three years ago, I was closing the restaurant and cleaning dishes and the bar. I saw something move in the bushes outside the kitchen. Then, there he was," she said.

She paused. Laura bit. "Who?"

"He had a bandana over his face and was holding a gun," she said.

"Right here in the jungle? On this dirt road with all the ginger and the sound of frogs?" Jack asked.

"Yes. His hand was shaking," she said.

"Why the bandana?" I asked. "You couldn't hide yourself in this village if you were invisible."

"I know," she said. "I knew exactly who he was. I recognized the eyes. I asked, 'What do you want?' He said, '*Dinero!*' So I said, 'You must be having a really bad day. I am, too.'"

"You?" I said. "A bad day?"

"Yes, I have them, too." She smiled. "I asked him, 'Why are you doing this? You're in a very small town, and everyone will know you as a thief!' He said he hadn't eaten in three days. So I said, 'How can you not eat surrounded by banana, mango, and papaya? Well, if you're hungry, come in, and I'll make you something.'"

Jack was visibly horrified. "Uh, I know we just met, but you're crazy." Jack pointed a finger in the air for emphasis.

"Bad things can happen in this world, but Louis and I always expect good, and we usually get it. Everything will always be fine. This bandit wouldn't do anything to us," Françoise said. "This isn't New York or Toronto. It's Pair-o-Dice Village. It's Pura Vida! He put the gun in his pocket, and I brought him in the kitchen. I showed him how to make the dish so that he could cook it for himself. We sat and talked while he ate. He never took off the bandana, but he knew I knew who he was. When he left, we gave each other a big hug. It was one of the best days of my life."

Jack came alive. "Françoise, I admire your story. I really do, but what if that guy shot you?"

"He didn't."

"Right. I know. But what if he did? If I ran a restaurant, I don't care if it was in the middle of a Buddhist temple, I'd have a gun. And if someone pointed a gun at me, I'd have laid him out," Jack said.

"Have you ever killed anyone?" I was shocked at Françoise' question and was a tad concerned that Jack was actually Thai Buddhist.

"No, ma'am," Jack said.

"Good, because speaking of Buddhism, the next day, someone would do the same to you! No matter how bad the situation and no matter how scared you are, you can always turn a bad situation into one that helps someone else. And you must do that for your own good. I don't do it because I am a saint. How can I expect to live in a world that takes care of me if I don't take care of it?"

"But you don't understand," Jack said.

"Mr. Jack. We both understand things in different ways. And that's fine. I think if you left your place and lived here, in a year or two, you would feel the same as I do," she said.

Jack looked at me as if to say, "Talk some sense into this woman."

The thought of Françoise with a gun struck me like Edith Bunker with a flamethrower.

"Jack, I totally get you because I came from where you do, but I have to be honest. Now that I think about it, if somebody pointed a gun at me in Pair-o-Dice Village, I'd surely give him money because that's what I'm conditioned to do. Honestly, though, I would never expect him to shoot me," Laura said.

"This is just not that type of place. It's a place of Pura Vida," I said.

"That's it! I lost both of you forever," Jack said.

Laura and I shot each other a concerned look.

"By the way, Françoise, Jack is Thai Buddhist," Laura said.

Jack grabbed his gut. "Yeah, and after this meal, Jack's got the belly to prove it."

CHAPTER 19
You Had Me At "Oh, no!"

A friend is someone who gives you
total freedom to be yourself.
Jim Morrison

OVER THE ENSUING five days, we took Jack and Dora on the best whirlwind tour we could, now on a bit of a mission to convince them of our sanity. "Jack wants one, dude!" He ran back and forth from edge to edge, taking in the views.

The lot was about three hundred fifty feet up with a quarter mile of valley below leading to the ocean. It was basically a peak that had been scalped flat with a building pad large enough for a rather large house and a smaller pad just below it for a two-bedroom guest house. It also had a large mango tree and a towering mountain behind it. Fruit trees were of great importance because they were like an enormous natural bird feeder, not to mention they attracted monkeys and other climbing mammals.

Jack and Dora's tour also included Nauyaca falls, a family-run attraction halfway to San Isidro—the town of 45,000 inhabitants and the closest traffic light. This was an eight-mile horseback ride to a large waterfall where we swam and lunched. We also took them to the beaches that were just a turn away on every part of the *Costanera*.

Wiped out on the last day of Jack's visit, Laura and Dora turned in right after dinner. "I think it's time to finish that bottle of whiskey," Jack said. We sat outside.

"Buddy, I've just gotta ask you again now that you've been here for over a month now. Do you have a better answer for me about why you came here than a story about a Magic Rock and some surfer dude you met for less than a day?" Jack made that tough grimace after a sip of whiskey like in cowboy and cop movies.

Damn! Here we go. "C'mon man. You know there was more to it than that!"

"Yeah, I do. Now that I've seen it, it makes so much more sense to me. But there's still that part of me that worries you two went completely off the deep end. You had so much going—not that you can't turn Pair-o-Dice Village into a huge success—but man, to walk away from all that? I fucked off in school, you know? I didn't go to college. But I did the best with what I had created for myself. I got a maintenance job with Pan Am to travel like a freak on discounts. And then I heard that CPD was looking for recruits, and I grabbed it with two hands. And this is my life plan. I put everything into being a copper. I've got a guaranteed pension. I couldn't walk away from it in a million years. You guys busted ass too. And then one fine day, you come to me and say you are moving to Costa Rica. You know what? First thing I did was run over to Jeremy next door and told him, and we were like what the fuck? I knew you were working hard. But *you*—you're a straightlaced dude. And when I found out it was your idea, all I could think was that you had gone insane from all the work."

"Naah, it's nothing like that."

"I actually want to finish my thought cuz I don't disrespect the idea. But I don't have a lot of people I am close to, especially serious people like you. I mean I'd take a bullet for my partner and close copper friends. But we ride around and call each other jag-offs and go boozin' and chasin' skirt. At some point, you need something stable. For me, that was you two. And now I just don't want to get a call from you sayin' you bought a lion shelter in the Serengeti."

I almost choked on my whiskey with the unexpected laughter. "Now that you put it that way, this isn't too far off from that, is it?"

"No, it's not. In fact, Jack sees the edge of the Earth just over that hill." He pointed. "Don't wander too far, dude."

"Well, look. While you were talking, I realized that I've got to level with you. There isn't really much more to it than what you already know. That's the thing, Jack. I get concerned because coming here for me seemed too natural. When I was here and thought of it, it seemed like riding a bike, and we went back. Rational life took over. But then when we came back here in July and saw it again, I was back on my bike ride. But you know, now that I'm here, I recognized a few more factors that might have brought us here but that I may not have realized at the time. You want to hear them?"

"Please." *Sip, sip.*

In 2002 two friends from our core group in Chicago honored us and three other friends by inviting us to be in their wedding. It took place in Delhi and Chandigarh, India, and was the ritual multi-day celebration. We were dressed in traditional Indian wedding garb for the ceremony.

During one of our days touring India, we had lunch in an outdoor restaurant in Delhi. A palm reader sat in the corner. We had a while before our driver was to return, so one by one, we decided to kill time by getting our palms read.

"Dude! I asked for a more stable reason."

"Look, I'm giving you all I've got. So Abdul, you know Abdul, right?"

"Yeah, you're Paki-Saudi friend."

"That's not what he calls himself, but Abdul, who turned out to be the best man in our wedding, went first. He didn't believe in fortune telling, and he was going to go first so we could all save our time and money."

"Abdul came back shocked, like he had seen a ghost. The palm reader had identified the number, age, and gender of all his siblings and an accident he had just been in, plus countless secrets about his life. All the others had the same reaction. Laura was amazed. I went last, and he shocked me with his true revelations."

"The one key potential inspiration revealed to me was that my most important time would be between the age of thirty-three and thirty-six. This was when I would be starting a very successful writing career. Of course, I was skeptical, but at the same time, given this man's apparent skills, I was excited beyond belief. I knew I was a good writer and wanted nothing more. However, to make it happen, I needed to keep a mind open to all possibilities."

"So you came here to write a book?" Jack was now desperate for logic.

"No, not at all. I mean I have a blog that I'm writing, and people are starting to wait for the next installment with baited breath, but that's it," I said. "And so now I'm thirty-six and in the last year of his prediction, I think now it's a little late, so I don't think I'll miraculously be a writer in the next year. But my mind is surely open. I mean, look at this place."

"Yeah, no shit. But c'mon man. Give me something good to go home with. I've gotta tell Jeremy that you're not as fucked up as he thinks." I had no idea Jeremy thought that but wasn't surprised. His favorite expression was, "Everyone out there's just nuts, man. I don't even want to leave my house." And he was only our age, not old and life-worn.

"OK, here goes another one that probably won't help," I said. "A week ago, we had dinner at the house of a couple who's our age." I pointed toward the ocean and their house. "They mentioned a new documentary we *had* to see called *The Secret* about the Law of Attraction."

"Kid, Jack's mastered the Law of Attraction." He flexed and presented his muscles.

"You've also mastered megalomania." I explained the Law, which says that if you visualize your goals every day and are prepared to act on opportunity, you could have anything. It seemed too contrived, but as they explained it further, I was struck with a meteoric revelation. Every night before bed for the prior three years, I had envisioned Laura and me living in a house overlooking the ocean. Once we had committed to the move, life took over, and I discontinued the visualizations.

"I think it worked, Jack."

Two

"God dammit! I'm just going to have to tell Jeremy you two are fuckin' Fruity Pebbles. But look. Your reasons are fucked up and weird, but I told you I get it somewhat," Jack said.

"So the people here—they're crazy, but they're back home crazy, not Costa Rica crazy. I see there's a difference. When Indira dropped trou next to me, I thought she was a freak. But then I'm thinking I'm in the jungle. Who's going to give a shit? Some chimp? So bang! I'm sitting in the middle of a stream with her in my drawers. And then what still gets me is those fuckers are biting the shit out of that little kid, and she's sitting there bummed like she missed a Bears game."

"Yeah, nothing fazes her. Makes me want to have been brought up here, at least a little."

"Probably just a little, dude. Anyway, and then Françoise with that story. I swear to Christ I would have shot that guy without even thinking about it. But that's what I know. What I know doesn't work here. But neither does what you know."

"Thanks, Jack," I said appreciatively.

"No, but see, you've decided, fuck it. One year. For better or worse. And you know that if you hate it, it will be over and you tried it. If you love it, by the end, you'll know what I don't know. And it'll be right for you. And Allan wants you to help him sell those lots?"

Allan did seem to have a lot of confidence we'd move some product. "Seems to, yeah."

"That mountain's so steep, when I was on one of those lots, it was like I was on the nose of a cruise ship looking over." He leaned forward with his arms out.

"Well put. I'll have to use that as a selling point," I said.

"That's going to sell like hotcakes, dude. And the stock investing has been just smokin', right?" he asked.

"Never been better, thank God. But you could throw darts blindfolded in this market and do well. Probably means it's going to fall apart in a year or so, maybe less." I said.

"OK, but you know that, though. So you do that shorting shit you were trying to explain to me." He symbolically looked out into the blackness of the valley.

"Yeah, you chose quite a spot. *Everything's* like a postcard. And even if you don't find any other great friends, which you will, Indira and Hal are top-notch," he said.

"Thanks, bud." I was getting a bit emotional.

"I'm sold. Not for Jack, but for you," he said. He beautifully executed one of his pregnant pauses for effect.

"One thing, though, kid."

I anticipated another lighthearted joke.

"Laura's transparent."

"What do you mean? Like open and honest?"

"No, dude. That weight she's lost is whack. I'm not going to be one to tell a woman shit about stuff like that, but you've gotta figure that out. Not normal," Jack said.

I revealed to Jack that we knew something was awry since day three. And recently, we had found out from the villagers that *giardia lamblia,* a water-born parasite, was rampant because the village water mains broke twice a week. We were convinced that was what she had. The villagers had drawers full of the one-week regimen of pills to get rid of it, but call us North American, we felt like we should get a diagnosis from a doctor before we went popping oral pesticides like Cheese Doodles.

But it was getting bad enough that her intestines were so sore, she would groan on every bump—of which there was no shortage—on the village roads. And Bergers wouldn't even let you hear them sniffle until streams of blood were jetting out of their ears. I told him about the giardia theory.

"Sorry, dude," he said regretfully. "But, it's good you know what it is, kid. So she should just take some of those pills and kick its ass. If not, she could drink some of this." He held up his whiskey. "That shit will come right out of there screamin'," he said. "And you? How are you feeling?"

"Good. Why?"

"You're not as bad as her, but I'd consider putting some rocks in your pockets, too, or you'll get blown to Panama."

At 153 pounds before we left, I was already a notorious lightweight. I knew I had lost some weight since arriving, but I had no pain. What's more, the village people told me it was natural for newcomers, with the loss of electrolytes and all the sweating.

"That shit with my dad is always in the back of my mind eating me alive is all. Fuckin' male Italian drama we both have. I've tried sending a few e-mails, and he never picks up the phone when I call, nor do I really know what I would say if he did. It's a problem," I said.

"Just watch it dude. You know, I kick ass and arrest shitheads and hang with a tough bunch every day. I shouldn't feel comfortable around people like you, but I do and can't explain it. Thanks for that. It's an honor to know you and to be able to tell everybody I have friends who did this. I'll always love you both. You're the best."

"Thanks man." I got up and gave him a big hug.

"All right, not too long," Jack said. "Wouldn't want those horny frogs to see Jack getting excited."

CHAPTER 20
A Reptile Dysfunction

"Adopt the pace of nature: her secret is patience."
Ralph Waldo Emerson

December 15, 2006

The local gringo veterans of the jungle continued to stress it in roughly the same way: "People see the charm and peace of the tico smiles and the beauty of the jungle and the ocean. This place is a temptress. It's love at first sight. They want to move here right away." *Just like I did.* "It can be totally worth it, but most come escaping things and thinking that this is one hundred percent paradise. It's not. Those people don't last."

Laura was a fairly "present-moment" being and generally loved her life in Chicago. I knew full well that I was the primary driver of coming to Costa Rica. Her agreement was partly a desire for exploration, but mostly an act of love. I wasn't yet convinced I hadn't come to run from my self-imposed work ethic and the boredom of a routine-driven society. If so, it would be ironic that we came to a place that had less readily available entertainment out of a sense of ennui.

Hal famously put it best: "People come here wanting the sense of adventure and then don't want the adventure. So they retract from what the country offers, and then they get bored."

If we didn't learn to self-entertain, we'd be in the crosshairs of a failed attempt at life in Pair-o-Dice Village. And obviously, we were thirsting for outlets of entertainment, proven by Dora having left a copy of *The Lovely Bones*. Laura was so excited and devoured it cover-to-cover in two days. "That was awesome but gone. What do we do now?" she asked.

We took our repaired truck through the tico village below the property we owned and up into the hills that would hopefully someday be our neighborhood. There, we joined the "Lagos del Fuego Hiking Club."

A pioneer who built the first house in the development, Doctor Bob, ran the club. He lived there with his wife and son, almost in solitude, with very few other houses around.

Former president of his national board of physicians, Bob went home several months per year to practice medicine. But when he was in Costa Rica, he spent his time working wood in his workshop by his house and hiking the untouched jungles behind the development. This was genuine primary rainforest with rivers and waterfalls running all through its tall mountain-lined gorges. The Club collected annual dues from hikers who didn't want to store mountaineering gear. With the money, he financed a central gear depot—all carried from North America by other gringos. He attracted participants for hikes three or four times per week. Any profits were donated to the tico schools in the village below the development.

"Be here tomorrow morning at five thirty," Bob said the previous night. He had a South African accent and an extremely calm and controlled demeanor, with a deadpan dry wit. We weren't happy about the imposition of the brutal bugle call the next morning. Nonetheless, we could tell Bob didn't mess around when it came to hiking, and he would leave without us if we were late. We showed up bright and early.

Our mission was to hike a river to set permanent hooks in a waterfall at its mouth so that Club members and guests could conveniently and repeatedly rappel down its rock face. We had been told that rainy season would end like clockwork on Thanksgiving. This year was a clear exception. Laura and I were lent Bob's son's ATV, on which we slugged through the mud to the hike's starting point.

Our route was thick jungle at its finest, with huge trees—vertical and fallen—hanging vines, lush moss, air plants, and orchids everywhere. They were all set in the constant acoustic backdrop of trickling and sometimes raging river water.

Bob was, in essence, transforming the jungle into an ecologically sound theme park for outdoorsmen. He would name points of interest after a feature or occurrence—like Peccari Ridge, named after the wild boars that were spotted along its top.

We hiked up a mountainside on switchback trails cleared by Bob's former guests. "This will be the hardest part," he said. Then it was mostly downhill or across the jungle along the gorge walls.

Bob carved peach palm stalks, extracting the hearts for us to eat. He also broke open hollow tree thorns as resident ants scurried out. He named trees and flowers. His jungle persona was exemplified by his big bushy beard and the well-worn machete strapped to his side.

"Woohoo! This is so beautiful!" Laura said. She was weak from her continued intestinal bouts. Nonetheless, as soon as Bob put us waist deep in a pristine, cool jungle stream, she was exhilarated and surprisingly in her element.

The course was a stair-step chain of pools three to eight feet wide, one emptying downward into the next. Like the water, we would travel across each pool and down into the next one. You could smell and see the deep hydration of the jungle everywhere. Everything was green except for tree bark and the slippery rocks under our feet.

We both still had only our Timberland high-tech boots bought in the States. This particular hike validated the villagers' claims that they were useless as I did my best Bambi impression, slipping about.

"Bet you spent a pretty penny on those," Bob said pointing at my boots as I lay just fallen in a stream.

"Yes, and we are *so* proud," I said.

"Go to San Isidro for rubber snake boots like these," Bob said, pointing to his galoshes. "You can get good ones for about twenty dollars. They grip the rocks much better, and you need to cover those shins. You look like a scrumptious viper snack," he said.

He looked at Laura's concerned face. But clearly he wasn't one to hold back. "*Bothrops asper*. Sometimes called the ultimate pit viper. Hunts at night when it's cooler and tends to sleep during the day. There are actually more venomous vipers around, but these are the most dangerous to humans because they live so close to human habitats. You'll probably never actually see one over a year's time, but they're around. I've seen three in my ten years hiking. But you need to be ready," he said sternly. "Oh, and speaking of snakes, buy machetes." *We know. We know.* "We're going to be clearing a lot of paths now that you're part of the Club. When we hike, we're like lawn mowers, and you're not going to kill vipers with your camera." I looked down at the dry bag that we had checked out from the Club gear closet.

Continuing the hike, we descended less frequently as the terraced pools became wider. I was so comforted to actually be losing myself in the jungle. I loved to look at nature, but it didn't have much of a calming effect. I wanted Costa Rica to give me that ability, and now I was feeling it for the first time.

"Whoa! Back!" *Clank, clank!* It sounded like a clash of swords had erupted ahead.

"Shit! Oh, my God!" Laura yelled, quite a bit farther ahead.

I sprinted over the edge of the next pool, swiping vines out of my way. Our small group stood in a circle. I recognized the five-foot snake at the center from an e-mail sent by a coworker before we left. The subject line read "Just Watch Out for These."

"What is it?" Laura said.

"Well, now you've done it! We installed that one last week, and you already lopped its head right off!" I could see his humor was camouflaging his angst. Bob took in a deep breath.

"*Terciopelo*, Laura," I said.

"Aaahh, very astute, young Glen," Dr. Bob said.

It was laying curled up on a wide, flat rock about three inches in girth— its neck sliced about three-fourths through and bleeding.

"I thought you said you saw only three snakes in ten years," I said.

"Four," Bob didn't miss a beat. "Yes, snake boots would be brilliant, you reckon? Laura, you would probably have been his target if old Gordo here hadn't saved the day," Bob said.

"Why? I was fourth in line!" Laura was now sprung with vitality and adrenaline.

"They have no ears, and so they sense your approach by vibration. So it's easy to startle them—hence, their tendency to bite humans. Big ones like these have been around a while and know they only have a week's supply or so of venom to use to hunt at any given time. They're more patient than the younger ones. He senses the first three people pass, tension escalating, and thinks, 'Well, maybe I can wait this out.' By the third or fourth, he's all-in, and snap! The good thing is that the big ones also know exactly how much venom to put in you to make you go away. But it's the same venom—still loaded with gangrene-inducing bacteria. Go untreated for any significant period, and they'll be removing large chunks of rotten flesh or a limb from you one way or the other."

"I walked right past it!" Laura said.

"As did I." Bob was number two in line. "Just didn't see it. Blends in with the rock well, aye?"

We left the serpent's corpse in its resting spot. I felt bad for it. It didn't wander into our habitat—quite the contrary.

The river quickly became too rugged and any path we tried to clear too lush. We were wiped out. "Well, we'll make another go at this," Bob said.

We walked across a long ridge and found a path exiting the jungle. We soon arrived at a flat plateau jutting out over the valley and stopped for the view.

"Hmm." Bob became distracted by a tree behind me. It had a large, muddy tumor on its surface with what looked like streams of dry clay radiating from it.

"Take a taste," Bob said to Gordo.

"Do you know the variety?" Gordo asked.

"Not sure yet." Bob broke open one of the veins, and several insects crawled out. He immediately pressed one with the tip of his index finger and down the hatch it went!

"Hmmm," he said. "A bit nuttier than the ones last week."

Gordo dug into another vein and began feasting. "Mmm," he said, satisfied.

"Have a try, Glen," Bob said.

"All right," I said.

Without a thought, I broke a mud vein, captured a squirming victim on my fingertip, and *crunch.* I felt bad for him too. It was like popping the orange flying fish roe in which sushi is rolled—if those eggs had legs.

"How does it taste?" Bob asked me.

"Like wood." *Probably could have guessed that.*

Laura looked at me as if I had just eaten one of the local giant cockroaches with fork and knife.

We rode the ATVs back to Bob's house for tasty and colorful Costa Rican eggs and toast and then bid our fellow jungle marauders farewell.

"I want to do this at least once a week," Laura said as we stole down the hill. "That was the most amazing experience! I loved it!"

"You weren't freaked out by bugs and spiders and the snake and all?" I asked, surprised.

"Not at all until you decided to have your snack. Everything was a surprise and so interesting! It was like sensory overload. I forgot all about the spiders," Laura said. Laura's greatest fears were fire and spiders. We had already experienced her fire fear in Costa Rica; she wouldn't light our gas stove—which had no pilots—with the matches it required. She also froze every time she saw a spider, which was every morning. About twenty golden silk orb-weaver spiders about four or five inches in diameter were strewn across the back doors of the FlawedShack. Even more were in the windowsills, which I had to evacuate during Operation Screens.

"And Bob's there, so I don't worry. Hal's great and all, but he's a wacky jack of all trades, so I wasn't completely comfortable on the hike the other day. Bob is a man of the jungle. I even forgot I was sick! I can sit down on our patio and have wildlife come to me or I can go to it. The difference here is that I am active. And my mind isn't on who I want to be when I grow up or the fact that the water's out," she said.

"OK, I ask again. You weren't fazed by the snake? I mean I was—not in the creepy crawly sense, but more in the 'I could lose a leg' sense," I said.

"Fazed, yes. But what did we expect coming here? I worry about those things being around with Skippy and Rugby maybe getting out, but I was on top of the world at breakfast. I even felt comfort—like we found the reason we came here," she said. "To be one with nature."

"Well, we can self-entertain, I guess," I said. "One of the most important criteria. Check that off the list!"

We returned that night after knocking off several chores. The climb up our driveway, which was in desperate need of repair, was turning into a bull-ride simulation.

With buckets of rain dropping, we quickly got all our belongings and ran toward the house. There was a patch of darkness between the driveway and the back terrace because the outside spotlights seemed to burn out after a week of use.

I high-kicked through the puddles and felt a long object slithering up my leg. *Oh, God. "The Terciopello hunts at night," Bob said.*

I ran a few steps to get away. As I turned around, I felt the same thing but could see nothing. It felt to be at least three feet up my entire back calf and lower thigh, to where the hems of my shorts began. *Still with me. Run!*

After ten more suicidal steps on the wet, glazed Spanish-style tiles, Laura asked, "What are you doing?" *No time to answer.*

I turned to face my aggressor, expecting to maybe see something several feet behind in the dim light coming from the kitchen. Again, n*othing!* And then I felt it again.

I dropped my backpack to the ground and bolted toward the pool for a possible jump. "Whaaat the heeeelll is gooooing oon?" I yelled in a wavering, terrified voice.

I stopped before a final desperate jump into the pool. I felt nothing now but still saw nothing that could have created my prior sensation as I looked back.

"Glen, what are you doing?" Laura asked, now impatient and clearly frightened.

"I don't know. Just give me a minute," I said, "and don't move."

"What is it?"

"Look, I was being chased by a snake, OK?"

"Shit! Again?" She clutched her belongings tighter on her chest.

I calmly and methodically went back toward the terrace. I didn't see anything. *With that kind of length, he must have slithered away. I would have seen him.* "I don't see it now, but I'm telling you, I felt it all the way up my leg. Lucky it didn't bite me," I said.

"Yech!" Laura said with a frightened full-body shake.

I went back to gather the belongings I had strewn about during my escape.

You've gotta be shittin' me! My laptop backpack—open and unzipped—lay on the ground getting soaked. My power cord trailed from the outside pocket.

Laura laughed so hard she fell in a puddle because she couldn't stand.

We ate dinner and prepared for bed.

"Yeah, keep this up, and you'll be in the self-entertainment hall of fame," Laura said.

We resumed our laughter and couldn't stop.

Three

CHAPTER 21
The Truck Stops Here

"Again, you can't connect the dots looking forward; you can only connect them looking backwards. So you have to trust that the dots will somehow connect in your future. You have to trust in something—your gut, destiny, life, karma, whatever. This approach has never let me down, and it has made all the difference in my life.

Steve Jobs

December 20, 2006

Over a month had passed since we had hastily bought the two trucks. As feared, they had not been in the driveway at the same time for one second during that time—constantly in shops either in San José or locally. Of course, this created huge lifestyle problems, as there really weren't any establishments within any reasonable walking distance. The nearest one was the grocery store in the village, and that was at least a forty-five-minute walk. Also problematic were the phone calls we'd receive from the mechanics saying that more problems were surfacing as they tried to solve others. The bills kept increasing, and we really had no choice but to pay them if we ever wanted our cars back.

Laura suited up for Jihad with the mechanics of Costa Rica, but speaking only tortilla minestrone, she channeled said war at—and through—me.

She serenaded me with multi-day marathons of vulgarities, a vocabulary set that she seemed to be developing quite rapidly, also because of her ailments.

I had already come up with names for the trucks. Laura's black beast was the Montalloper. The previous owner had determined he could save money by replacing every malfunctioning part on this Mitsubishi Montero with ones from a Hyundai Galloper.

My green truck was called the Monterror, for its general pain-in-the-ass nature. Together, they were the Car-Cinomas, a label chosen over a close second—the Montumors.

One day at six in the morning, Luis drove the Monterror to us after a long stay in the ICU in San José. This was fortuitous because the Montalloper was typically at the bottom of the hill with a dead battery.

Upon Carlos' arrival, we took the "good"—those quotes taller than a giraffe riding an elephant—Car-Cinoma to visit its ailing cousin.

"It's the alternator," he said shaking his head. "These damn cars."

These were *"buen carros"* a month prior. Hearing these words made it painfully appropriate to run him over with one of them. Notwithstanding, I was owning my decision to buy two trucks to learn some desperately needed lessons.

Again, ticos are brilliantly resourceful. "This battery just needs a charge," Carlos said, stating the obvious. "You need to drive me to the bus station in San Isidro so I can return home. I've got it!" He put the dead battery in the Monterror to charge on our drive. Pretty smart!

We pulled off the *Costanera* Northeast up the mountain roads toward San Isidro. After twenty-five minutes, we hit road work—pothole patching. It surely was a picturesque traffic jam—mist rising from the lush mountains amidst a chorus of chirping birds. We inched along, and after five minutes, I released the clutch too fast. It stalled. I looked at Carlos like I had lit a match in a dark closet full of explosives.

He giggled. "Start it. It's a new battery and should have some charge by now. I put it in myself," he said.

I tried. Nothing.

Carlos' look said, "Get out, you daft gringo. I'm driving." I—no longer Don Glen but rather Don Dummy—symbolically put my hands up as if dropping a pistol and got out. Señor Sourpuss took the wheel.

"It will start in reverse." I contemplated whether I had processed his Spanish in error, and the scenery began passing us in the opposite direction to which I had been accustomed. He had pulled into the opposite, oncoming lane of traffic in reverse. Luckily, this solved the issue of the blind mountain turns as we were traveling with the traffic flow in front of us and had no cars behind us.

When satisfied with his speed, Carlos would pop the clutch to start the engine. And none of the cars in front of us honked or cursed, but rather followed us as if our ordeal was a spectator sport.

"What are you doing?" I asked rhetorically, my heart racing.

"Eh, it's fine," Carlos said. "We have to drive to get to a garage anyway. Why not try to start the car on the way if we can?"

And then it dawned on me. Why the heck did we install the dead battery in this truck if I was going to have to drop it on a charger in San Isidro anyway? I eyed the perfectly good battery he had removed in the back seat, along with Carlos' twelve-year-old son, who seemed completely undaunted. *OK, now Carlos is an overly resourceful tico!*

The Monterror had power windows. Shut, and without electricity, they fogged profusely as the temperature rose dramatically in the truck and I began perspiring buckets.

"José!" Carlos threw his son a rag. "Clear the windows!" He looked in my direction. "You too!"

I cleaned my half of the windshield and window as Carlos miraculously managed to do the same. I then dove through the back seat all the way into the tailgate area. The son and I scurried about, clearing the windows. I slammed up against the tailgate a couple of times as he released the clutch. *Is he trying to get rid of me?*

After about ten minutes, we approached a very sharp turn even *he* was too scared to take backwards. Of course, he couldn't stop the truck in the lane he was in with a stream of oncoming traffic in front of him, and there was no shoulder on either side of the road. What's more, this curve was on a flat. We had lost momentum. I got out of the truck and pushed as he veered it into our original lane right in the curve! Cars were now veering around our truck from behind into oncoming traffic on a blind turn.

We both got out of the car and weighed our options. "You stay here," he said as he directed traffic. *Uh, where could I possibly go? And where the hell do you think you're going?* "I'll go to the nearest garage. Please watch my son," he said, pointing to the boy wandering into a grassy roadside plateau slightly up the road.

Carlos hitched a ride up the hill from a random driver. Glen became GDOT (Gringo Department of Transportation) for an hour. With no cell signal, I couldn't call the cops to help. So I stood in the curve and did everything short of set myself on fire to prevent cars from totaling the Monterror— which would have ironically been my greatest fortune. Meanwhile, scores asked if I needed help. Two offered to sell me batteries from the trunks of their cars, but I had no idea which type I needed. I had the lives of many in my hands.

I looked over my shoulder to monitor the son. He was standing on a rock wall over which I couldn't see but I knew looked pretty steep and high up over the valley.

"Excuse me, kid, but please come by me over here." My Spanish must have been bad that day. I must have said, "Hey kid, please do your best impression of a highly caffeinated kangaroo," as he began jumping onto and off the wall playfully.

So I can walk over and get nasty with the kid, leaving the biggest speed bump any unsuspecting family would never remember in the curve. Or I can explain to Carlos that his son bungeed the ridge and forgot he was born without a cord. I evaluated each scenario for potential loss of life and decided to continue my GDOT role.

Carlos finally arrived with someone else's battery, which he quickly installed in the Monterror. We now had three batteries in our possession.

The boy had wised up to his father's approach and was by my side when he arrived. *Cheeky niño!*

"Give me a second," I said to Carlos and ran to the rock wall. My lower digestive tract tightened like an oyster on a shucking table. That drop was at least three hundred feet, and the kid did a Baryshnikov on it for over an hour!

As I returned to the Monterror and saw Carlos in the driver's seat, I remembered my new Don Dummy status and got into the passenger seat. The diesel engine started with a roar.

We returned the battery to its rightful owner up the hill along with a gigantic tip. I marveled to Carlos that no cops had been on the road. He shrugged his shoulders as if to wonder why I would expect any.

"The battery in the back seat is too dead. It will need to charge overnight," Carlos said as we drove. *What happened to "It's a new battery. I installed it myself?"* I had our cell and no way of telling Laura. She'd take me for dead, likely more appealing to her every day. "And I have bad news," Carlos said. Over the past month, he had already become the Tom Brokaw of bad news. "Your battery—that's not the same battery I gave you. Someone must have switched it."

I was done. "I'm buying a new one in San Isidro."

We proceeded toward San Isidro in the region of Perez Zeledón. The small towns had little *sodas* (restaurants), *abastecedores* (convenience stores), *talleres* (mechanics), *iglésias* (churches), purveyors of *rotulos* (signs, of which there were a shocking number of manufacturers) and *supermercados*. Children in uniform walked to and from school laughing and smiling as farmers peddled their succulent fruits from roadside stands.

Just before San Isidro, we approached a large sign on a curve saying "in Perez Zeledón God is the General" and then, wham—the expansive green valley with San Isidro cradled in its base.

A periphery of larger furniture shops, car dealerships, and coffee factories surrounded the more intense bustle at the town's relatively small heart. One-way streets ran along one-story storefronts housing the hallmarks of a developed town—paved roads, larger grocery stores, banks, utility offices, and appliance and home stores.

Conspicuously absent was any decorative architecture, even on the large white church presiding over the town square—all white with flat plaster walls and a cross perched on the roof.

Carlos installed the new battery, he and I parted at the bus stop—nearly in tears of joy—and I began the ride home.

I pondered our plight and solutions to the dilemma I had created. *It probably would be cheaper to sell both cars and hire a full-time driver.* In one month, I had two machines that were doing nothing but consuming time and money. *This is not what we came here for!*

Nonetheless, I got a grip and began to ease into tranquility, with the gorgeous landscape passing and the Monterror shuffling along surprisingly healthy. As I veered potholes, it was a good time to go slow—to breathe the pristine air and take in the orange glow of the sunset over the ocean to the west.

This is what it's about. Just a spoonful of nature helps the bankruptcy go down. I was awash with a natural calm, a drug to which I longed to be addicted. *We just need to sort this problem out, and it can be the land of the new, peaceful Glen.*

About twenty minutes from home, the oil light turned on. *Paradise is going to kill me.*

CHAPTER 22
Crappy New Year!

For last year's words belong to last year's language
And next year's words await another voice.
And to make an end is to make a beginning.
T.S. Eliot, "Little Gidding"

December 30, 2006

The New Year was upon us. "Everyone's been so gracious in inviting us for the holidays, but I really need to be close to friends and family now," Laura said as we reminisced over our recent holiday experiences and strategized how we would celebrate the turn of the year.

Thanksgiving had been spent at Allan's house.

"Hey! Laura, Glen! Happy Thanksgiving!" our friend said as we arrived at Allan's.

"Hi!" We were taken aback by his drunken state. Of course, this wasn't completely out of the ordinary in the village, but we had never seen *him* this way.

"Where are you going?" Laura asked.

"The folks inside sent me to come find you," he said. "We thought sure one of your sick ponies blew a knee again." The Car-Cinomas had legendary status with the village people. "I couldn't find my keys, so I just started walking."

"On these dirt roads in a highly seismic area? You could have spilt your wine, my good man!" I gestured toward his glass.

He belly laughed. "Ah, come to think of it, you guys are expendable," he said, waving his hand behind him dismissively as he had already turned to weave back up the road toward the house. I envisioned guests leaving one by one, like in a zombie apocalypse, each to go find the last, until all that remained was a big table of food and no one to eat it. And an abundant table it was—a standard feast of turkey and all the trimmings. Oh, and then there were my two dishes—Moroccan lentils and borscht. I always had to be unique when I cooked.

I spent the first part of that day the way I normally spent Thanksgiving—cooking and distracted. On this particular day, I longed to go home and fix things up with my family, which was clearly not possible.

For Laura, it was a time of lack. She would normally spend Thanksgiving playing board games, talking, and horsing around with her family. I always marveled at how they could sit inside an entire cold Pittsburgh day, deep in conversation, without moving a muscle. Rather, Laura spent this Thanksgiving silent, swinging out on the hammock and missing her family. We intentionally didn't fly home because we had only been away a few months and also we had no one to tend to the Boys.

For the same reason, we stayed in the Village for Christmas, which was just as difficult for Laura and a little more for me, since, unlike Thanksgiving, no one had invited us anywhere. Hence, I couldn't cook to pass the time and avoid any thoughts of loneliness and my lingering alienation from my dad back in Miami.

On Christmas Eve, we went to our favorite pizza restaurant. Erwin, the eccentric German owner, had the only brick oven for miles. His restaurant was in the valley, like the rest in Pair-o-Dice Village. There wasn't a written word in the restaurant listing his food items or prices. He'd merely offered mixed greens salad, meat pizza, veggie pizza, lasagna, and roast pork. These were the only things he served forever and ever, every day.

"Well, things sure are different here. I never thought I'd be sitting in the jungle with no one around on Christmas Eve," Laura said.

Three

Back home, huge Christmas trees stood in the department stores, and tiny white lights lined Michigan Avenue. There would be no big dinner table feast and no excitement on loved ones' faces from opening presents. One unbearably cold day could have made us truly feel the season was upon us—but one would surely be enough.

And then there was that trade-off in our minds. Christmas trees were weeds compared to the green of every outdoor glance at any moment. And our weather was so much better.

On Christmas morning, Hal and Indira invited us over at the crack of dawn, likely realizing at the last minute we'd be alone. We were thrilled and prepared, already having gone to town to get some toys for Nako.

A couple weeks before, we had discussed the optimal Christmas in Pair-o-Dice Village, and aside from flying in family, that was it. Hal and Indira were already loved ones.

We spent Christmas at the little *casita* with their view and a small decorated outdoor tropical fruit tree, watching Nako take in her presents. I cooked pasta and sides, and we chowed. It was a day of rest, laughter, and good friends. A lousy, dreary, experience turned delightful.

And yet, as we turned in that night, we returned to what was missing. All in all, the holidays had been a negative to our life leap, revealing front-and-center how removed we were from family and a life we had worked so hard to build.

We approached New Year's Eve with a mix of dread of those blue feelings coming back and hope that we would get invited to some big party where we could meet new people.

The hope panned out when we were invited to Erik's house at the last minute on a "referral" from Hal and Indira. He had arrived from Switzerland several years before and built a magnificent house with one of the rare views that rivaled Hal and Indira's. You would ponder how Erik pulled off his building project, especially in years past when nothing was accessible—until you met him. He was the emblematic European engineer and project manager—a regimented perfectionist.

162

Erik had somewhat cursed himself by bringing his best European belongings along—all the best pots, utensils, knives, appliances, furniture, and electronics. How he got it all through customs and the resulting taxes he must have paid gave us migraines.

Word unfortunately spread of his material rarities. On an isolated road with only four houses, the thefts began, and Erik unexpectedly became a prisoner of his wondrous home. He was rumored to fire rounds into the air once a week, reminding any interested to tread lightly.

To alleviate his exile, Erik built a few *cabinas* and rented them. His customers watched his place while he made a little money, capitalizing on his highly desirable view.

The party began at five, just in time for the magnificent sunset over the ocean with two uninhabited rock islands in the foreground. We knew Indira, Hal, Brenda, and Paul—with whom we had spent a significant amount of time since our arrival—quite well. But as people arrived, we noticed we were at least acquainted with most of the gringo community. And this party was not even in Pair-o-Dice Village, but rather fifteen minutes north.

The food was impressive. Erik provided cocktails and crustaceans like he owned a shrimping company. I was dismayed not to have asked about the potluck as others brought in their goodies.

Laura and I mingled for a few hours and then retired downstairs to the pool area below the house, which was built into the hill just like Hal and Indira's would soon be. On the first floor, we were basically on the first row of bleachers to his view.

We sat in the near dark on lounge chairs, watching the two rocky islands floating in the beautiful moonlit ripples of the ocean.

"So did you think this time last year we'd be sitting here to start 2007?" Laura asked.

"Of course!" I said. "I also envisioned being the world's sexiest man. That panned out, too."

Laura looked at me with a wise-ass smirk.

"You know, Hawaii is still just a tad more beautiful, but what an amazing place" she said. "Everything's a painting. It's all so calming as long as I can stay out of my head and forget about all the critters."

"I know what you mean," I said.

"I'm very disappointed in myself," she said abruptly.

"Why?" I asked. In defense against the "most marriages go home in a body bag" claim, we had used our 10/10 technique almost every day. As such, I knew about everything Laura was thinking and feeling, so it wasn't a complete surprise for her to say such a thing. But still, she usually would react to adversity by pumping herself up, not bringing herself down or dwelling.

"You're in your element here," she said. "I can tell how much you love it. This is your place. Your eyes light up when you wake up in the morning. The last time I saw that was when we first started dating. You were at the top of your game on that project. Should I be scared that you were so in your element in a tornado shelter under corn fields?" She smiled.

"Yeah, I do love it here. You're spot-on," I said. "I'd love it more if things worked mechanically and logistically day-to-day. But it's my type of gig. There's a new culture, and you know me—always doing impressions and making jokes about stereotypes. I'm a culture junkie. And the unpredictability is thrilling."

"And then I come along and screw up the rotation with my sickness and intolerance of things," she said.

"I wouldn't say you mess things up," I replied. "And wait. Intolerance? You never told me this." *Where's this coming from.*

"Look, I'm sorry I haven't been up-front, but I'm having a real hard time. And it's more than all the weight loss and pain. I just didn't want to screw this up for you," she said.

"Screw it up for me? How bad is it?"

"When we meet most gringos, the husband *and* the wife turn to you to ask what you do. They hardly ever ask me. And you know we left the States with our work as our identities. I didn't think so then, but I definitely know it now. I'm obsessed with it. And a year ago, I was making more than you. I never cared about that, but in that moment when they ask, I remember, and it matters. And it's so stupid, but it hurts. And Hal proves that they wouldn't even understand what I did if I told them. It's all mental ego bullshit. But it still bothers me."

"Listen, you've always been strong, and we'll be up and running with Allan soon," I said.

"You think so? Look at me. I can't do anything on my own now. All that comes out of my mouth is the tortilla minestrone. And the sad thing is the few times I've tried, people understood me! I can communicate and don't! But the ticos ask you if you're tico when you speak. So I think why bother?"

"I don't know what they're thinking," I said.

Laura laughed. "You're incredible," she said smiling. "Can you ever take a compliment? Since when do people not know what their native language sounds like?" *Guilty as charged.* I'd argue with the Ace of Cakes if he accused me of baking well.

"I spend all day mad at myself—telling myself I should be doing this and that. That I should be adjusted to our new life here already. That I should be working for Allan when I don't even have the energy to walk sometimes. That I should be speaking more Spanish. That I should not be so dependent on you. That I should be strong because right now I feel as if I am fading into the background. That I should be working with you through our ordeals. That I should be taking more advantage of nature. That I should explore the coast by myself even if I'd get stranded in the jungle with the Montalloper. I mean it's not like no one would find me."

She stared at the ocean throughout her soliloquy, her eyes beginning to moisten. Laura was a person of direct contact—a master at interaction. She couldn't even look *me* in the eye.

"OK, so resolution one for 2007. We are going to go back to the doctor and accept nothing but a cure for an answer." I had already told her about Jack's concerns. "We have to start there."

"OK, but there' something else I need to get off my chest with you. You have to work out this drama magnet thing you've got going," she said. *Wait, uh, hello? What? I thought this was about you!*

Three

My personality was indeed making two contributions to our predicaments. The first was always being ultra-sacrificing for people to the point of anxiety, coupled with the anger of getting myself in too deep and causing myself the anxiety in the first place. Why did I cook ten-item buffets for dinner parties when my ingredients were nearly inaccessible and our kitchen was a floor model from Toys R Us? I took too much care of other people and not myself, to the detriment of the two of us.

Second, I could never sit with my own thoughts. Even in Chicago, I needed action to stave off the boredom. So I was prone to creating huge, almost unrealistic projects and problems to fuel my energy. These factors were much more pronounced in the jungle by ourselves with every known distraction abruptly removed.

"You don't need to create drama. It's here. I mean you and I have reversed roles completely. You have to be the logical problem solver, and I'm being driven by emotion. And now we've got a crap house and the two crappiest cars in town. Pretty big coincidence, don't you think? I wanted to spend just a little more and get a better house, but you didn't. Dra-ma. Drama that you create."

In truth, we had toured crappier houses around town and we knew people who had worse cars, but they didn't have two.

"And then this other calamity you're dragging out with your dad. It's killing you. I can tell, and every time I see it on your face, I have to remember that I'm the cause of it," she said.

"You're not the cause of it," I said.

"Look, whatever. If I weren't around, none of this would be happening. That's the bottom line," she said.

"It's more complicated than that. It's stuff between him and me that has finally come out."

"It's not. I'm between you and him, and I need to be removed. Start talking to him!" she said.

"He won't—"

"Fix it! And from this day forward, if you're creating any more drama—

even a smidge more—it needs to stop. And I mean now! I need none of it, and I won't have it!" *Crappy New Year!*

"Point taken. Sure," I said. I was still hopeful for a tender midnight kiss. "Drama-free New Year."

"I mean look at your history with cars. It's ridiculous! Now unbelievable!" *Uh, I agreed with you. Hellooooo!*

"You know as well as I do—"

"I told you we shouldn't buy the Monterror, and now you've been the proud owner of four disasters."

"Uh, one of them's yours." *Stupid, stupid, stupid!* I will remember that look for the rest of my life. "Could you please just look over there?" I pointed toward the ocean. "I'm turning to stone. All that can't be a coincidence. You're right," I said.

"I don't give a shit if I'm right!" she said. She never did. *All she cares about is what I'm going to do to fix it.* "All I care about is what are you going to do to fix it!"

"I already thought about it. We sell both of them," I said.

"You're out of your mind."

"Well, look, it's pretty clear that they're just going to suck us dry. But I don't want to commit to buying anything else until we decide we are going to live here. We go back to renting. I'd rather pay less and drive something new at this point. I have the perspective," I said.

"How is it that you couldn't think this way a few weeks ago?" A vein in her forehead was reaching a critical pressure point. She paused a moment.

"OK, what's done is done. They go on the market tomorrow."

"Deal."

"OK, can I offer one more thing?"

She sighed. "OK, sure. What?"

"We came here with American needs and expectations. Our reality is different. We don't even have stable water. Everyone's been telling us, just like they told us not to get two cars, that we need to reduce our expectations," I said. "Things don't always happen and work the way we want them to here. It's time we accepted that."

Three

"The Richardsons will hopefully pass by while here, and we can totally terrorize them. But until any of these things get fixed, we have to accept them. We've survived until now with the bats and the suicide showers and pumping out of the pool. It's not the end of the world." I said.

"All right, but you really turn the screws on them," Laura said.

"Me? What about you? They speak English!"

"Ooooh no. You know I'd normally jump at the chance." *She would.* "But I've listened in on a few of those phone calls. They're passive-aggressive to the nines. I'd flip my lid in five minutes," Laura said. "OK, so agreed. The functioning of our house is no longer going to bring me down."

"Good. Me neither."

"OK, it's New Year's. I'm sorry I brought this down, but 2007 is going to be awesome if we can keep these commitments. Now, what's positive?" she said.

Now this was Laura's usual. She always looked at the glass as half-full, whereas my glass was always half-broken. *Speaking of role reversal.*

"We've done something here that so many people dream of and would be too scared," Laura said. "Think of all of our friends seeing us ditch the same life they had worked so hard for to go to the jungle. And they were so supportive." She paused. *She's gonna get choked up.* She got choked up. "And now I barely have a phone to talk to them." She forced herself through the words. "OK, I'm focusing on the positive now. This has been such a learning experience. I mean think about the perspective we will always have on life, even just from the last two months. No matter what life throws at us, we'll look back on our courage. We'll be able to do anything," she said, getting excited, tears clearing.

"We're doing 10/10 every day. That's a positive habit," I said. "And who do we know who sees something like that," I gestured toward the ocean, "hundreds of times a day? And we can pull over and hang on the beach whenever we want. And the nature," I mused, "we're like friggin' Tarzan and Jane out here. That's such a treat!"

"And you know people come here and have the sense of adventure and don't want the adventure!" Hal's voice boomed over the apparently increasing volume of conversation upstairs. "Like Laura and Glen, for instance!"

"Hey! *Cállate*, Don Hal," Laura said.

"Ha, ha, ha!" Hal uttered his typical innocuous all-knowing laugh. "I knew I'd find you in a flash if I said that out loud. I am personally insulted you thought a party could go on without you. What are you guys doing? Planning on taking the local hardware store public?" He was dripping with sarcasm.

"Be up soon!" I said.

"Better come quick. I'm losing my will to live without you!" he crowed back.

In her true coaching fashion, Laura turned to me and said, "OK, so what are we taking out of this conversation?"

I scanned the immediate past. "Absolutely get you better, sell the Car-Cinomas, fix this Dad thing, lower our expec—"

"Five, four, three, two, one, Happy New Year!"

Laura looked at her watch. "It's only 10:10! Do they think they need to practice?" Laura asked.

"Who knows? Must be some kinda gag. I bet Hal's at the bottom of it, maybe even for our benefit." I looked at Laura in the dim moonlight. *Damn, my wife is hot.* "I'm glad you told me what you did. It's important. Now put these things in the 10/10's every day. That's what they're for!"

"I love you," she said. *Beat me to it!*

"I love you too," I said.

"I still can't believe we're doing this," Laura said, looking into my eyes closely.

"All right, let's take in the view for ten minutes before we go upstairs to the bedlam," I said.

When we went upstairs, Brenda and Paul were washing dishes. A couple of others were clearing the large banquet tables. Everyone else was gone.

"Where is everyone?" I asked.

Brenda turned with her sweet smile. Paul was visually bewildered at our appearance. "I thought you bailed on us," he said.

"Happy New Year," she said. "I was going to come down, but I thought you guys might be having a moment."

"Not the kind you're thinking of, unfortunately," I said, winking. "But it's only ten."

Paul smirked, knowingly. "Yeah, it's our first New Year's here, too. Shocked us. Midnight was too late for the sleep schedules here. They agreed to call it at ten."

We're thousands of miles from family and friends, and we couldn't even celebrate with the fine folks of the El Toucan Assisted Living Facility?

We said good-bye and sped down the coast, anxious to get to the Flawed-Shack for a phone signal to talk to those back home.

I put my keys on the dining room table. "Give me the phone. It's New Year's in Pittsburgh in ten minutes," Laura said. We were an hour behind Eastern.

I reached in my pocket.

"It's not here! I bet it fell out of my pocket by Erik's pool," I said.

"Oh, come on! I bet it's in the car."

"OK, but if I don't come back right away, I'm going back to Erik's," I said. *There's no way I'm going to be able to get that phone back here in ten minutes.* "Shit! Then we won't be able to call at midnight!"

It wasn't in the car. When I arrived at Erik's house, the lights were all out. I looked at my watch. *11:10! People don't stay up for shit around here!* I didn't know Erik well enough to get him out of bed. My heart sank. *Completely disconnected—no Internet and no phone.*

I turned around and went home, defeated. I walked into our bedroom where Laura was drying off from her suicide shower. "I feel horrible, but the lights were out when I got there," I said.

Laura began to cry. "I'm sorry," I said.

"No, no," she said. "This can't be your fault. It's something bigger. These holidays are just cursed."

I had a sudden dreadful thought. *If I lost that phone, Ricardo's sister will drag this gringo through San José behind a horse!*

I washed up for bed but couldn't possibly cleanse myself of the melancholy I felt for Laura. The holidays were just so important to her.

"Look, don't worry about it. It happened. We had a good conversation tonight. Let's think about that. I'm numb," she said.

Thank you. Suddenly, a large pink bolt of light appeared through the window. "Wow! He really *is* doing it!" I said.

One of our neighbors across our ocean-side valley view had just launched his surprise that had been rumored around the village all week.

"Our own personal fireworks show!" Laura said as the colors of the professionally choreographed rockets danced off the ocean and across the valley.

I put my arm around Laura and there we sat on the balcony, the most blessed and helpless couple in the world. "Again, we have nothing, but we have this. Everything's unexpected."

CHAPTER 23
The FlawedShack Redemption

A house divided against itself cannot stand.
Abraham Lincoln

January 1, 2007

"You know the Richardsons are supposedly leaving town in two days. I have no idea how to contact them," I said, sitting at the entrance of Lagos del Fuego waiting for Dr. Bob and his friends.

"It's New Year's Day. We'll worry about that tomorrow. I just can't believe I did that. Seven waterfalls!" Laura said.

"Do you remember the conversation last night about turning the screws on them?"

"And I used to be afraid of heights! I can't believe it! How awesome!"

Frankly, I could understand my wife's excitement. We began 2007 at 5:30 a.m. with a thrilling rappelling trip with Dr. Bob. The three-hour hike included seven tall waterfall rappels.

I surely enjoyed it, but I was weak and without balance—not for lack of snake boots, which we both now had. But we were anything but cover models for *Outdoor* magazine. Yes, from the knees up, we were decked out with helmets and harnesses. Yet the rising temperatures going into rainy season called for swim trunks, and all I had was basketball shorts. Hence, tall soccer socks were needed to avoid skin irritation on our shins and calves. Add my very own machete and I looked like some love child of Crocodile Dundee, Pelé, Dr. J, and a school crossing guard on a rainy day.

My sickness was a sensation like nothing I had ever felt before. I listed my simple symptoms of weakness, lack of balance, and underarm pain to Dr. Bob, who had no access to any diagnostic equipment.

"You'll be fine," he said. "Just go into town and ask them for this." He wrote down an antibiotic. Most medicines were over-the-counter. Bob grabbed his gear and headed for the door.

He turned on the way out the door. "Incidentally, I once had a patient with your exact same symptoms."

"Oh, and?" I asked.

"He had flesh-eating disease," he said.

"Hey, wait! What's that?" I sounded like a high-pitched Yorkie with a habañero up his keester.

"OK, must be going now," Dr. Bob said.

"You're just going to say that and leave?

"Where are my keys?" He smirked and faked oblivion to my despair.

"Wait, wait!" I plead.

"You'll be fine. I'll be around if it gets worse. See you in a couple hours." He walked out.

He was referring to our trip to the Danza de los Diablitos ceremony two hours away on the Boruca reservation. The Boruca Indians once ruled the Pacific Coast from Puntarenas to Panama.

We were to caravan there in ten SUVs containing Lagos del Fuego gringo inhabitants. Alas, ten SUVs might have been enough to carry all the town's gringos.

As we awaited the caravan, I thought about the end to my wife's fear of heights. New fears had surfaced, and old ones vanished. The prior night's conversation also proved that some hopes were evaporating without being replaced.

I pondered my own personal changes. It seemed my persona was shifting so fast, the only tangible development was an awakening boldness I had never before exhibited. This was in the face of increasing impatience with house, car, and health-related problems that just seemed to persist.

The caravan arrived, and we were off. Costa Rica has the most microclimates in the world aside from Kauai, Hawaii. As we ascended the mountains, everything became arid, dry, and cruelly hot. It felt to me like 120 degrees, but I knew some of it was my illness. Unfortunately, our friends had decided to tailgate in the middle of a shelterless dirt parking lot. I was desperate to escape the sun but stayed put to be social. It was a prime opportunity to make new friendships and fortify others. Try as I may, however, I became too weak to string together a conversation.

Nonetheless, I roughed it out long enough to see the parade. It reenacted the historic Spanish Conquest of Costa Rica. The men wore the beautiful, colorful, and ornate Boruca wooden carved masks—a token item at every Costa Rican tourist shop. They fought a bull, another man in a large wood frame wrapped in burlap and painted with a bull's face with horns mounted on top. The box reached down to his waist. He would stand, walk several steps, and then crouch so the box was resting on the ground.

The mask-wearing devils migrated between households, dancing on their porches, drinking *chicha*—a corn liquor—and eating tamales. At the end of the parade, our version was one full of demons drunk beyond belief, stumbling all over one another.

We entered and exited the parade route for pictures with the participants. Each photo led to an invitation to join the procession. I never would have survived. We rushed home as soon as the parade finished. Because it was New Year's Day, I couldn't get any antibiotics from the closed pharmacies.

I might have been coated in Sterno and lit ablaze the next morning. I was a human Charbroil with no air conditioning.

Regardless, Laura and I agreed, I should talk to the pharmacist. Ordering drugs in her best tortilla minestrone might prove precarious.

Laura: *"My husband is very hot."*

Pharmacist: *"I'm free Saturday night. Here's my number."*

I staggered in with 103.5 fever, barely standing. I had a splitting headache and frightening joint pain. Every sprain, tear, or surgery healed long ago seemed fresh from the prior day.

"Oh, you have the crush-bone flu!" the pharmacist said. *I hope that's an upgrade from flesh-eating disease?*

Then a thought made me shudder. *Allan had dengue fever and said it was called crush-bone!* Allan was the only person we had ever met who had had the rare mosquito-borne ailment. The kicker was that he had managed to contract malaria as well.

After asking if she had the drugs for me to self-administer à la Kervorkian, she told me crush-bone *fever* was dengue. Crush-bone *flu* was a local strain of simple flu that attacked the joints. She confirmed the high fever was normal, and I'd get better.

On the couch that afternoon, it felt like someone was shucking my joints like oysters. It was too painful even to make our one flight of stairs.

"Hello!" A man's voice came from the open front door. In such a remote place, this was the equivalent of blowing an air horn in my ear as I slept. Luckily, I didn't have the strength for a heart attack.

"Uh, hi." He was a gringo, advanced in years and weighing even less than me. My concern dissipated. "Do I know you?"

"Yes, I am Don Richardson, your landlord," he said. *Where's his wife?*

"Oh, Don. I just saw it again! I am going to have a stroke! We must deal with this immediately!" A woman of equal age in somewhat formal slacks—the first I had seen in the village—appeared in the doorway.

"Oh, hi," I struggled to sit up. They stood stationary and expectantly. Particularly impaired at that moment, I couldn't connect the synapses to proceed with the conversation. Instead, I just stared at them. At a loss, they stared at one another. Then in complete synchronicity, they both leaned forward to signal their desire to enter.

"Laura!" was all I could muster.

She came downstairs drenched in sweat. The Richardsons introduced themselves. *Laura gave me a look of conviction that said, "If you have a cell of energy, find it."*

Three

We were already familiar with their dynamics. Always both present on the phone, he did all the talking. But she owned the house. After sorting out our items of business, I'd ask for decisions and resolutions. He'd say, "I'll have to ask my wife and call you back." It was like he was a marriage apprentice, first day on the job. She was a marriage therapist.

"Hi, I'm sorry, but I'm extremely ill and contagious. It's probably not a good time." Despite my wife's nonverbal pleas, I was struggling to sit upright.

Without a word, Mrs. Richardson proceeded farther into the house. He followed meekly, newly demoted to whatever is below apprentice.

"We must discuss repairs," she said.

God, we've been wanting to do this for weeks, but I can't now. Laura, please get them out of here, my face shouted.

Mrs. Richardson looked toward the Bears game I was watching—a rare luxury. "Um, OK, that needs to be turned off." She winced, pointing at the TV. *Damn!* I aimed the remote at the TV. "And now, let's put these chairs in a circle." *Good afternoon Pair-o-Dice Village. This is Dr. Helene Richardson. I'm listening.* Her husband complied and in a flash I, on the couch, was surrounded by three chairs.

"You don't understand. I have near one hundred-and-four fever and am rather incapacitated," I said.

"Oh, don't worry, I'm discussion leader." She sat, crossed her legs, and folded her hands on a writing pad.

On a tour of the house, they had noted plaster falling from the walls, interior and exterior, warping of all the windows and exterior doors, and a broken stair banister. The ceiling over the guest bathroom toilet was also rotting from a water leak, and varnish on one of the steps was being dissolved by some substance.

"The substance you speak of is the bat guano we clean up every morning. And now I have a few questions," I said. She gave me a face that expressed irritation at the interruption. "Um, how do you know what's wrong with the inside of the house?"

"Oh, we've visited three times."

"Inside?" Laura asked.

"Yes, you've been out a lot," Mrs. Richardson said.

"You're supposed to ask first," Laura's tone escalated.

Through a condescending laugh, she said, "Oh, come on! This is Costa Rica! Pura Vida! Live a little!"

"Yes, Laura. You see? Here, appointments are optional—like screens." The conflict was energizing me somewhat.

Mrs. Richardson glared at me. "OK," I said. "Second question. Aside from the plaster part, how many of those things on your list are ones we haven't told you about?"

"Um, let's see." She scanned the notes once more. "None."

"Mmmm. And now you've got this list, and what we wanted fixed is about twenty percent of it. Before you couldn't be bothered with it, and now it *all has* to be fixed yesterday?" I asked.

"Well, when you see it all, it's a horror," she said. "Yes, all this must be fixed. I'm even going to rebuild all the doors. You'll love it. I'm sure." She fanned herself with her pad as if to avoid fainting. I would have looked around for hidden cameras if anyone in the village could install them.

"Let us assume for a moment that you did all this work. How long would you think it would take, and where would you accommodate us during the work?" I asked.

"Oh, I talked it all over with Beto, and he said it can be done in two weeks." Laura emitted a laugh as I did a rough tally.

"Who's Beto?"

"Oh, he's wonderful. He knows how to do everything—masonry, plumbing, carpentry."

I knew I should have gotten Kervorkian drugs. "This place has twenty-four exterior doors and about half as many windows," I said. It's not like we lived in a mansion, but the builder used doors as a decorative element. Sixteen of them bordered the living room alone.

"But Beto said—"

"How long have you spent in Costa Rica?" I asked.

"About two weeks," she said.

"Yes, right. We've been here five times that long, and I tell you your projects will take no less than four months," I said.

"According to you," she said dismissively.

"That's right, and my last question is . . ."

She sighed.

". . . is running water on that list of yours? Or the broken burglar alarm?" I asked.

She pursed her lips. "No."

"Yeah, I didn't hear you mention them. Coincidence that those are the only two things that don't deteriorate over time? That you could just fix when you decide to retire?" *Where the hell is all this coming from?* I looked over and saw a proud smile on Laura's face.

"Well, um." She fumbled.

"Yes, so this is a lot to take in," I said. "Why don't you let us ponder all this?"

"No, I don't think that will do," she said. "It's almost time for us to go back to the U.S. I couldn't possibly go home with my house in this state."

"Yes, rather inhumane, isn't it? Look, I can respect your terror since we've experienced it for a while now. But see, you have tenants here now."

"So when can we come back?" she asked.

In twenty-two days?

"Can you give us two days?" I asked.

She stood up and walked out without a word. Mr. Richardson shrugged his shoulders and followed.

Despite Laura's praise, with time to ponder the implications of the interaction, I started to panic. Before, we needed things fixed, and they didn't care. Now they wanted to fix things we didn't care about—that would make the house unlivable as they were fixed.

But how could we say no to them? That word wasn't in my vocabulary! I once moved from Miami to Chicago on my own dime to double my salary only to arrive and be told by my new boss that my salary was actually to be the same as I was making in my old job. All I said was "OK." Confrontation was my kryptonite!

We shopped our predicament around for the next few days. Feedback from everyone was to tell the Richardsons where to stick it. Hal told me to "knock that Mr. Richardson on his ass" until I revealed his age. I spent those two days trying to convince Laura that we couldn't say no, knowing full well that what they were proposing was insufferable. As the moment of their return approached, I practiced my thoughts and delivery as if I was to deliver the keynote at the White House Correspondents dinner.

The conversation upon their return to the FlawedShack was like none I had ever had in my life.

"So here's how it's going to go." *Just channel Laura. Channel Hal.* Two days had passed, and the crush-bone hadn't let up a bit. "Screens and appointments are optional in Costa Rica?"

"Yes," Mrs. Richardson said spitefully.

"OK. Well, rent must be too."

"Now you wait a minute!" she said.

"No, hang on. We'll pay what's fair. But you are changing your side of the bargain. Quid pro quo. Each month, we'll calculate the percentage of the house's livability during that month. We'll give you the corresponding amount as rent. With two cats and a jungle out there, any time a door or window is off the hinges will be a zero percent day. And from here on out, days where the rest of the village has water and we don't will be counted as fifty percent, at best."

"If you don't pay rent, we'll just evict you!" This was the first time the husband spoke.

"Many of the houses on these roads are charging rent as somewhat of a formality. Truth is that you need someone in this house to watch it while you're gone." I folded my hands in my lap. "We'll take our chances."

The look from both said, "You smug, snot-nosed asshole."

"Are you finished?" Mrs. Richardson asked.

"Word of advice would be if you want to maximize the rent check, leave the interior projects until our lease is up. And we will require a written schedule of your planned maintenance activities two weeks before starting. Oh, and no other work starts until the house's water system is repaired," I said.

She turned to her husband. "Honey?"

He clamored with the baton just passed. "Yes, you will hear from us within a week."

"OK, thank you. I look forward to more civil interactions going forward," I said.

"Yes, right." He hesitated. "Good-bye." They left the house.

Having *never* spoken to anyone in that way, I felt like I had just disarmed a psychotic terrorist. "That was awesome!" Laura hugged me as my heart raced.

"Yeah," I said below my breath, "awesome."

The next day Adèle notified us of her firing and replacement by a woman whose boyfriend was doing some of the construction. She was thrilled beyond belief. "This house was a mess. I know. We lived in it. And I wanted to help you two so much, but everything was so impossible with them," she said.

It already felt like a new year on so many levels. We supposedly had traction on the FlawedShack Redemption. But we would now be in the middle of the only nuisance legendarily worse than cars in Costa Rica—construction.

And what was happening to me? Glen 1.0 got stepped on every once in a while, but everyone liked Glen 1.0. Without ready-made ways to solve issues and a wife in a compromised mental and physical state, Glen 2.0 was now born from circumstance. Would anyone like him? Was he a hero or an asshole?

One thing for sure—my personality was adrift. When it would anchor again was anyone's guess, hopefully sometime in 2007.

CHAPTER 24
A Matter of Wife or Death

I told the doctor I broke my leg in two places.
He told me to quit going to those places.
Henny Youngman

January 10, 2007

I figured the house would get better if God wanted it, but Laura needed to get healthy at all costs. Our defining moment was a hiking picture we put on our blog. I had my shirt off, and Laura was in a sports bra. "For God's sake! Remember to eat!" someone commented.

Jack had already pointed out that I had lost weight, but I still felt fine. Then one day, I walked to a cooler at the grocery store, grabbed a bottle of Coke Light, and my shorts fell right to my ankles to the astonishment of four fellow shoppers. I might have cared if I could have stopped laughing. I then stepped on a scale. I had lost seventeen pounds in two months and Laura fifteen.

With the only medical practice on the Ballena Coast, Dr. Nando had been working Laura's case. He was the most passionate practitioner we ever met. About our age, he drove from San José every week to his individual practice. We were initially sure he'd carry the torch for the country's celebrated health care system. Unfortunately, his aptitude was outshined by his zeal.

Three

He had prescribed rhino pills of every shape, size, and girth and shot Laura in the butt with a lance of a needle that left her sitting sideways for three weeks. After five visits, we were skeptical. But like drones, we kept going to him instead of the capital because *all* the village people gave us the consistent diagnosis of *giardia*. We needed a professional to confirm it before initiating treatment.

We finally concluded he needed coaching. Like cybercondriacs, we poured over horror stories of death-by-diarrhea at the intermittentnet café. We learned that *Giardia lamblia* was a parasite that colonized the small intestine, reducing the body's ability to absorb nutrients. Out of respect for my lovely bride, I'll leave the side effects to your own intermittentnet searches.

One day I marched into Dr. Nando's office just about determined to water board him into a diagnosis of *Giardia*. Having become somewhat joyless and devoid of a shred of charisma, Laura was with me but too weak and sick that day to muster much fervor.

His office was located in a little strip mall of three storefronts in Cordiál, about twenty-five minutes to our north, not far from Allan's new development.

We sat in the waiting room, a small hallway with no windows and one door leading to the dirt road outside and the other into Nando's office. It was the only place in the Ballena Coast to be frozen out by air conditioning.

Dr. Nando escorted a patient out. "Oooh. Ms. Laura, Mr. Glen. How are you today?" He spoke very good English with a thick accent.

We shook hands and sat down in front of his desk, a host of diplomas and certificates behind him—like Bernie Madoff showcasing his Asset Manager of the Year awards.

I leaned forward in my chair. "Doctor, we have been here five times. Laura is no better. In fact, she's worse."

"Yes, I see the more thinning and pain on her face." His voice faded as his face drooped like an overripe jack-o'-lantern. We were frustrated, but I felt bad for him.

I began my case. "Laura has a sore stomach and cannot ride in a car without literally crying."

"Aaaaah. DEEs is a vEry impOrtant fact," he said, rubbing his beard. When in diagnosis mode, he would inflect his words in that accent like some William Shatner/Ricardo Montalban amalgam.

I rattled off more of symptoms he had heard from us before. He took notes. "DEEs is a fAct we nEver consEEdered een de pAst. And gEEven the rUling out of de GiArdia and Oder bactEria tEEpically cOlonissing de digEstive trAct, and wEEth dEEs new facts, we can Only conclUde de extrEmely rAre contrAction of vegibrocolococcus!" I can't remember the real name of it for the life of me.

"No, that's not it!" I was now getting heated.

Nando's face changed. We shot each other respective two-thousand-yard stares, no more than one hundred inches apart. He was taken aback. *Glen 2.0, engage.* "I want you to tell me why this is not *Giardia*. Right here. Right now. Tell me the specific reason!"

"I have to go to the restroom." Laura winced and exited the room.

"EEt is so sEEmple! We tEsted her for eet, and she was nEgative!" he said in a dismissive manner.

"Right! You tested once. *Giardia* can only be proven through three separate tests!"

"No, no. DEEs ees not rIght." He reached for a book, puzzled at my knowledge.

"Nando—can I call you Nando?" I asked. He paused at odd length, as if I had just asked him for his sister's hand in marriage.

"Yes." I could see his convictions vanishing into defeat. But his guard was still up for Glen 2.0.

"Nando, I like you. I don't want to yell at you. But please listen. We left family and big jobs to come here. This is a completely different place with different customs. We're strangers in a strange land. And Laura's illness, two sick vehicles, and a disaster of a house are really beating us down. And *Giardia* can become chronic. Look at her! How much worse can we let this get?"

I could tell he felt for us. Laura came in and silently sat back in her seat.

"All the people of Pair-o-Dice Village have had *Giardia* at one time or another with those pipes always breaking."

Three

Glen 2.0 wasn't fine-tuned yet. I began to sweat in the cold air conditioning. *Was I having a panic attack?* My mind suddenly went blank. I needed a moment to collect my thoughts.

"Can you guys give me a minute? I have to go to the bathroom," I said. I actually did go to the restroom so that my excuse would be convincing.

The following has been authorized by one Laura Berger—just barely. I entered the bathroom and knew I had evidence to prove my case. The weak water pressure left "evidence" behind. Magnum P.U. was on the case.

I marched back to Dr. Nando, throwing the door open for effect. "Nando, with apologies to Laura, please walk into your bathroom. I challenge you to come back and tell me that is not *Giardia!*"

Nando perked up like a deer hearing a twig snap. He opened his drawer and pulled out a set of latex gloves. *Uh, it's bad, but it's not a homicide, Doc.*

"Oh, God," Laura said, burying her head in her hands onto her knees. "Aaaahhhh! How humiliating!" She started to cry. Laura had been intensely embarrassed in front of me over the entire course of her illness. Especially troublesome to her, there were no ceilings on the bathrooms at the Flawed-Shack. Otherwise, with no air conditioning, dying on the commode would be a certainty. I told her repeatedly I didn't care, which only reinforced her theory that all men were obsessed with farts and poo.

"He's a doctor, Laura," I said.

"So what? What do you think those gloves were for? He's in there handling my poops!" she yelled.

Now it was Nando's turn to throw the door open.

"II have fEEgured it Out!" he said.

"Ms. Laura has lost fEEftEEn pOunds!"

"She is cOnstantly tIred!"

"Her intEsteenes are sOre!"

"And from what I jUst saw, it EEs EEn my Expert jUdgement that Ms. LAura has the cOmmon pArasite, GiArdia LAmblia!"

You've gotta be shittin' me! Ooops, unintentional pun.

Dr. Nando walked proudly to his desk, brushing against Laura's head. She slowly looked up through tears of disbelief.

"III know the exAct cUre for dEEs!" he said. With that, he picked up another book and read us the treatment for *Giardia lamblia*, exactly the pills that the village people ate like bon-bons.

He scribbled the name on a pad—not that we needed a prescription—and we went to the pharmacy immediately next door.

How could something so simple have been so complicated? In an area where expert opinions were often inaccessible, we concluded we couldn't look to professionals in ways to which we were accustomed. If we were to live in Pair-o-Dice Village, even in matters of health, we were going to have to place trust in our fellow village people. We were longing for community? *That* was community.

But that night at dinner, we learned that community could also be found through strangers hours away. The rains had subsided rather abruptly, no longer propelling us out the door in boredom. But it only took four nights of cooking in our Playschool Cool Crew Play Kitchen, in which it took forty-five minutes just to boil a pot of water, to send us to restaurants for dinner again.

We stumbled upon Rich y Jan's. Aside from Catharsis—which had invested heavily in aesthetics—the valley restaurants had a somewhat adventurous nighttime feel. With no elevation from which to see, from your table, you'd hear a symphony of thousands of creatures through a curtain of complete darkness. It wasn't as if howler monkeys swooped from the trees to steal chicken wings. Nonetheless, I *was* once warned by a restaurateur to pay heed to the viper that had been in the men's room an hour before I was to use it.

Rich and Jan were the only ones at the restaurant that night. Two-year veterans of the village, they seemed to walk on air. They told us about how difficult it was living in the lowlands full-time, having endured hoards of mosquitoes, breezeless heat, and quite a frightening flood.

"But it's all worth it, guys. It really is," Jan said. "North Americans aren't used to this life, but if you can stop needing to always be doing something—to always have some distraction—you have no idea how much better you'll feel. You learn that happiness is in here," she pointed to her forehead, "not out there." Of course we were both experiencing that same reality, but the road in between was trying.

We told them the Dr. Nando story. "Yeah, you should have just trusted the villagers and taken the pills. Experience goes a long way here," Rich said. "But the health care is really quite good, especially in the capital."

"And sometimes there might be forces at work that give it that extra push," Jan said. Rich smiled at her. He knew exactly what she was going to say next.

Rich had become very sick shortly after their arrival. The hospital in San Isidro sent them to San José for more comprehensive tests. San José diagnosed a very advanced and life-threatening tumor—it was very likely inoperable, but more radiography taken that same day would confirm that. An elderly Costa Rican woman sat next to them in the hospital's waiting area where they anxiously anticipated the results.

Jan said the frail lady just "oozed happiness" without a word and prayed a rosary nonstop for hours. Then they learned from her that she knew their situation, was praying for them, and was there all by herself.

"Just then, the doctor came to get us," Jan said. "He sat at his desk with this amazed look on his face. I asked him how bad it was. He said the tumor was gone."

"What?!" Laura exclaimed. I was also stunned and looked to Rich who smiled in universal appreciation.

"Wait, wait. That's not all," Jan said. "I asked the doctor how it was possible. He showed us the image with no tumor. In the moment, we almost forgot to thank the lady for praying. I mean what do you say? She was totally modest and hugged us excitedly. Then she left. Never saw her again," Jan said.

"What a story! Can you imagine having that type of healing power?" Laura was on the edge of her seat.

"And you know what?" Jan asked. "We found out after she left that she had lost her husband to cancer that very same morning."

"Get . . . out!" I said. Both of us teared up.

"I know," Jan said. "You said that you really needed to rely on the community here. You probably don't know yet even how much. There's hardly anyone here. You see the same people all the time. We all know each other's secrets, strengths, and faults. Nature constantly has our full attention. And once you get in the groove where you connect into all that, everything just works."

"Well, that would be a drastic shift from our experience, frankly," I said.

"No, I know what you're thinking. You've got car trouble. We heard." I didn't even know they knew who we were. "And I'm sure you're having trouble getting a phone, and the village water is a problem."

"Right," I said.

"No, that stuff won't go away. But it won't affect you as much because after you experience the force of a close community in the cradle of nature, things much more important work out. That life that you might not even know exists beyond machines and TV and computers works. You get back to realizing what really matters."

We paid our check and waved to them with profuse gratitude for their perspective as we backed from the driveway.

"I am so glad we went out tonight," Laura said. "The trucks and the holidays and the Richardsons have been a bit tough. It's good to know that there is still reward at the end of all this. But I hope I don't need divine intervention to get better."

"Well, it might be easier that way. So you don't think being here has been rewarding?" I asked.

"No, I'm still really glad we came, and that getting in the cycle of nature thing is exactly why I did," Laura said. "There are days where we do such magical stuff. But on the days where I get to stop and think, it's sometimes rough when I'm all in my head. And it's just a process of peeling back the layers of the onion. Every once in a while another layer comes off, and I find out another thing about myself I didn't know. I'm learning so much. I think we're going to be peeling for a long time. And it's not just our layers we're peeling. Everything's new. The people around us have layers. The land has its layers."

"How ironic that when you peel layers of an onion . . ."

Three

"You cry?" Laura finished my sentence.

"Exactly. I guess nothing in life comes easy." I said.

As I pulled into the driveway, Laura put her hand on my arm and looked into my eyes. I saw an air both of mild despair and calm hope. "But if we're patient and follow through on this, everything will come."

CHAPTER 25
We've Got Green Cards, Yes We Do. We've Got Green Cards, How 'Bout You?

"If at first you don't succeed, try, try again. Then quit.
There's no point in being a damn fool about it."
W.C. Fields

January 20, 2007

Our tourist visas required us to leave the country every ninety days for three days. We chose Panama City for our first sortie. Its large malls, posh restaurants, casinos, and big-city feel reminded me of a slightly lesser-developed Miami. It also unexpectedly rekindled our desires to buy things and make life progress that had been diminishing in us since we arrived. These habits came back as if we were former smokers in a cigarette factory.

As we were landing, tears of joy filled Laura's eyes.

"What is it, Laura?" I asked.

"It's traffic. I see traffic." She pointed as I looked down to a highway three lanes wide packed to a standstill with headlights.

Another tell-tale sign of how batty our removal from big city life was making us was when we were in a large department store. Laura ran to me excitedly saying, "Oh, honey, look! Thumbtacks! We need thumbtacks!"

Three

"When was the last time you used a thumbtack?" I asked.

"Um." She looked upward in thought. "I don't know."

That question left us rolling in the aisle laughing, only to be outdone when I exited a fitting room to model a T-shirt for her. She pointed at my chest with sides splitting. I looked down at the slogan I had completely ignored in the name of comfort and fit: "Body by frijoles."

Regardless, we spent several insanely affordable nights in the air conditioned Hotel Plaza Paitilla overlooking the bay. And even then, we concluded that the Ballena Coast was the most beautiful part of Central America we had seen. We did, however, carry home this need to improve our first-world luxuries.

Upon our return from Panama—we had learned to concentrate on one task at a time for our mental well-being—we turned laser focus to getting our very own cell phones, at least until Laura's family arrived in a week when we would be too occupied to do so. After all, Ricardo's niece now had our current device on her personal balance sheet as income-producing property. Had I not found it on the pool chair at Erik's, she might have tried to repossess the Car-Cinomas—with my condolences to her.

We had made a number of visits to the ICE office south of us in Castillo—for both a home phone and GSM cards—waiting an average of thirty minutes each time only to hear *"no hay."* As such, the two cell phones we had also bought in Castillo sat in our trunk, now for forty-five days, possibly someday being useful as paperweights.

Being a one hundred percent people person, Laura recommended we go to the intermittentnet café to shop around our plight to the fellow gringos there. Our intermittentnet café of choice was a rather ingenious business creation. Intermittentnet surfers unsuspectingly performed their daily computing surrounded by property listings hung on a glass wall with a realty office on the other side. It was in a strip mall with a grocery store, a hardware store, tico restaurant, another realty office, and souvenir shop. Also in the dirt parking lot was our local Banco Nacional branch—an ATM hanging out the back of an unoccupied, haggard Winnebago.

The café had intermittentnet—the only type available—because it ran via satellite. Luckily, the storms that frequently blocked the signal on a daily basis had cleared. However, as expensive as they were, the satellites were often shared by various businesses, with signals beamed horizontally across valleys. From one day to the next, the aggressive jungle foliage would grow into the path between transmitters.

"We're back on dial-up," a customer would announce to a resounding groan that filled the room. During these conditions, the smallest e-mail would take sometimes five minutes to transmit, with twenty people sharing just one phone line.

One added feature of this particular café was that its patrons were sometimes followed out, pulled over by police, and questioned about the establishment's goings on. Gringos speculated at length about the criminal behavior in which the owners had become tangled, but it was all conjecture. We did know, however, that the owners had imported two brand-new beautiful diesel Ford pick-ups of countless tons—as rare as a four-leafed clover in the area. After three months, they were parked off the road in the jungle. This could only mean they had snuck them across the border without paying duty, and someone had tipped them off that the vehicles were on a search list.

Appropriately the gringo community at-large had a saying, "Costa Rica is the land of the wanted and unwanted. Which are you?" Of course, they were talking about their own community, not the ticos, but that saying was true. We unknowingly shared meals and beers with a couple that was extradited a year later for having kidnapped their granddaughter in the U.S., bringing her to Costa Rica. We shared company with a few people who were plucked out of the jungle for being part of an antitaxation activist club of some sort. Uncle Sam obviously came a long way to collect. But it was all very "don't ask, don't tell." In fact, we spent more time in the intermittentnet café than we would have liked and nothing seemed strange.

Our inquiries at the café revealed that those possessing cell phones had them for quite a while. Any newcomers had also been unable to get one. Of course, this was nothing new.

Three

But after a couple days of asking, a customer walked up to me and said, "Hey, I heard Brenda and Paul got a line at the ICE office in Cordial . . . ." We must have been in the truck before he finished his sentence because I don't remember the end of it.

We flew up the hill to Brenda and Paul. "How is that even possible?" I asked Laura. "There's no ICE office in Cordial, and if there was, we're friggin' idiots." Cordial was a tiny surfer resort to our north, but we were there almost every day at our two favorite lunch restaurants. One was outdoors and doubled as a Rasta nightclub, serving the freshest tuna steak anyone ever tasted for less than six dollars—and it was absolutely huge. The other was on a bluff about twenty feet over the ocean with a view down the rocky coast toward Panama—also amazingly good and affordable.

"Hey, guys! Great to see you!" Laura said as we approached Brenda and Paul's tiny, freshly built house. She had met Brenda over the Internet back in the States, and we had seen a lot more of them since Erik's New Year's party.

Brenda was a postal worker and Paul a construction contractor—both retired—from San Diego. The housing market had boomed back home. The Ballena Coast had striking similarities to the Pacific Coast Highway. Brenda and Paul, like, countless Californians, cashed out for a cheaper, earlier retirement.

They had been married for decades and had the devoted manner about their relationship of a couple that had endured a world of triumphs and sorrows together. In Costa Rica, they had upstart frustrations like ours, but they laughed at the eccentricities and flaws that times like these brought to the surface in each of them.

Their house was about two hundred feet over the ocean with basically the same view as Erik's—with the two rock islands in the foreground. They were about ten minutes north of Pair-o-Dice Village in thick primary rainforest dripping with sloths, monkeys, birds, and bugs of every type.

I quickly learned from them that I would rather be fed a sandwich of poison dart frogs every day than build a home in Costa Rica. Unfortunately, Brenda and Paul's developer had convinced them to pay him in full before arriving from the States and prior to finishing the house. Paul, a lifer in construction, was on the verge of a homicide with an unfinished pool and gaping holes for windows.

"He won't return my calls! I want to shoot the guy, but he's the only one who can get me those windows!" Paul said.

They slept in a storm of insects every night. Brenda even had the honor of being stung on the bridge of her nose by the infamous bullet Ant as she slept. Its name comes from its Smith & Wesson stinger, loaded with venom, non-life-threatening but painful beyond measure.

"I could have beheaded myself to make the pain go away," Brenda said. "Luckily, it did, but I've never felt anything like it."

Paul was deathly afraid of insects. "If I could buy a full-body mosquito net, I'd wear it all night," he'd say. But in a country with more insects per square inch than dirt, he seemed to take it somewhat in stride. Brenda poked fun at his bug fears, and he seemed to enjoy it—only because it was her delivering it.

They also lived up a road with only five houses on it, none previously having a telephone line. This meant they had to buy all their own poles, lines, and all other material to get a phone in their house. ICE, the national telephone and electricity utility, was beginning to install phone-based Internet, which was obviously very important to them. We'd bump into Paul at the store after being stiffed on an appointment or delivery or after having gone to ICE. Realizing his odds at success were becoming worse than sitting in front of a broken slot machine, he'd be blathering frustrations into the open air like a dingo leaving a meth lab.

Unlike us, however, Brenda and Paul *had* to make Costa Rica work. They admitted their life leap was financially irreversible. In an odd way, we could see a blessing in lack of the choice to stay or go. There was something about facing a challenge and saying, "I have to make this work," instead of "What does this mean?" or "How does this 'score' our decision?" like we would ask.

We loved sitting on their back deck by the empty pool, taking in the view of the ocean while chatting. Brenda was always so smiley, and Paul was so satirical about their predicaments—much like me.

Three

Our visit on this particular day had a targeted purpose, however. For once, we hoped we'd have reason to make it quick.

"So this may be the craziest thing you've ever heard me say, but word at the intermittentnet is that you got a GSM card in Cordial yesterday," Laura said.

"Yeah, ICE rolled a trailer into town," Paul said. "They have tons of cards. Hey, wait! Where are you going?" He laughed, knowing full well.

We knew we might more easily get a permit to bury fifty metric tons of enriched uranium in the jungle than get a simple cell phone before our year was up. We were basically in the car before he finished the sentence.

And there it was in Cordial—a trailer with the letters "ICE" emblazoned across the side, parked along the dirt road. (Can we just agree that from now, I don't need to put the word "dirt" in front of the word "road?")

"No hay," the guy said. They had given out almost a hundred the day before. They might have them in eight days *si dios quiere. A week-ish! Promising!*

Since Brenda and Paul's house was on our way back to the FlawedShack, we stopped back by to have our usual daily visit.

"Hey, you guys flew out of here so fast, I didn't get to tell you about the colors," Paul said.

"Colors?" I asked.

"Yeah, we got an extra card just in case, and they gave us a green SIM card. It doesn't work here. We found out everyone in this neighborhood has a pink card. We need pink. This thing is no good to us," he said, holding out a phone to Laura. These colors were a new slant in the cell phone saga.

"If it works at your place, you can have it." Brenda was so sweet. *So this is what it feels like to be approved for an organ transplant.*

"Wow! Thanks!" Laura said.

"We'll call you if it works!" I proclaimed exuberantly. "Oh, wait a minute. Sorry."

"Yeah, quit while you're ahead." Paul shot me a cautionary look.

Down the hill to the highway, then up our hill, onto our pool deck, dial a number, hit talk, and zilch, zippo, bupkis. The same words were appropriate to describe the phone's signal meter.

I immediately opened our rental phone. *Pink.* "OK, we need a pink one, too. Square one if they have only green ones in Cordial," I said to Laura. *Why didn't I just open it up back at Paul's?* This was becoming part of the "jettison any sense of time" phenomenon we were told would happen to us. Having now spent months in the midst of Pura Vida and *no hay*s, we were being much more forward-thinking. The day took you where it pleased. You'd wake up in the morning thinking you'd spend the day on the beach, and you'd go to five people's houses for meals and drinks and get back in time for bed.

The next day, someone at the intermittentnet café seemed to know a thing or two about the card rainbow. According to this fellow, the government had invested in converting the entire country to pink cards. Midway through the project, the pink company was discovered to be bribing officials and was fired. "If you're in a place that can see only a pink tower, and you have green, you're screwed," he said. Then another gringo interjected. "I have a blue one. Anyone have a blue one?" *What are we—dying eggs?*

Being in Cordiál anyway, we knocked on that trailer door every day. And every day, the answer was *no hay.*

And why did it matter? We were already there. What we didn't think about was the mental effect of constantly hearing *no hay*. Someday soon we would realize just how poisonous being busy just for busy's sake would be to someone trying to adjust to Pair-o-Dice Village.

CHAPTER 26
Costa Freaka

There are some people who live in a dream world,
and there are some who face reality; and then there are
those who turn one into the other.
Desiderius Erasmus

February 3, 2007

The Berger family alighted from the Hyundai van at a gas station just north of Pair-o-Dice Village in the fresh early evening darkness. As grown adults in our mid-thirties, we openly mused about why people's impressions of our decision mattered so much to us. But they did—especially family's.

Each Car-Cinoma seated seven, but a driver brought them to the village. We would have had more faith in two Tonka trucks than our mechanical steeds to transport them from San José after such a long flight. And anyway, the Montalloper was in the shop yet again.

Like when Jack arrived, we began to see our surroundings through their eyes. "Wow! This place is off the map!" Tom, Laura's brother, exclaimed.

"It's so dark. There are hardly any street lights," Jeanne, Laura's sister said.

"Everything looks old," Little Laura, our four-year-old niece and Tom's daughter, proclaimed.

As we drove them up to the FlawedShack, the family recounted the daredevil driving they saw coming over Death Ridge. But at the FlawedShack, where we ate the first dinner I had made in quite a while, they seemed not to be able to sustain their excitement and became rather quiet.

"Everyone's a bit freaked out about the weight loss. Both of you," Tom explained the next day. The family called him FBI. Although maybe not perfectly aligned to its intent, this was his nickname because whenever someone had a secret in the family, he would always be the one to let it slip. I told him that Laura's bout with *Giardia* was over—mostly true aside from a rare flare-up, which meant the parasites were likely still there to some degree.

"You're not going to say anything to her, are you?" I asked. "She's really beating herself up over having gotten sick—don't really know why—that she's missing a professional reputation here, and that I'm taking care of most things. She doesn't need to hear that she's withering away physically *and* mentally."

"Are you kidding?" Tom said. "No way! We've been picking things up on the phone too. She's hiding stuff. I try to be funny about it to get information without being an ass."

"Yeah, she really got a kick out of that Costa Rica F.I.N.E. thing. Good job." I said. Tom had asked Laura how she was doing a week before on the phone. Laura said she was fine. Tom asked her if she was "normal fine or Costa Rica fine." When Laura asked him what the latter was, he said, "Fucked up, Insane, and Neurotic, Every day."

Everyone headed to their respective sleeping areas to unpack and prepare for bed. *Zzzzt!*

"What the fuck?" My fair maiden began launching expletives from upstairs through the darkness of the power outage.

Where were the usual three flickers before it went out? It was ironic what a dependable hallmark this was of an undependable power grid.

"No big deal, everybody. Welcome to Costa Rica. I'll grab the flashlights," I said. I went to the window. *Everyone else has power. Explains the missing three flickers. Not good.* Then it hit me. *It's our house! The breaker box or the meter?* If I was right, we'd be on our own to find an electrician and have him show up. The Bergers would be in the dark for their entire stay, almost certainly.

Three

"I'm going to go check something out real quick." Under no circumstances was I going to reveal that I was going down onto the road to check our electric meter as Laura knew the implications as well as I did. They'd know soon enough, however, from the roar of the diesel engine.

I checked the breaker box on the way out. It looked fine. Down on the road, I shone my flashlight on the meter, a part of it still smoking and smoldering. *Welcome to the Pair-o-Dice Village Shits Carlton, Mr. and Mrs. Berger! I will be your steward, Glen. Yes, I know it felt like your shower water was electrified, but try it now.*

I then saw the most beautiful three letters—ICE. *Is it an ICE box? Maybe they're responsible?* I went back up the hill and broke the news.

Jim, Laura's father laughed.

Laura carpet-F-bombed the village in an all-out blitzkrieg.

I, as had become my natural M.O., was cool as a guanabana milkshake. I dialed ICE. "I am so sorry for the problems, sir," the delightful ICE representative said on the other end. "We will be out immediately"—no invocation of the Lord's desires, no rough estimates of days, no *mañana*. I was at a loss for what this truly meant. Time would tell.

"Oh, sure, immediately! Immediately could be some time in 2008! This never happened before! Why now when my family's here?" Laura said hysterically. "First it was the holidays. Whenever we have a special occasion, it just gets shit on!"

"I bet I know why. We've never had this many people in here. When it's just us, we can't take a shower and run a ceiling fan at the same time without tripping a breaker. We had every light on, two showers, and the laundry going," I said. "Probably bypassed the breaker and melted the box."

"I'm telling you something that you know as well as I do. My family travelled fourteen hours to live in darkness for a week!" Laura continued. By all indications, especially knowing the problem was on our own property, I assumed her prognosis to be one hundred percent spot-on. But that wasn't acceptable. There had to be a way. *Pull out all stops and see what happens.*

After ten minutes of Laura's family watching her pace and assuring her that they would have a good time regardless, Glen 2.0 emerged. "Enough! Everyone is going to bed right now! It isn't up for debate! We will have power in the morning!"

"But—"

"And you, Costa Freaka!" I pointed at Laura. "I can't fix anything with you ballistic like this! To bed! Everyone! Now!" I yelled.

"You—"

"Now!!!" I nearly screamed.

Everyone left the living room without a word. Had they had tails they would have been tucked so far between their legs, they would have poked their own eyes out. The family retired silently, shocked that such a historically mousy bloke had thundered such an edict. I paced our bedroom thinking that Laura's family could not go home thinking this was their daughter's way of life, especially since they knew it was my idea to drag her out here.

I set my wristwatch alarm for 11 p.m., giving ICE two hours to arrive before I called back.

At 10:15, *could it be?* I heard trucks—big trucks, utility trucks. I went out on the balcony, and although I couldn't see the road, I could make out the movement of spotlights. *The Bergers had the gods of* hoy *(today) with them, and they had vanquished the demons of* mañana!

At 11 p.m., Laura squinted at the sudden brightness of the restored lighting.

"See what I mean? Just have faith, and things can happen," I said like a Sunday preacher. *Fake it until you make it, I guess.*

The following morning, we went to magnificent Ballena Beach, with the two rock islands dancing in everyone's view just a hundred yards offshore. It also had a cool freshwater stream that descended from the mountains behind the beach and cut through the sand into the ocean. It was like having the ocean and a pool literally bordering one another.

Troops of white-faced capucin monkeys traversed the mangroves as we ate at a beachside restaurant. Our waitress, Emilia, showed Little Laura a sloth hanging from the trees.

Three

After some touring and a day in the life of Laura and Glen, we returned to the FlawedShack for a swim well in advance of sunset.

"If I lived here, I'd never leave the house. The roads are horrible, and with your view and the pool, why would you leave?" Jeanne told me as everyone was changing for the pool. *I could list the reasons, but we don't have time.*

I slipped out to the grocery as everyone leapt into the pool. I returned to hysterical laughter. When Kathy, Laura's mom, really started laughing, she often couldn't stop and would turn some heads.

I asked what happened, walking over to the pool with my shopping bags. Laura looked petrified. *Everyone's in stitches, and she's terrified. Spider or fire.*

"Take a look over there." Her finger trembled as she pointed.

I had to get closer to believe it. "Yeah that's a tarantula." It didn't strike me as extraordinary to see a tarantula, even though we hadn't seen one yet. What was extraordinary was that it chose to show up at this rather imperfect time. *After the transformer last night? Now this?*

"So did someone almost step on it while running around the pool or something?" I asked.

"No!" everyone shouted in unison.

Kathy explained between fits of laughter. "And then out of the corner of my eye, I saw this thing fall out of the sky. I pointed to it and asked what it was. Jeanne went over to look, screamed, and started beating it with her shoe."

"But it already looked like it was just about dead before I hit it." Jeanne was now poking it with a stick to ensure it was a goner.

Jeez, the timing. Now I was especially surprised because this was a true rarity. "I know what this is," I said. A local had told me about a wasp that stings a tarantula and flies it back to her nest to lay eggs in its abdomen. The larvae feed on the spider as they grow. "For some reason, the wasp must have let go or something, but if it already seemed like it was dying before Jeanne got to it, that's probably it." *Just another day in paradise.*

"Nature is amazing," Kathy said, which confirmed they knew I was serious. Of course, tarantulas falling out of the sky was probably not the jungle welcome wagon we were hoping would meet them in paradise.

They had had a wonderful swim in the pool, in awe of a view like ours available every time they peaked over the ledge. The spider was more of a curiosity than a shock, Laura's reaction notwithstanding.

As the sunset ripened, Tom positioned himself for better viewing.

"You want to see the green flash?" I asked him. The Berger family's heart was always in Hawaii, where people awaited the rare and coveted green flash from the sun as it completed its dunk into the ocean.

"You can see it?" he said.

"Oh, yeah, it's best from right over there," I said. "Over there. Move to the left. OK, a bit to the right." I moved him toward a specific spot on the very edge of the pool deck with the road far below. *Tom's a brilliant guy. He's not going to fall for this.*

There he stood, waiting. Like clockwork the first bat came out of the roof and whooshed by his head. He didn't notice. Another one. No reaction. *He needs a little nudge.*

I started humming "The U.S. Air Force Song," as a hint. *Off, we go, into the wild blue . . . Whack!* He smacked himself in the head. Without a word, the concern I had been watching for appeared on his face.

Despite his sharp intelligence and wit, Tom was the prime target for this joke, if I could pull it off. A tough truck driver, he weighed north of two hundred twenty pounds. When the Steelers had recently won the AFC championship, he hugged me out of impulse, nearly popping every disk in my back like water balloons.

"Ah! What's that?" he asked five seconds later as another passed. I stayed silent. Another. "And that!" He waved his arms in the air, almost dropping his beer, never leaving the flight path. "Whoa!" he nearly punched himself in the head on the next one. *OK, now he's going to knock himself out and fall down the ridge.*

"It's the Costa Rican Air Force," I said, laughing. His look told me that I had a few moments to spit it out or I'd end up headlong in the valley. "Bats. Every night, hundreds of them fly off into the sunset."

He motioned toward his backside. "It's time for you to visit the bat cave, pal," he said. It was rare to pull one over on him. I basked in the moment.

"Jeez, the only thing left is snakes! You see any around here?" he asked.

"They're around." We told the family about the terciopelos. "We've never seen any on the property, though. You're safe. Just don't walk in tall grass without our boots, and no strolling outside at night without a flashlight."

That night, we had an amazing dinner at Catharsis. They agreed that you'd be hard-pressed to find better food back home. And the next morning, I delivered a curse-inducing 5:30 wakeup for a hike with Dr. Bob. He took us on one of his novice hikes. We walked for two hours in the flat riverbeds that received the water from the falls on the hills and mountains we'd usually hike. Even though it was a lighter hike, there were enormous boulders and fallen trees across the stream that had to be scaled and descended.

Dr. Bob must have anticipated the difficulty that inexperienced North Americans would have with the jungle. I assumed this when he—possibly already of retirement age—decided to put Little Laura on his shoulders. "This will keep us from having to wait for her and give everyone two free hands to catch their falls," he said. She stayed on those shoulders for the entire hike.

"What is he, a superhero?" Tom, a linen truck driver who slung around wrecking-ball-sized bags of sheets and tablecloths at five every morning could barely believe his eyes. I suddenly felt ancient.

"You know, I don't know what it is—maybe the clean air or just the aura of the place, but you see people who back home would consider a flight of stairs an obstacle accomplish some crazy physical feats here," I said.

The hike ended at a low-lying waterfall that emptied into a deep gorge. The Berger family basked in it, reminiscing about swimming in Waimea and Manoa falls in Honolulu when everyone was younger.

Dr. Bob encouraged all of us to swim under a rock resting flat between two others, elevated about two inches over the water of the pool where we swam. Having eaten termites and led most of this hike with my machete in hand, I was becoming rather daring, but something about what was under that rock intuitively gave me the willies.

After finishing our swim, we reversed path, hiking exactly the way we came. "Sorry I didn't swim under the rock, Bob." Bob was amazingly giving of his time to take us on these hikes. On this one, he was responsible not only for us but for another large group that was visiting Lagos del Fuego. He didn't get paid a cent for this. I never wanted to turn down any opportunity he presented to experience something new.

"All right, Glen. You can do it some other time. You missed a very unique experience, though."

"Damn! What?"

"Well, a bunch of bats hang upside down under there during the day," he said.

I got chills. "But that rock is like a couple of inches off the water!" I said.

"Oh, it's concave underneath, there's at least six inches between you and them," he said.

"Look, uh, maybe you and I should have a talk about exactly how quickly I plan to progress toward my jungle badge," I said, laughing.

So far, the trip had been adventurous and marvelous at the same time. The family had experienced a little jungle rawness—with the power outage and hairy spiders being dropped from the sky by an insect a fraction of its size. They had also witnessed the spectacle and proximity of the wildlife and the jungle beaches—plus our routine hiking the pristine gorges of Lagos del Fuego.

"It's really been perfect," Laura said as she and I walked toward the Monterror alone with our guests following. "I mean when that power went out, I thought their whole trip was sunk, but it's going really well. I am so thankful we are able to show them this. In this moment, it really feels like all this was meant to be."

CHAPTER 27
Seize the Day

I love my husband. He loves me. There are monkeys in the trees.
Thomas Berger

February 5, 2007

"Costa Rica is my favorite place!" Little Laura said on the way down the *Costanera* to lunch.

Laura and I looked at each other with amazing satisfaction.

"I'm so glad. And there's lots more to come!" Laura said.

"Yeaaaaah!" Little Laura bounced in her seat.

As we drove to lunch, I made arrangements for an overnight hike and camping trip in the rainforest. We still hadn't taken them to Hal and Indira's, our property in Lagos del Fuego, or Allan's new development, so breathtaking we were regularly spending half-days there. We were becoming incredibly well acquainted with Allan's development. Nonetheless, the couple of stabs we had made at convincing tourists in the village to come see it had proven fruitless. I continued to work the stock market, but our efforts to energetically sell property in the midst of all our logistical concerns were obviously falling short.

Today, lunch would be at one of our favorite spots—a restaurant at a tilapia farm about seven miles south of the village. The tilapia farm was quite unique—a primitive, unassuming Japanese garden of tropical flowers. But the real draw was yet another waterfall across the road and down a five-minute path. Above the pool sat a boulder the size of a tour bus that the waterfall presented at its mouth proudly like a hockey player after winning Lord Stanley's Cup. The current had been unable to dislodge it, but doing so would undoubtedly precipitate a meteoric splash in that pool and the certain demise of anyone below. This was furthest from my mind as I took my in-laws to swim there.

When we had first found the falls, a tico explained that a few years prior, an enormous tree grew from one of the banks along the river above the pool. One night, a large storm passed as the locals heard debris crashing down the river in the darkness. That morning, the tree was gone, and the rock was lodged in the mouth of the falls.

The path to the falls was owned by the proprietors of the tilapia farm and restaurant. The understanding was that, on your honor, lunch at the tilapia farm restaurant was the cost of admission.

At the waterfall, the family talked about how much the area looked like Hawaii, lending legitimacy to the motivations of our life leap. "But it's certainly more hostile," Jim asserted, referring to their recent brief encounters with the elements.

"I just silently thanked God again that we have these moments to share with our friends and family." Tears streamed down Laura's cheek as the family had water fights in the pool and took minihikes up the river.

I put my arm around her and watched in satisfaction. *Yes! The ultimate payoff. Gratification is so much sweeter when you risk so much.*

At lunch, Tom characteristically discredited his status as elder sibling by staging a puppet show with our leftover fried tilapia heads. He could slay a librarian at an abbey with his humor.

After lunch, we toured the pools of the farms. "There's one! There's another one!" Little Laura pointed at the fish as if she was playing Where's Waldo. Tom held her by the waist as she sat in his lap on a bench that he leaned toward the pond for a better vantage point.

Three

Laura was still smiling with deep satisfaction. *Caution!* This instinctive thought was planted in my brain from goings-on in our peripheral vision. *Something's wrong.*

It looked like Little Laura was trying to dive into the pool, her father hanging tight to prevent it. The wooden bench was tipping into the pool. "Laura! Stop!" Tom said. "Cut it out! Now!" He stopped her momentum and righted the bench quickly. "I said stop!" He grabbed her face and turned it toward him.

"Oh, God! Seizure, seizure!"

I heard Little Laura begin to choke—gasping for air—with her eyes purely white and rolled back.

I launched off my bench like a rocket, keys already in hand, running up the hill with Tom following right behind me carrying Little Laura like a football. Being a single father, Tom and his parents had full responsibility for her and were mobilizing a plan they had executed once before. Laura had had a seizure in Pittsburgh. The doctors said it was from high fever and would go away with age. But because they could be rather damaging to the brain and it had happened only once, the family was to get her straight to a hospital should one happen again.

I looked back. Laura and Jeanne were keeping up, but Jim and Kathy were trailing quite a bit.

"The nearest hospital is forty-five minutes away! Move your asses! Move! Move! Move!" I yelled. Glen 2.0 was back.

I flew down the dirt road—blind turns, cows, and their herders be damned. I silently weighed potential outcomes: (1) Little Laura dying in the car, (2) having a head-on collision with an oncoming dump truck delivering materials to one of the construction sites, or (3) T-boning a cow—pun intended. I never slowed, surging through shallow streams, potholes, and other obstacles. The Monterror took to the air at least three times. I sounded the horn constantly as a warning, surely futile given the lax modes of the locals and my current speed.

"Arrive alive, Glen. Arrive alive," Tom said and then turning to Little Laura, "Breathe honey! Breathe! Just stay with me! You're going to be OK." Tom was very obviously forcing calmness for her sake.

Little Laura began gasping for air between sobs. "I'm scared, Daddy!" she managed to say, choking. *Good! She's breathing.*

We turned into Lagos del Fuego, on the way to the hospital, to see if we could ring Dr. Bob from someone's house because we didn't have many numbers stored in our phone. We sped up the road ten minutes and arrived at the first house belonging to people we knew—one of the tax-evasion couples. Dr. Bob didn't answer the phone. This failed gamble set us back a half hour.

We drove another thirty minutes to Cedro, a town big enough for a bank, an ICE office, and a couple of small grocery stores, but most importantly, the local hospital. Little Laura now seemed OK, but we feared what might happen to her next.

The hospital was made of cement block coated with years of clear gloss paint. It had an old linoleum floor. This lack of updating made sense because a brand new hospital complex was being built ten minutes closer to the village. A nurse immediately called us into a room with nothing but a bed and an oxygen tank. It all seemed discouragingly primitive, reflected by the concerned looks on the family's faces. Little Laura seemed exhausted but somewhat back to normal. After a couple minutes, a young woman entered.

"Hello, I'm Dr. Fernandez," she said in Spanish, shaking Laura's and my hands as the entire family watched anxiously. *She thinks we're Little Laura's parents.*

"Hi," I said in Spanish. "I'm Glen. Tom here is the father. I can translate."

"Very well," she said.

"Please tell me what is happening." Dr. Fernandez's hand was under Little Laura's face as she smiled sweetly into her eyes.

I had contemplated my lack of Spanish medical vocabulary on the way into town. This was going to be rough. I'm sure what I said translated into something no more coherent than: "The little girl's head suddenly drooped and began bologna marshmallow cow tail. She cried for her Jehova Marsala cherry tire irons. It sounded like coronary condominium dust muffin."

Three

The doctor tilted her head like a dog watching the pope pole dance. "I speak English. Please proceed in English."

Tom explained the events to Dr. Fernandez. Within minutes, Laura was brought into a hallway. Three technicians wheeled over the oxygen tank and got to work. She was given a mask decorated to resemble a purple dragon with inhalants. She was given shots, her blood was drawn, and vitals were taken. Little Laura didn't have to move a muscle.

The frenzy of tests was so pronounced, Laura and I became concerned. I pulled Dr. Fernandez aside. "Is she OK? She's getting so much treatment."

"Oh, she'll be fine," she said. "She has an ear infection. Her father said she was outside in the sun all day. That, with her fever, induced her seizure. We'll give her antibiotics. Just keep her out of the sun for a week."

"Thank you, doctor." I shook her hand.

"Of course," she said. Tom had one concerned eye on his daughter and the other glazed one on Dr. Fernandez. I went back to the family and relayed Dr. Fernandez' diagnosis and recommendations.

"And Glen told the doctor my mom says I'm a catch!" Tom said. *Ah, crisis over. Back to humor and fun.*

A technician handed me two prescriptions and directed Laura and me toward the pharmacy window. "Well, it was great while it lasted," Laura said. "I just can't believe it. I thank God my family is having such a great time and less than an hour later . . . ."

"Yeah, I know—a big slap in the face. But she was susceptible to febrile seizures, and your parents said she was complaining about her ear before she arrived," I said. "So really, what she had came from the States."

Her smile was meek and defeated. I felt bad, knowing she was going to feel this anguish for a long time. Still feeling a bit responsible for their situation, I went to pay the bill. *If we can pay to keep two Car-Cinomas on life support, we can pay a family medical bill.* Luckily, I was in a hospital because I almost fainted at the amount due: only forty-three US dollars. For that, we had spent two hours in an emergency room and filled two prescriptions with no insurance.

Now knowing that Little Laura would be OK, our anxiety levels decreased, and I was able to take an objective pause on our ride home. Despite its ups and downs, Costa Rica made you proud to have chosen it as your temporary home. When your car was in the ditch, someone grabbed a tractor to drag you out. When a fight between spouses registered on the Richter scale, you went out on the deck to the most amazing natural theater you could ever want. And when your niece had a seizure, the medical care was first-class—and for a pittance.

We reentered Pair-o-Dice Village beaten and despondent and came upon Los Desemparados, our sibling gardening dynamic duo. I stopped to speak with them. I would have regardless, but for the first time, they had missed an appointment for the special *chapea* we had arranged for the family visit. The yard was rather jungly at the moment.

"*¡Buenas, amigos!*" I said enthusiastically.

"Hey, Don Glen! It's a beautiful day, *gracias a dios!*" one of them said.

Unprompted, they entered into an explanation for their absence. I smiled and nodded, interjecting empathy every so often as they spoke. "You don't say?" I said. "Oh, that's horrible!" I sympathized. "Well, I hope they feel better. So you will come tomorrow?"

"Of course. If God wants it, we can fit it in at seven in the morning," they said.

I rolled up my window and continued up the hill. Laura harbored a distinct disappointed look. *She understood it all.*

The Berger family tended to be a curious lot, especially in new lands with new cultures. They were always inquiring and learning. "They seemed very kind and happy. What was that conversation about?" Kathy asked. I explained their having missed the appointment.

"And why didn't they come?" she asked.

I recited what they told me verbatim, that they were in San Isidro waiting for a delayed bus toward Pair-o-Dice Village. One of their two daughters fainted, and they had to rush her to the hospital.

"Oh, that's terrible." Empathy was one of Kathy's most pronounced traits.

"Mom, wait for it," Laura said.

"Wait for what?" Kathy said.

"Then, at the hospital, the other daughter fainted," I said.

"And you believe them?" Jeanne asked.

"No," Laura piped in. "But that's what I told you to wait for."

"Why didn't you say something?" Kathy asked.

"Because that was a pretty ornate story, no?" I asked.

"Yeah, but it's impossible," Jeanne said.

"Impossible, no. Improbable, yes," Laura said.

"What are you guys, sheep?" Tom asked.

"And why didn't you say something? Kathy repeated.

"Well, see, if we are to get on here, the priority has to be getting along. That's why they went through such an effort with the story," I said.

"But they should show up if they want to get along," Kathy said.

"Yes, that's one way of looking at it—our way, by the way—but there are other dynamics behind the scenes. They probably couldn't say no to someone else at the same appointment time. And they probably do it to other people other times, unbeknownst to us when they show up for our appointments. But that's the key. Saying no is not acceptable for them," I said.

"Mom, if you lived in a world where time didn't matter, would you really care if they showed up or not? We live in that world now," Laura said. "I mean in my mind I don't live in that world, but outside my mind, that's the reality."

"The bottom line is patience," I said. "The only thing stopping us is our North American tendency to always stress that time is finite and that lying is *always* a sin. But what are the consequences around here? It's grass and a few bushes, and here, time is all anyone has. There are no obligations or expectations. So they'll come tomorrow. Then again, maybe not."

"But they lied to you," Jeanne persisted.

"Probably," I said. "But if we are going to live in their culture as guests, we are going to have to value the same things they do. Peace and friendship is more valuable. If I call them out, I have violated the main cultural tenet, and we're out some good gardeners—hard to find, by the way. How does that help us?"

"Laura!" Jeanne pled.

"It's a different world, guys," Laura said.

"How can you live like that?" Kathy asked.

"We didn't think we could. We still barely can," Laura said. "But they live with it just fine, so we know it's possible. And besides, we'd be pitting what we *think* is right against an entire country's culture."

"I'll put a hundred thousand down on the culture," Tom said.

"Exactly," Laura replied. "And in the end, we have to remind ourselves it's just that—culture. It's not right or wrong."

We ascended the rollercoaster driveway in a truck full of puzzled family members coupled with a mixture of pride and self-doubt.

Earlier, we had woken up to a glorious morning and the family's complete fervor for the village. In the span of eight hours, they were likely ready to charter an airlift out of the war zone. And they still had four days left.

CHAPTER 28
Two Flakes and a Snake

You know, you can touch a stick of dynamite, but if you
touch a venomous snake it'll turn around and bite you and
kill you so fast it's not even funny.
Steve Irwin

February 5, 2007

"I'm afraid for Laura," Tom said at the FlawedShack over Erwin's delicious pizza pies later that night. "What if it happens again? It's just us and nature here. The hospital is so far away."

I felt bad for him. "You feel like you've brought your daughter into a shit storm and can't protect her."

"Pretty much," he said.

"Just shower, get ready for bed, and tomorrow will be another day. My sense is the country's hazing is over. Welcome to the frat." Like all my other reassurance over the past several days, this one had no reliable basis whatsoever.

Everyone began preparations for sleep and the family's tradition of evening tea. Laura and I spent the next half hour revising the family's itinerary to keep fever-stricken Little Laura out of the sun. Naturally, I was under strict orders to cancel the night hike and camp in the rainforest. As we were finishing, *thump, thump, thump.*

"What was that?" Laura asked.

"Sounds like pounding on the wall." Then we heard Tom's voice. I couldn't make it out. In the past, I had been able to understand him from across a crowded Walmart. This was an intentionally muted whimper, as if the guest apartment were adorned with sleeping crocodiles. And it was Tom whimpering, the guy who lived a respectable portion of his adolescence on the streets—with the Popeye forearms and the spine-snapping bear hug.

"What's he saying?" Laura asked.

"Snake, snake, snake." The pounding continued.

Laura's face flushed white. "You've gotta be—"

"Just stay here, and don't tell your parents. If it's not poisonous, we can get it out of here without everyone else knowing," I said.

"How will you know if it's poisonous?" Laura asked.

"No idea." I immediately went outside to tell our serpentine neighbor we were fresh out of sugar. The interloper was situated smack dab *on the welcome mat* of the guest apartment. Regardless, after three months of chaos, you could have groomed my nose hairs with a weed whacker and induced nary a flinch.

The snake lay there motionless, about ten feet away from me. Tom's wide eyes darted between the snake and me through the window, as if he just heard the first sounds of hissing in a gas chamber. "I can't believe it. I opened the door to go to the main house, and there he was. Imagine if I didn't look down!"

"Daddy, Daddy! I want to see!" Little Laura said, running toward the door.

"Stay in that bed or you won't leave it until we go back to Pittsburgh!" he yelled back.

"Remember when we had the talk about the jungle being safe with a few exceptions?" He nodded anxiously through the glass. "Tom, meet Exception. Exception—Tom," I gestured.

His speechless eyes pled for more information.

"*Terciopelo*—aka ultimate pit viper. Just stay put until he goes away." I turned heel. Tom seemed fine with my proposal.

Think fast. What do you tell the others? I went back into the main house.

"What happened?" Laura asked, the rest of the family now with her for tea.

Damn! Little Laura's going to tell anyway. "We have a *terciopelo* on the welcome mat. He'll go away," I said calmly.

"You're kidding," Laura asked.

"Nope," I said, "but I forbid anyone to do anything about it. Seriously, it will go away. We now know the hospitals are cheap, but that's no reason to go back."

"That thing could kill Skippy and Rugby!" Laura said.

"Forget Skippy and Rugby! My granddaughter is out there!" Kathy said.

"Skippy and Rugby and all of us are *in*side. The snake is *out*side. Let's keep it that way," I replied.

"You've got to kill it!" Laura said.

"No, I don't," I said.

"Well, then I will," Laura replied. *What the . . . ?*

"No you won't! We came into *his* habitat, not the other way around!" I plead forcefully.

"If you don't go out there, I will," Laura advised.

"And if she doesn't do it, I will. The only thing between that snake and my granddaughter is a door!" Kathy said.

"Precisely!" My tone was emphatic.

"I'm going." Kathy started scanning the room. "What can we kill it with?"

I looked at Jim, who, as he dunked a Mennonite cinnamon roll in his tea, looked at me calmly as if to say, "Good luck with *that!*"

"OK, well our snake boots are in the bodega. You'd have to walk right by Mr. Snake to get to them." Of course, in my mind, this was a fine deterrent.

"You mean the laundry room, right?" Kathy said, heading through the patio door.

"Stop it, Mom! I'm going," Laura left in a flash.

What the hell? Laura makes me fetch the laundry because she's afraid of the jungle night. Kathy's high school aspirations were of becoming a nun—not the

214

stereotypical vocation of a snake slayer. Now they are going out into the blackness of nature to rumble with the greatest pariah in this hemisphere?

Laura returned immediately and began donning snake boots.

"OK, everybody stop! I'll go. But for the record, you all suck and will for a very long time!" I said.

"These are your boots anyway." Laura handed me the footwear. "I got the wrong ones." *Ah, how conveeeeenient!*

I donned the boots and cruised by Jungle Enemy Number One to fetch my machete and flashlight from the Monterror.

Mr. Snake, meet Wyatt Twerp—one hundred forty-one brawny pounds—lollipop stick legs poking from his boots, machete gracing his right hand and flashlight in the left. The mere thought of killing a fellow earthly inhabitant made me queasy and uneasy.

I gave him stink-eye and assessed my next move. He suddenly made a break for it—tail disappearing around the corner adjoining the exterior walls of the laundry room and the guest apartment. I assumed he was seeking shelter under the tall bush in that corner. *Game on, I guess.* I bolted instantly, whacking fiercely with the precision of a guy in the middle of a Lasik procedure.

I lifted branches and dead leaves with the tip of my implement, examining the ground under the bush, briefly seeing his tail again, only for it to disappear into the leaf pile. *He's cornered. Oh, God. I really have to kill him now?* I continued my examination.

No sign of him, but I did see blood on the machete. I contemplated momentarily going inside to fake triumph. But I had been hired—obliged, rather—to carry out a hit. The boss-ettes inside would demand to see a stiff.

"Is he dead?" Tom called from inside.

"I don't know," I said. "I lost him."

Tom exited the guest apartment to coach me from behind with his own flashlight. Jim, swaddled in his robe, provided air support from the balcony above whilst enjoying his evening cognac.

"He had to have gone up that bush," Tom said.

Three

"I haven't seen him come out. He's still somewhere in the corner," Jim said. *Sip, sip.*

"I looked everywhere, and he's not here. And this type of viper doesn't climb trees!" I replied. *Now how exactly do I know that?*

Laura looked down from the balcony, holding a glass of wine. "Did you kill it yet?"

So glad the spectators have concessions! Panic came over me momentarily as I realized I had no idea where he was.

"Look, man," I said to Tom, "a retreat is in order. He has to be here, but we can't see him. We're just going to poke around here until one of us gets tagged."

The Pennsylvania tribunal above voiced their sentence to the gladiators below.

"Find it!"

"Kill it!"

"Get it!"

I began cutting away all the low branches. "Tom, hold this machete and watch for him." I grabbed a rake leaning against the wall. Rake, rake. No snake.

"There have got to be holes in the wall," Tom posited. "I looked at everything with the flashlight. He's not here."

I entered the guest apartment on the other side of the wall—*nothing there.* Then I switched to the *bodega*, filled with obstacles like luggage, pool hoses, and a washer/dryer from which he could jump out at me. *I'm going to end up in the hospital tonight.* No snake.

I felt daft and anxious. Laura "the Enforcer" and Kathy, "Mother Superior of the Holy Order of the Sisters of Lack of Mercy," would be none too happy.

"He's gone." I was thrilled for the snake.

"I'm telling you I was standing here the whole time watching this corner. He's not gone," Tom said.

Aw screw it! I jammed my head into the bush, branches resting on my shoulders, entering myself in the contest for World's Stupidest Human, 2007. *Nothing!*

216

I stepped back. "All right, let's calm down and use both flashlights," I said. Our united glow scanned from the base of the bush upward.

At neck level, an interesting pattern appeared behind a clump of leaves. I had a flashback to the funnel cake shape behind the glass of the Deadly Snakes exhibit at the Serpentarium by my childhood home.

Like I said, they climb trees!

Although I don't recall, Laura claims I uttered a fervid soliloquy of hysterics. All I remember is using the word "varmint" for the first time in my life. Could it have been that it was two inches away from where my face had been less than two minutes before? Can you say, "Good-bye right cheek?"

Now I was incensed. Survival instincts and a good dose of rage drowned my compassion. This guy absolutely had to be offed.

"Give me," I said to Tom, my hand extended toward the machete.

I brandished my jungle blade like Hercules. It was more like Quirkules, hitting everything but the snake—sparks shooting from the cement. Noting my deficiencies, he didn't flinch a millimeter. *He has a brain the size of a Coco Puff and can still tell I have the martial prowess of potpourri with this thing!*

I aimed my blade full-force and squarely hit his perch. But after my repeated errant strikes at everything but the snake and my brother-in-law, the machete was now blunt as a hammer.

I hit it again. The branch finally fell to the ground. I struck at the *terciopelo* a few times, chopping almost clear through his back third. Releasing my tense muscles, I analyzed my work. He was motionless—dead.

Tom looked down at him, paying his respects.

"OK, I'll go get a trash bag." I turned to walk away.

"Wait! He's striking!" Tom said.

I turned, and he was retracted, aimed at my heel. I swung blindly, like taking as many pictures as you can of the Taj Mahal knowing you'll get a at least one good one. But I saw nothing. My eyes were closed.

"Wait, stop!" Tom's command paused my apoplectic tirade.

"Look at this! He committed suicide!" The light of the flashlight shined on the snake's teeth sunken into its own flesh.

Are you kidding me? After a near cheek amputation and the abandonment of all compassion, he couldn't bear our ineptitude and decided to end it?

"Why couldn't he have done that twenty minutes ago?" I asked.

Now confident that the risk of an errant beheading by my blade had ceased, the Pittsburgh nobles descended from the tribunal to deliver their performance assessment.

Until that moment, Tom had only spouted reason and guessed the snake's ultimate location—up the bush. However, the moment he declared, "I'm gonna pick it up," I knew we were both just two flakes and a snake.

"Like with your bare hands?" I asked.

"Yeah, he can't do anything to me now," he said.

"Dude, Dr. Fernandez wasn't *that* good-looking," I said. "Plus, she won't want you with parts missing."

"He's dead," Tom stressed.

"Tommy! No! Leave the snake alone!" Kathy exclaimed.

"Ma, it's sliced three places!" Tom bent toward the snake.

Whack! Kathy smacked him in the back of the head. "Thomas Berger! I said no!"

You put that snake down this instant, and we'll go in and cut the crusts off your peanut butter and jelly and have a nice glass of juice! Tom yielded, head drooped.

I laid the corpse across the tip of the machete. "Here, gimme," Tom said, hurling it over the side of the property to the depths below, "Taps" echoing in my head with Kathy yelling, "Thomas Berger!" in the background. Everyone reentered the home to resume pre-bed activities. Jeanne, the competitive couch napper, slept through the whole thing.

"Well, maybe the country isn't done hazing you yet," I said as I passed Tom's bed to get something out of the bathroom. "But hey! Get a good sleep in. Pick-up soccer match with rabid wild boars tomorrow bright and early."

And then a trucker from blue-collar Pittsburgh showed me a bird I had not yet seen during four months in the jungle.

CHAPTER 29
A Family Who Hurls Together
Stays Together

Illness strikes men when they are exposed to change.

Herodotus

February 6, 2007

Jungle threat level was at orange. We dared only to show the Bergers our property and Allan's new development. Even this proved to be adventure enough for them when at one point, I took seven loved ones in an SUV up an incline that felt like I was scaling the underside of a bridge. "Arrive alive, Glen," Tom said again.

Tom had assessed the implications of the seizure and snake episodes. As far as he was concerned, his family and daughter were under assault from the jungle. "Can you get antianxiety pills without a prescription? I mean the strong stuff."

The family ended up transplanting their usual activity when together— sitting in deep discussion every waking moment—into the jungle. Jeanne got her wish to not have to leave the house anymore. Objectively speaking, when one didn't have to deal with all its issues, I could see why. It was basically a resort setting without staff. And staying at the house and chilling was ironically quite fitting. After all, we really didn't know when we'd all see each other again. Things could have been worse—especially if we ventured out and risked our next unknown calamity.

And then the village graced Tom with crush-bone flu on the last day of his stay. Laura and I were once again overcome with a sense of guilt for these hardships. We instinctively cancelled the van for their return and decided to accompany them to San José. I tied all the bags to the roof of the Monterror the next morning, and off we went.

Getting out of the truck at the McDonald's in San Isidro, I saw Jeanne vomiting into her own hands. Despite the long drive, I assumed she hadn't done this just to pass the time. We had another fallen soldier. Grandma and Grandpa were the only two visitors left unscathed.

"Do you think my Dad's OK?" Laura said, scanning the McDonald's menu of *McNíficas, McPollos, and Doble Quarto de Libras con Queso.*

She had reason to be concerned. He was uncharacteristically quiet, and Jim and illness went together like Tidy Bowl and tapioca pudding. If you want to see fifty shades of grey, talk about hospitals, doctors, aging, or ailments in his presence.

For instance, years ago, he was diagnosed with angina and was a candidate for emergency exploratory surgery to determine the extent of risk. It was November. The holidays were upon us.

Jim was told that they didn't have any slots for angioplasty available at his doctor's hospital of choice until the New Year. "What if you find I need more extensive surgery?" Jim asked.

"We'd have to transport you to another hospital," the doctor said.

Jim calmly delivered the solution. "Tell you what. I'm going home to celebrate the holidays with my family. If I'm still alive after that, we'll do the procedure." In January, he got his exploratory and needed the angioplasty. Laura didn't know about it until it was over.

"I'm fine," Jim repeated over Death Ridge.

"Yeah, Dad. Are you America fine or Costa Rica F.I.N.E.?" Tom asked. Even crush-bone couldn't stifle his humor.

And then the Monterror's clutch—replaced just two months prior—started to gag. In hindsight, I could have set my watch by these occurrences.

Another watch-setting benchmark was getting lost in San José, which had quickly lost its novelty. After a half hour of rush hour traffic and an almost dead clutch, the infirmary was deteriorating in the back and becoming invisible in the setting sun. I resorted to stopping at Pizza Hut for directions to the hotel. The three employees rattled off Costa Rican directions. "Take a left by the lady with the hairy mole on her right ear." I whipped out *colones*, and within ninety seconds, we were following an exuberant delivery guy on a moped to our hotel. His excitement stemmed from the fact he was delivering a pizza right around the block so this was going to be *"doble propina"* (double tip).

We had tried this once before with a taxi driver, asking him to run the meter so that we could just follow him. "I've got it! The perfect business idea," I told Laura. "We buy a tow truck, rent a little shack in Cartago," the first town on the periphery of San José, "and charge people to take them to their final destination in San José. We'd make a mint."

"You lost me at the part where you said we buy a truck," Laura said.

I lay awake all night that night, unable to sleep over Tom's groans—even though he seemed to be sleeping just fine. The next morning, we saw the infirmary off to Pittsburgh. A call upon their landing confirmed Jim's illness, which he could no longer hide in transit. Only Kathy had survived the trip unscathed.

"What the hell was that?" Laura said in the Monterror going back to the hotel.

I couldn't begin to explain it. We began discussing whether karmic or supernatural forces might be working against us. I always had this sensation that the jungle was so much bigger than Laura and me. Of course, on the surface this was physically true, but hopefully you catch my drift. I reminisced about the last few months, trying to pinpoint ways we might have hurt nature or done wrong to the country's inhabitants. I had harassed only two landlords from Arizona, and I quickly assumed they did not have supernatural influence in the country.

Three

That afternoon, we found a new certified Mitsubishi mechanic in San José to fix the clutch. When he called the Monterror a disaster, it was like telling us that when you take a shower, you get wet. Had he actually said this, I could have said, "Well, at our house, not always."

When he gave us the first—with emphasis on *first*—estimate, our bind became as real as ever. We were unable to sell either truck and needed to keep both on life support at sky-high prices to have a shot at someday getting rid of them. The repairs would take two days. With his certified status, at least he could get parts.

Day three came, and a litany of *mañanas* ensued. The bill grew along with the new mechanical anomalies discovered.

We had left a pile of food for the Boys at the FlawedShack that would last only four days. Laura was straightjacket-ready, with the Monterror disassembled to the point it wasn't drivable even if we wanted to go back. "We have to call Indira and Hal." The issue was that, like us, they had no home phone. In fact, the only place they got cell signal was at a mango tree on an empty lot five minutes from their house. Indira would sit on her ATV in a friend's lot taking in one of the nicest views on the coast as she tethered her cell phone to her laptop for Internet. A not so occasional herd of cows would pass in her midst. We didn't have that type of cell phone, unfortunately. Of course, there was no answer, despite Laura's calls every ten minutes.

"If you had to ask me my three core values, taking care of the Boys would always be at the top of the list. And I leave Pair-o-Dice Village with no contingency plan for them? I am completely changing—and not for the better! Indira doesn't even have keys!"

"Well, you were actually forward-thinking. You already left a four-day supply," I said.

"OK, around here, that's not forward-thinking. That's impulsive," she said.

And God bless the hotel owners, dear friends of ours who brought all the fresh fruit and refreshments we wanted every day to drown our anxiety. They also took us to lunch and talked with us for almost four hours, clearly helping us to unwind and deal with the stress. The fact they took that amount of time from running a busy B&B meant the world to us.

Finally, at the end of day five, Indira called. "Hey! I got your message. Relax. I didn't have to break into the house. Did you know that you can get through any door with just your index finger?"

"Makes sense. I noticed last week that all the doorknobs are installed backwards," I later explained to Laura. "Unfortunately, I hadn't noticed the collateral security risk. You know what's intensely curious is that everyone talks about petty theft being rampant in the village. We've had a brand-new TV in plain view a fingertip away from a break-in, on a completely isolated property, and not a thing has happened." I was starting to buy into Hal's theory that our personal risk might be higher in Chicago.

Of course, now with word out in the village that we were stuck in San José, we became flooded with errand lists from the village people. And finally, on day seven, we decided to go to the shop to monitor the work and motivate them to get us back home. We laid fifteen shopping bags on the mechanic's shop floor and sat in two plastic chairs in plain view of the Monterror. Oblivious to it at the time in our near-psychotic state, it was probably the most insensitive thing we could have done. Dump fifteen bags of consumer goods still in their packaging with arm-length receipts poking out of their tops sneering mockingly at the jumpy army of mechanics. Meanwhile, they tried desperately to get all four wheels back on properly.

They finally finished around 8 p.m. The bill was adorned with new discoveries and markups over the past day. I threw a fit, about as well received by the shop owner as a maggoty fish. He stood his ground, our alternative being to check back into the hotel for God knows how many days while he pulled the new parts out and put the old ones back.

On the way home, we did everything we could not to review the events the village had produced for the Berger family. Whatever was the opposite of a welcome mat, that's what was rolled out for them.

I began to lament that all the hours that Laura and I had put in back in Chicago earning enough money to come here were now dissolving in mechanics bills. Before leaving the States, we made sure that we had enough money to make it through the year under any reasonable circumstance. Unfortunately, all the scenarios we had made up did not amount to my purchase of two old Car-Cinomas. For the first time, I actually considered just abandoning them somewhere.

We arrived at an impassable bridge. Flashes of weld shot into the night air ahead as it was obviously being fixed. This was common on the northern unpaved portion of the *Costanera* south of Quepos.

"Can I do this?" Laura asked.

I looked into her eyes. "Look, I will agree that this feels a bit like the beginnings of a spiral, but really, our luck only really turned when your family got here for some odd reason."

"No, that's not all of it. I'm tired of fighting to get stuff done. I'm tired. I haven't slept a good night in a week. I just want to sleep."

I was silent, not knowing what to say. *Am I in the cheap seats here with all my "adventure is my muse" and "magic rock BS?"*

"I do know what that's like, you know? I almost flunked out of grad school my first semester because I was sleeping eight hours a week," I said.

She started to cry, and I felt like I was just punched in the stomach. "I lay awake at night, and the same thoughts go through my head, *over* and *over* and *over*. How could I have put myself in this position—where my husband takes care of everything? Why don't I just go out there and speak Spanish? Why doesn't anyone respect me around here? And then when I think that, my first impulse is to go out and start working. But the *Giardia* isn't completely gone, my hair is falling out in clumps, I have headaches—which I've never had before—and these crazy itchy eye allergies!"

The allergies were an abrupt and unfortunate development. She woke up with them one fine morning, and indoors or out, her eyes would now tear and itch. She even resorted to wearing swim goggles around the house always—during breakfast or cleaning or watching TV—looking like a Mark Spitz mutation of The Fly.

"I'm falling apart. And I don't have a vehicle to even start working. I'd leave every customer stranded in the middle of the jungle every damn day!"

"Remember, the fact that we even came here was a huge step that no one else would have taken. Be proud of that," I said. *Maybe I'm reaching.*

"Come on, Glen! I can't find a bathroom around here without you. And all the wives are dependent here, even if they speak."

"Indira's not," I said.

"OK, great. One person. I don't know. Maybe I'll grow from this. But this is unfortunately exactly the way I pictured it," she said.

"OK, then why did you agree to come here?" I asked. Bad road. Redirect.

"Because I saw that there was something in you that needed to be here. I say we followed the signs. They were your signs. And I spent a year rationalizing this whole thing and putting together the logic I needed to make sense of coming here. But that's the problem. You can't force logic when you're a logical person. Either it makes sense or it doesn't. And I made up this big story in my head so I could feel good about coming, I'm just stupid. Stupid, stupid, stupid!" she yelled at the top of her lungs.

"Thank you for doing this for me, however it turns out," I said.

"Yeah, well, we'll see now, won't we?" she said.

"If it means anything, you did use logic," I said. "You told me Hawaii was too far from family. You wanted to see if we could live here so that we could build on our property in a gorgeous, peaceful place in the middle of nature. Family could come visit, and we'd be close enough to visit them. So you weren't stupid. Logic got you here. You were ruining it for me because I just wanted to jump and come. Maybe I should have used some logic, but you know that's no fun for me," I said. "So who is the real stupid one here? The one who just flies blindly or the person who is a bit forward-thinking?"

"And how did that logic pan out? How can I enjoy my surroundings with hardly any means of communicating with anyone? Without running water? And how can I visit family waiting hours and maybe days for broken bridges like this one?" She pointed ahead.

She's right. I thrive on chaos so I can deal with this.

"You're right," I said.

"I don't care about being right!" *OK, that worked.* "I care about what we're going to do about all this! Before we came here, we arranged for Costa Rican bank accounts, bought a ton of basics and packed them, and put everything in Chicago in storage. And then we went through all that crap from Chicago to set up our residency, and we arrive, and all the rules have changed. So now—poof!—just like that—no residency! We organized everything, and four months later, every day it feels like we're still moving in! Every time I think we've made progress, the next big thing hits that's missing. Everything's an uphill battle! All I want to do is relax! Just for one day! For a few hours! You know what else I think about when I'm awake at night? You. You don't care about comfort. If I were more like you, then I wouldn't be awake and tense. And then I get tenser because I'm angry with myself for not being more like you. It makes me nuts. And I shouldn't be comparing myself to or competing with you! I should just go with the flow!" I could hear hoarseness in her voice now from the escalating yelling.

I had nothing. There was so much there that only the dumbest husband would try to fix through words. What I did know was that Laura was seesawing, and it was tough to watch. Nonetheless, I knew why. She was resilient. She was ultra-competitive—both with herself and others. And in the midst of adversity, she always dug up the positive. In times of crisis, she'd always ask me, "So what are you thankful for?" and wouldn't stop until I identified something that was inevitably there. She was like a swimmer caught in a whirlpool. She was vacillating between being on the verge of swimming out of it and being pulled in again, only to have to fight harder to reemerge the next time.

It took them five hours to fix the bridge. We got home at eight in the morning.

The phone rang right as we entered the FlawedShack. It was Laura's family, who sensed now that they had escaped some type of poltergeist and left us behind. Little Laura got on the phone.

"I can't wait to come back," Little Laura said with the cell phone on speakerphone.

"Oh, I'm so happy to hear that!" we both said. Laura was thrilled.

"Yeah, but I asked Grandpa when he'd bring us back, and he said, 'Neeever agaaaiin!'"

We couldn't blame him, but what would this mean for us living in Costa Rica? Would we now be fully detached from family unless we went to Pennsylvania?

We hung up the phone and milled about the house in silence, preparing for a nap. Would taking a long trip to the States—extremely difficult with the Boys—now be the only way for either of us to come in contact with any family? Until that moment, I had never known such a feeling of detachment and solitude existed.

CHAPTER 30
With a Little Yelp to Our Friends

Wishing to be friends is quick work,
but friendship is a slow ripening fruit.
Aristotle

February 25, 2007

Our spontaneous visit began. While stuck at the hotel in the capital, we had met Regan and John. They were a truly delightful couple exactly our age who brokered land in Arizona for winemaking. They had beautiful, upbeat spirits and were aggressive businesspeople like we had been.

"How is it that you are now inviting strangers to the FlawedShack when our first fight in Costa Rica was because I wanted to do just that?" I asked Laura after dinner at the hotel. I was all for it, but this was surely a flip in character that I wanted to investigate.

"I don't know. Maybe I'm starting to let go, and what better area to start than one of the things I love most—making new friends," she replied.

We gave them an express tour of the Ballena Coast over three days. We had deep conversations in the car, pool, and over dinner about our victories and defeats. Despite their business success, they had an extremely open mind to what life might bring. They thought our life leap was the coolest thing in the world. We laughed like idiots, so forcefully that it seemed possibly abnormal. "I can't believe how quickly we bonded," I said to Laura after they left.

"I know. It's like meeting Hal and Indira again, but this time these two left. I think having someone with us who admired the leap we took and yet could relate to our prior life was exactly what we needed," Laura said. I agreed.

Regan and John's visit gave us some much-needed perspective, and Laura and I decided to step up the 10/10 communication so that we could talk through our issues with the situation and each other to keep them from festering. Every morning first thing after breakfast, we would drive to the beach and write and talk about a key question in our lives.

Of course, it didn't hurt that it was a gorgeous setting where almost no one came except tico fishermen. Every morning, they laid their catch on the beach for the few ambitious seafood lovers wanting first dibs at *pargo* (snapper), *robalo* (snook), *atun* (tuna), and *dorado* (mahi).

Through our 10/10's and e-mails home, we determined what happened to Laura's family was not so unusual. Just recently, two of our friends visited Machu Pichu. These two were the most intelligent planners we ever knew. As corporate strategists, everything they attempted in life underwent strict written analysis in a series of notebooks they called *The Book of Life*. And in Peru they got teargassed when a protest broke out, he ended up in a hospital from stepping on a rusty nail and food poisoning, and she got stuck in Brazil with a bad visa.

The only thing expected is the unexpected. Especially in Costa Rica. Yet, we were optimistic heading back to San José to pick up our next batch of guests—Jane, Mark, and their son, Chase, from Arizona—that we could avoid major calamities.

Jane and Laura were joined at the hip and had raised hell in Hawaii in their teenage days. New crazy stories continued to surface that I could barely believe. Like how Laura had been ferociously attacked once by a cat that had gotten into a friend's mother's bag of cocaine. She also unintentionally broke a girl's nose who had picked on Jane, hitting her a bit harder than intended. A photo also floated around of Jane's bare butt squatting over a paper maché volcano in the middle of a pedestrian area at a popular hotel on Waikiki beach.

Laura left Hawaii for college in Indiana, and over the next decade, they lost touch. As Laura went to college and graduated, Jane lived her life free-style, a snowboard instructor living in her car in Oregon.

After a surprise reunion I had arranged as a birthday gift, they never looked back. By the time Laura and Jane reunited, she had met and married Mark, had two kids, and had moved out of the car.

Now Jane was an accomplished nurse and Army Reserve officer, despite the fact that ceremonious discipline and rules were oil to her water. Mark was a physician's assistant from Portland—serious about life but a thrill to be around because of his intelligence and goofy sense of humor. He was an Army Reserve captain. He had Swedish/German/Japanese roots, a look at which the ladies tended to gawk, all hot and bothered. Sought by elite doctors around the States, he was also very diligent about organizing and planning finances for the life Jane and he intended to have together and for their kids.

Before exiting the Ballena Coast for San José to pick up our guests, we came upon a man standing in our lane, waving branches for us to stop. His car was in the other lane, a trail of three cars behind his.

I got out of the truck to see if I could help. "Are you OK?" I asked.

"Oh, yes, *gracias a dios.*" He pointed fifteen feet down the road.

"Laura, come here! Get out! Get out!" I saw a tawny-grayish blob coming out of the grass on the roadside. It looked like a cross between a Koala and a raccoon.

"What is it?" asked Laura.

"I don't know," I said.

And then it clicked. I remembered our zip-line tour.

"It's a sloth!" I said.

Ticos jumped out of their cars, always fascinated and protective of all wildlife.

"You've never seen one?" the tico who stopped us asked.

"Not up close," I said.

"Oh, then you'll want to walk up to it," he said proudly, assuming the role of tour guide for his country. The three of us walked over to the animal, standing right in front of us and staring up.

"It looks like it's smiling!" Laura said. It did. "Oh, my God, it's so precious!" The black fur around its eyes, made it look like it wore some type of Lone Ranger mask.

Where it got its name was plain as day, or the word *sloth* came from the animal itself. It had the same movements of any other animal, but at one-third speed. It struck me that the only reason we were able to get so close to it was because its top speed was so snail-like. Watching a sloth cross the street was like watching a movie in slow motion. It was like our whole world was slowing.

"Can you pick them up?" I asked my new friend.

"Yes, but I wouldn't. You see those claws?" I nodded in agreement, taking in the pencil-like picks coming out of its toes. "Those are designed to get them up very tall trees, and when threatened, they just want to climb. He might be fastened to your head quite quickly."

We waited for the sloth to finish crossing, took several close-up photos, and watched as he smiled at us upon reentry into the forest.

"It almost looks like he wants to wave," Laura said.

We continued on and arrived at a B&B in San José—where we would overnight with Jane and Mark. We arrived midafternoon to relax on the grounds and have what always proved a therapeutic conversation with its owner, Jacqueline. She was an extremely spiritual person and not afraid of any discussion topic. Our victories and failures were all laid on the table.

Just after dark, we fetched our guests from the airport. We gave them the standard Costa Rican greeting. "Pura Vida, you guys! Welcome!!! Now let's go to TGI Friday's!" Well, that was the gist. We hadn't had an American-style burger since Panama. I had ordered one on the coast one day and was brought a patty of ground ham with a slice of cheese. I called it Burgerless Cordon Blah. Tonight, I wanted the real thing.

Jane and Mark were shocked to see Laura's weight change. She hadn't gained back a pound even though the *Giardia* seemed to slowly be going away. The allergies and a headache, now constant for two solid weeks, unfortunately persisted.

Nonetheless, Laura was visibly overjoyed to see them. We told them of all the amazing things they'd see as they sat across from us, their enthusiasm building.

The next morning, Jacqueline put her hand on Laura's arm and said, "Honey, I hope you don't mind, but I made an appointment for you with a friend. You really need her help. I see it in your eyes."

"Who is she?" Laura asked.

"She's a shaman," Jacqueline said.

"OK," Laura said.

I couldn't believe how quickly she succumbed to the idea. My silent alarms were triggered immediately. Laura's favorite expressions were "*I can't* means *I won't*," and "You're responsible for your own actions." Granted, the conversation with Jacqueline the day before had indeed ripped the scab off some recent wounds. In fact, under the circumstances, such a visit might have been beneficial, but I knew Laura would start beating herself up over going to see a shaman sooner or later.

Jane and Mark awoke, and Laura was already long gone. "Hey, guys. We'll need to hang tight a bit. Laura went to see a shaman," I said.

"OK," they said like it was nothing. *They're such awesome friends.* I wondered what they must have thought. If their visions were anything like mine, they were watching Laura go off to a strange house in the middle of their vacation. Bead curtains hung in every doorway, a visitation room was adorned with lava lamps and a toucan-shaped bong in the middle, and dead monkeys and poultry hung about.

In the meantime, Jane, Mark, and I self-administered a four-hour cardiac stress test with several pots of Costa Rican coffee for four hours.

En route back home, Laura relayed her experience with the shaman. "I waited in a garden outside before being invited into a private room. The room was naturally lit from a louvered window, smelled of incense, and had a chakra chart on the wall. I sat on a massage table and she asked me to explain my situation. I told her that I have not been sleeping and that I'm only comfortable at the beach or reading in the hammock. I try to relax and enjoy the surroundings, but my mind is in a flurry thinking of all the things that need to get done. I worry about Skippy and Rugby getting loose, money, no income, and lack of stability. I have constant headaches and sometimes feel like I am going to throw up from the anxiety. I can't deal with all the unknowns today and in the future and don't know how to take control of the situation. It keeps getting worse."

I was glad I didn't need to explain Laura's backstory. Jane had spent many an hour on the phone and over e-mails with Laura already, talking about what she was going through. My having to explain things to them in front of Laura would have been a mine field, at best.

Laura continued. "She told me to lie down and start inhaling through my nose and exhaling from my mouth. She did it with me so I could focus. At first I did it quietly because I was embarrassed. Then I really started to experience a bit of relaxation. She shook some type of rattle with feathers around me. She chanted, shaking the rattle and beating the same rhythm on a drum repeatedly. She danced around me with my eyes shut the whole time. I focused on the drumbeat, but it was hard. Concentrating on the drums did help. The whole ritual lasted about 10 minutes."

"She then said my energy was imbalanced. Luckily, Costa Rica was my place of purification and connection with the spiritual spheres. All life forms are interconnected and interdependent. I was blocked and needed to open up my mind, body, and spirit. All this anxiety was making me resist my surroundings. I needed to embrace nature, myself, and others. I felt extremely calm as I left but was very tired."

"I know she's right but how do I open myself up, especially since I'm so angry with myself for not being able to snap out of this funk! I feel lost, trapped, and confused about who I really am. I'm changing so drastically and quickly, and I think it's for worse."

"Laura," Jane said, "sounds like if you can just take a month or two to sit back, regroup, and not judge yourself, you might just get your rhythm back."

"I can't believe I went to a fuckin' shaman!" Laura said. *OK, silence is golden.* It seemed like Jane and Mark had the same thought as the shaman visit was dropped for the rest of the ride.

At the village, Jane and Mark, like everyone else, loved the retreat-like setting of our house—so much, in fact, that they discussed a potential property purchase with Allan. We took them on the usual tour—the properties, rain forest zip-lining, the hike to Indira and Hal's waterfall, and the Pair-o-Dice Village restaurant circuit. A special moment for me was running old Tae Kwon Do forms with all three of them on the beach for the first time in fourteen years.

We spent a day fishing with "Fisherman Matt," who had become our go-to guy for the sport. His name was typical of the region as, since it was such a small community, people were named after their hobbies and professions—Tennis Mike, Concrete Jerry, Liquid Lenny, etc. I never understood why the latter name was pegged on Lenny, as his love of drink was rather typical of the community. The most curious of these names was B.J. Betty. Apparently the initials in her name stood for the "special services" for any man at the bar who would fix the latest thing that needed repairing at her house. At least I knew if the FlawedShack got bad enough, I had options.

Laura's love of the ocean, dolphins, and turtles—which swarmed the waters—as well as my affinity for fishing, made our days with Fisherman Matt some of our best.

A tour with Matt wasn't your normal deep-sea fishing experience. He had a twenty-five-foot dual engine center console vessel. Despite its smallness, the boat was adorned with equipment showing Matt was a serious angler. I was fascinated at how he fit it all in the cramped quarters, always out of sight.

A Californian, he lived meagerly on the revenue from tours for over ten years on a large property overlooking the bay where he was anchored. He likely bought his land at gumball-machine prices—now surrounded by actors and big-shot lawyers driving him completely mental, as he was deeply connected to the purity and simplicity of the Ballena Coast.

His property and boat were all he had. They were sources of pride and joy but a devil to maintain by himself. Asleep every night at 6 p.m., he'd rise at 4:30 each morning to prepare lunch and the rigs for his trips. When he wasn't out fishing, he was maintaining the large property.

A simpler guy, you couldn't find. He was young-looking—his hair long and body lean, sporting the standard flip-flops, T-shirt, and board shorts. But the lines on his face and his traditionalist and occasionally petulant demeanor gave away his true age.

Matt talked through everything out loud. "We're going to catch some live bait here and then drop them in the trash lines," he'd say. "I put this extra line around the bill of the Ballyhoo for more movement so they look like they're swimming," he'd explain of his less fortunate pre-rigged frozen victims. I appreciated his informative process monologues. And the primitive smallness of the boat made everyone a mate. "Fish on! Glen, take the wheel!" or "Laura, get the gaff!" or "Punch it! Punch it! He's heading for the boat!"

I became the object of some of his peevishness the day with Jane and Mark. "Oh, no. Either that's going overboard or you." He pointed as I gleefully munched a banana.

"You brought bananas?" Laura said.

"Yeah, what's the problem?" I asked. *Chew, chew, swallow. Take another bite.*

"Bad luck," Matt said.

"Yeah, bad luck," everyone said in unison.

"Wait! You know about this?" I said.

"Aw, heck yeah," Mark said.

"Everyone knows that," Laura reaffirmed.

"Yup," Jane said.

Growing up in Florida with a father who loved to fish, I felt like I was the butt of some practical joke.

"And the hell if you're throwing them overboard," Matt said. "I'm still gonna try like crazy to catch you something today, but right now, I can tell you it's your loss." Luckily my other comrades in fishing considered the banana mojo to be a fable and didn't hold it against me.

Three

We had caught tuna, mahi, swordfish, bonito, and marlin in respectable quantities on past trips. We couldn't have caught Ebola in a hot zone that day. While he tried to mask it, I could feel Matt's stare occasionally scald the side of my head throughout the day.

Marine life's aversion to fruit notwithstanding, the all-out skunking was likely a blessing. Laura and Jane had an entire day in the sun to remind them of their days in Hawaii and discuss life, a rare opportunity if we were to stay in Costa Rica.

The most important part of that visit, and all the others for that matter, was a declaration from Mark that was now becoming standard fare. "I've gotta tell you that when we heard you were planning this, we thought you were totally crazy," Mark said, "but now we get it. I mean I think you're clearly pioneering here, but in twenty years, with the growth that they're seeing, I could totally see us retiring here. Now our first choice would be Hawaii, but this surely isn't very far off from that."

"Everyone comes here and says that," Laura said as we raced back to the bay, "and it's so important to hear. For one thing, you and everyone else basically recite our logic for coming here back to us. And then they see the promise that we do. There are so many moments throughout the day here that electrify your soul. You'll see a sloth or a monkey in a tree. Or the mist will be rising out of the valley. Even the sounds of nature on the back deck with a nice cup of coffee just breathe life into you. And then you're in the middle of a long e-mail and the Internet goes out. The cell towers go on the fritz while you're having a deep conversation or you'll leave a truck stalled in the middle of the jungle. Those things are a punch in the gut that just takes all the wind out of you. Everything's an extreme around here. There's no in-between. And it's just the two of us here in a complete role reversal. It's like we're dancing, he's now leading," she pointed to me, "and the rhythm of the music is completely undanceable. I mean whenever we're approaching a problem, I'm thinking he's going to go left, and he goes right. And we see things in each other and ourselves that we never saw before, like he sees me crying sometimes and says, 'I didn't marry a crier,' and he didn't. And I see strength in him that I never saw before, too, which is so cool. Then again, he's going up against mechanics and salespeople where he has to negotiate and employ deep logic, and it's just not him."

"Yeah, I love it here, but we—well, make that mostly I—have made a few really bad decisions, and I always feel like I walk out of negotiations with a big honkin' wedgie," I said.

"Hey, look, you're onto something here. I just think you're trying too hard," Mark said looking at me, and then turned to Laura, "and you've had a run of sickness and bad luck, and are being too hard on yourself. I'm willing to bet the allergies, headaches, and hair falling out—basically all the sickness you're experiencing—is your body responding to what's in your mind. And I'm not one of those medical types who really buy into the Eastern philosophies, but you pretty much have *the* list of ailments I would attribute to stress."

"Yeah, I know it's hard to do because you're young and have so much life ahead that you think you could be messing up now, but take it easy and just let it come. You'll see. It'll all shape up," Jane said.

A raggedy tender boat driven by one of Fisherman Matt's tico friends whisked us back to the beach that night. "And leave the bananas home next time!" he hollered from the boat. I could tell that my comrades in fishing now were superstitious enough to hold it against me.

Early the next day, I began loading the Monterror. The lessons of what happens when you drive to San José were obviously lost on us. We planned to overnight with Jane and Mark, pick up Kathryn—another inbound friend from Chicago—as we dropped them off, and then return to Pair-o-Dice Village the next day.

After piling up three suitcases, I saw we had a flat. This was the one area where we had been outstandingly fortunate. The village people went through tires like beer on the primitive roads where building materials were dropped regularly from trucks. Yet this was our virgin flat.

I entered the guest apartment. "Mark, you got a second?"

"Sure, bud, what's up?"

I told him about the discovery. "I need you to watch in case the Monterror decides to grab me with an evil set of hands I have yet to discover." He laughed. "Seriously, this thing is so cursed, I'm afraid of everything I do around it. Just make sure it doesn't crush me or something."

He laughed. "Bummer. All right brother, let's go."

I looked to Jane. "And please run interference with Laura. Just keep her occupied until we finish." She giggled a bit nervously.

I pumped the jack upward as Mark watched. *You've gotta be friggin' shitting me! What is this? A go-cart jack?* Fully extended, it was a foot short of the underbelly of the Monterror. A squirrel could have used it as a pogo stick.

Mark began to scan and pace the driveway. "What are you looking for?" I asked.

"Something to shim the jack," he said.

"Awesome." *What does "shim" mean?*

He returned with a few paving tiles. "Help me get some more."

Matt—a veritable jungle MacGyver—then executed a plan of genius. He lowered the jack all the way, put it on a stack of tiles, and pumped the truck upward. Once at maximum extension, he created another stack of tiles that was tall enough to almost touch the bottom of the Monterror and lowered the truck onto them. Then he built a taller stack, put the jack on that, and repeated until we had a stack tall enough to get the tire raised off the ground.

I wanted to strangle the Monterror's previous owner later in San José, and then it hit me. The ingenuity of the ticos was undoubtedly bred from an environment where everything wasn't ready-made. It was a way of life I had never known. My ingenuity was naturally inferior to theirs. How could I blame anyone for not having given me exactly what was standard?

"How'd you know to do that?" I asked Mark.

"Spend enough time in your pop's repair shop—these things just come natural."

"What are you guys doing?" I heard Laura's voice behind me.

"Um, we're changing a tire. By the way, Costa Freaka called while you were inside and said she won't be able to visit today," I said.

"You've gotta be shitting me!"

"Yes, exactly what I said. But don't spend your last hours with Jane having an aneurysm. We've got this."

"Jane! You're not going to believe this!" She went back toward the house. *Oh, yes she will.*

The tire changed, off we went to San José to get lost. I was convinced some gremlin controlled the Etch-a-Sketch of the maps stored in our brains. "Hey, those two gringos are back. Should I shake it again?"

We dropped Jane and Mark at the airport and picked up Kathryn. We blew and quickly fixed a radiator hose on the way home, but that precedent didn't faze Kathryn. She just wanted to veg at our house all week. I couldn't help but think that she would be the perfect person to try what we were doing, completely content as she was reading or staring at the view all day.

Our two recent visits were near perfect, and so was Jack's. This gave us hope that the importance of sharing this new land with friends, if not family, would be met with great fulfillment. What's more, basking in our friendships was like tasting that one food your parents served to celebrate your victories as a kid. It was that one that brought a sense of calm and satisfaction no matter how old you were. It was much easier to picture our lives when they were around.

But as things quieted down over the next few days, I was able to sit and stew with a realization. It had been lurking in my subconscious since Laura had her moment of crisis waiting for the broken bridge to be fixed. And then on the way home from dropping off Kathryn, she said, "Maybe we do it like most of the people here—six months here and six months back home." Of course, this seemed impossible at our age, but I held my tongue for sake of not stirring up the pot. I could tell she was starting to back down from our plan.

We needed to stick to it. The only thing I wanted more than Costa Rica was Laura. I worried I might not be able to have both.

I immediately resolved to make this work for both of us so that *we* could live here happily—together. But could I enjoy the next seven months tending to this perhaps impossible task? And wasn't this really what I was already doing? And by making this extra effort, was I deviating from the plan myself? Surely a successful life in Costa Rica long-term wouldn't be me trying to make it work out for my wife full-time. And then there was the morality of secretly maneuvering to "make" her like it. Was that fair? I guessed unless I revealed my intentions, it would be a secret agenda. But if I did reveal it, Laura would feel the independence she cherished so much to be compromised. Then again, was creating a pleasant environment for my wife just a loving act by a husband? *So many questions and so much confusion.* I felt like a spinning top starting to wobble before it fell over.

But with everyone gone and not one more visit planned, time would fly. The road to the answers would only shorten.

CHAPTER 31
Deep Issues Massage

"Fall down seven times, get up eight."
Japanese Proverb

March 2, 2007

"We fell in love with this place as tourists, right?" Laura asked on the beach one morning.

"I like to think I was having an experience that went beyond tourism, but we were on vacation, yes," I replied.

"So then why don't we go back to that tourist mode while we are settling into being here?" Laura said.

The need to unwind from a life of few demands was curious, but I had to agree that if we could manage to abandon this sense of progress, we'd be better off. Then maybe one day we would realize that our souls had stabilized once again, and we could start hustling property.

After all, we still had six months to show that we could make at least a meager living in the village. We were so lucky that the stock market was raging the way it was, which surely helped cover at least some of our budgetary variance. We had come thinking that we'd be selling properties like hotcakes by December. That was Plan A. But we were finding that this would require some pretty aggressive marketing. Being such a remote place, tourists still came for its beauty—yes—but not en masse. What's more, every time we struck up conversations with some, they liked us well enough, but the local realtors had mastered the art of sniffing out a tourist with money. "We already are working with a realtor," they'd say. I silently considered a business model where we'd give clients a free tour of a bat-infested house in exchange for viewing property. And trying to sell property to the locals was futile as everyone was selling land on the side anyway—like a bunch of crabs trying to sell each other sand at the beach. Nonetheless, we knew we had it in us to put up a really robust operation, just not now with all we were experiencing.

We had no Plan B. So, instead, we decided to supplement our strategy to live like tourists with a little hedonism. Our newfound joy was massages.

We had been to a hotel along the *Costanera* on several occasions for massages. The luxury property was the unique brainchild of a German fellow who must have arrived with a payload of patience and gold bars wrapped in thousand dollar bills. Looking at such a place made his motivation level seem like a disease. The décor was an odd but curious mix between historic Costa Rican and medieval renaissance. The hotel had an elegant outdoor restaurant, an infinity pool, and several rooms on a bluff jutting out into the ocean. It even had two yachts used for deep-sea fishing.

I thought it would probably be easier to tee off from Myrtle Beach and make a hole-in-one on the moon than run a luxury hotel on the coast. Case in point, while we spent time there, employees would occasionally dart about in response to some small—or not so small—structural or mechanical calamity. But all in all, people held the hotel in high regard. This fellow's dream seemed to be panning out, but we had heard from the locals that it had been at titanic financial cost. *The best way to make a million dollars in Costa Rica is to bring ten million.*

Our masseuse of choice was Consuela. She was a tiny Costa Rican with a vice grip. What can I say? We liked it rough. She had blue eyes as big as quarters, was soft-spoken, and timid.

My massage ended one day as Laura waited. We obviously both couldn't have Consuela at the same time, but waiting for one another enjoying the hotel's setting was almost as good as the massage itself.

"OK, Glen," Consuela said softly, backing away from the table. "We're finished. Was everything OK?"

"Of course, as always," I said. "Thank you."

"Your towels for shower are there." Consuela pointed at a footstool by the massage table.

The shower was in the massage room and had no curtain or door. She left, and I hopped off the table and into the shower.

I ran the water at my feet to regulate the temperature. Once the hot water began to steam, I turned the cold knob. *Feels the same.* I turned it once more, spinning it a full turn. *Broken. Oh, well.*

I turned on the shower head. *Oh, that's hot!* I soaped up. *Ugh, skin frying. OK, maybe I'll screw with this a bit more.*

I turned the cold knob again. *Nothing.* I developed a rapid appreciation for what pasta must feel like. I spun it one more full turn in desperation. *What the hell is wrong with this thing?* One more spin, *pang!!!*

The knob suddenly flew off and struck my shoulder with great force, followed by a jet of water that pinned me against the back wall like a flyer for a bake sale. I shielded my eyes from the spray and tried to squirm free from this hydraulic reverse tractor beam. The force of the jet, completely cold, was actually starting to hurt my chest.

And in the midst of it all, I actually thought, "How the hell do they have water pressure like this?"

This is loud! Someone's going to run in here in seconds! I'm nude!

I lunged toward the towels as the stream of water flattened on the wall and sprayed about the room. The door opened. There I stood in front of Consuela, dripping, with towel in hand. I looked like a live model in a display window for a bath wares store in a red-light district—except for the model part.

"¡Hay, Dios!" she exclaimed and ran out. *Hey, what is that supposed to mean?* I wrapped up and walked out to the changing room. As I changed, I heard the emergency crew enter the massage room amidst expletives and clanging tools.

Outside in the lobby, I told Laura what happened. She hadn't laughed like that in months, which made it all worth it. *Whoever is up there, let us laugh like this more often, and we'll be OK here.*

Water was still gushing out of the massage room and down the exterior staircase to the parking lot as we walked to the Montalloper to leave. Consuela opened the door with a mop in hand. Our eyes met, and she immediately looked down timidly.

I contemplated my physique, not having weighed myself in some time but knowing I couldn't be a pound north of a buck forty. For that same reason, I had recently been reluctant to remove my shirt and was an astonishing beacon of whiteness. *I probably should have double-tipped.*

I certainly had a good, funny story for that night. Adèle, our former property manager, invited us to her new bed-and-breakfast for after-dinner drinks. We had had a fair amount of contact with her husband, Gerard, and her at the FlawedShack. But tractors and shiny, unpainted aluminum roofs were all we had seen of their budding construction project from across the valley.

After a sharp turn off our same road, we made what would have been a frightening climb four months prior up to their gravel parking area, where Adèle stood waiting. "Welcome. We are so glad you came!"

She gave us both a big hug. I felt we now had a certain camaraderie. They had survived living in the FlawedShack like us—so far. A pool sat between their house and the B&B's five rooms in a two-story building. They were still living in two of the hotel rooms since the main house was not yet finished.

We sat on the terrace of one of the rooms, talking and listening to the roar of the waves crashing into the rocks below. Although it was pitch black and invisible, I could tell by the proximity and tenor of the ocean water that whatever was out there was strikingly beautiful.

It was a glorious night. I broke the ice with my story about being hosed down like a street protester after a calm massage. We shared our impressions of the splendor and struggles of Pair-o-Dice Village. It was thrilling and therapeutic to laugh about the pain. Gerard told us about his adventures coming to Costa Rica for years—working during the off-season and spending his savings during the high season. He, again, had bought his land at gumball-machine prices years and years ago.

"One year, we come here from Canada in an old—how do you say—*ambulance?*"

"Exactly, ambulance," Laura said. "Why an ambulance?"

"We deed not have money to fly, and someone geeve it to us. It was ooooold," he said. Laura and I laughed in astonishment. "So de bordeur wis Nicaragua was not so secure, and we realize we just drive and drive, and we are in Costa Rica. And so we have de car unregistered. After de driving here, we decide to fly home. But what do we do wis de ambulance? It was register to me, and I did not want to pay de duty if someone find it. So we burry it."

"Burry it?" I wanted to clarify, thinking he failed in his word choice.

"Yes, like under de ground," he said.

"That's crazy! Where?"

"I weel never tell."

Laura told them a story Allan had relayed to us about a guy years ago who bought a lot from him in the village and built a house. The night he first filled his pool, a herd of cows wandered through his yard, and two of them fell in. The next day, they found the cows' owners, but the entire pool was destroyed and had to be redone.

Then, after three hours of great conversation, intense laughter, and an imprudent amount of wine, there it was—a moment you write into your bucket list after the fact. At 1:30, a glowing treasure trail reflected off the ocean, leading to the biggest harvest moon I had ever seen—reddish-orange with wisps of mist across it. It rose proudly into the air like the unveiling of a prized painting. Now fully visible, the view was even more amazing than we expected, with foamy water shooting up off the rocks and radiating in the moonlight.

Adèle and Gerard seemed used to the sight, but we wanted our watches to stop and to never see a calendar again. It seemed a hallucination in the middle of our own reality.

Three

"Today, when we were at the hotel, I realized that everywhere we go—I mean *everywhere* there's some amazing sight," Laura said. "People travel from all over for this, and we have it every day."

"I know," Adèle said. "Not too many people make it to this part of Costa Rica, but once you see it . . . . We risked everything to come here. Everything."

Shortly thereafter, I pulled an abdominal muscle laughing. We left at 2:30 because we literally couldn't stop cracking each other up, and it just got too painful.

That day was so symbolic of our experience in the village. As tourists, we saw nothing but tranquility everywhere we looked. The entire place was like one big meditation area. And now as nontourists, we were finding chaos even in massage rooms. But this new approach to life was fun for both of us, and in that, we were achieving our near-term objective.

Laura said it best. "Let's just have as much fun as we possibly can until the dust settles. And then, no matter what happens, we can look back and know that we enjoyed the heck out of these days."

As I walked toward our front door, I looked up and wondered how many moons might be hanging outside our window without our realizing it. What if we just took our minds off what we were missing and not doing and just focused on what we had for a while? Might we then have the clarity and energy to organize our lives and stabilize?

CHAPTER 32
The Phone Ranger

Failure is success if we learn from it."
Malcolm Forbes

March 16, 2007

Getting tired of hearing about us going to ICE every day to check on cell phone lines? Well, then you know how we felt *living* that experience. Every time I heard *no hay* I had to wonder (1) what the heck was wrong with us, and (2) why I was even trying in the first place.

We also tried our luck occasionally at scoring a land line—more difficult than finding a compatible liver, which I would soon need if I visited the trailer a few more times. Miraculously, after over fifty visits, we were finally granted a line. Minor, an exuberant ICE guy, helped us complete our paperwork in his endearing Pura Vida "my finger is permanently glued to the sky" enthusiasm. This guy had control of a hot commodity, and he let you know it. He was also young and had a great government job, a rare blessing.

I validated just how prized an office job was in Costa Rica making small talk with a representative at the bank in Cedro. "These jobs must be in high demand. How did you get yours, if you don't mind me asking?"

He smiled. "I'm good at soccer." He realized I required further explanation. "I was on a semi-pro team in San José. The regional soccer team here kept losing, so the branch manager came to the capital to find players and hired me."

"Wow! He hired you so that you could play on his favorite team? He must really like soccer," I said excitedly. "But how'd he get you on the team?"

"No, it's not the professional soccer team. It's the regional bank team. We started winning. He was very happy, and here I am now—working on your account."

Of course, it made sense in a coastal economy that the way to get a "traditional" job would be through connections or some ulterior talent that was of interest to the employer.

"*Buenas, Minor,*" I greeted him cheerfully as he appeared the next day for the installation site survey.

"*Buenas,*" Laura waved from the hammock.

Laura and I had spent the morning shouting over the deafening sound of the cicadas as it was the one-month season for them. The noise took over everything. When we called fellow village people, all either side could hear was cicadas. They were so pervasive that whenever we'd arrive at people's houses, their dogs would sound like they swallowed an electric shaver, mouths full of these raucous insects.

"Mr. Glen, we see if you can have telephone. You come with me," Minor said. He fired up a tiny Toyota pickup truck. The wobbly, fish-taily ride down our driveway in his two-wheel drive pickup felt like a crash landing.

"OK, so first we must find the box. Then we count poles," he said as we sped down our hill.

"I don't understand," I said.

"The box has plugs for your line. We see if a plug is free."

"Ah, I see. Thank you for coming, by the way," I said. "When we get back to the house, we can sit down for a Pilsen."

"Ah, no, Mr. Glen. I'm happy for doing this and no *cerveza* while I work. I like you! Are you interested in property?" he said.

"I have many good properties for you to see." In Costa Rica, there was no real estate agent's license. Everyone was an agent, and, of course, with all the people Minor met on a daily basis, landowners were wise to come to him in droves with their listings.

"Maybe we can talk about it later," I said.

"OK. You will love it. Big properties. Big farms. Big views," he said.

"Sweet. I look forward to—"

He slammed on the brakes and spun the truck like a weather vane pointing toward a wood pole. "There is the box. Go see the connections." He handed me a screwdriver.

"Me?" I asked meekly.

"It's easy," he replied. "Go, go."

I lifted the cover and saw an empty socket. "Here?" I pointed desperately toward a little vacant port.

He squinted and leaned forward in his seat. "Yes, Mr. Glen. That's it. You have a free socket."

Feels too easy. I was guardedly hopeful. His look said he had a reveal coming. "Now we see if you are not too far away. Get in." Rocks were spinning from under the tires before I could close the door, my foot dragging on the road. "OK, now you count poles," he said.

"*Uno, dos, tres* . . . Why am I counting?"

"I measure the distance by poles," he said.

"So they're all the same distance apart?" I asked.

"No." I knew that answer.

"What's the maximum?" I asked. *"Ocho, nueve."*

"OK, esstop," he commanded as the brakes locked.

He shook his head. "Too many. You are too far from the box. The most is eight poles. But!" he rubbed his chin.

"What?" I asked.

"There should be another box south of you," he said. "We count to that one."

We passed the opening to our driveway. "OK, esstart counting!"

"Uno, dos . . . seis . . ."

"OK, esstop!" He slammed the brakes and again slid the truck into a spin like a trained stunt driver—never mind the fifty-foot drop at the edge of the dirt road with no guardrail.

"Only six poles to the box," he said smiling. "This is good." I instinctively grabbed the screwdriver and headed toward the box. "See the slot?" I said. *This is it!*

"You can have telephone!" he said. I could have smooched a dead octopus.

We sped up the driveway. I couldn't wait to get to Laura.

"We're getting a phone," I said to her on the patio.

She leapt out of the hammock. "That's awesome!" She hugged me with a big smile. "Thank you, Minor!"

"My pleasure, Miss Laura," he said gladly. "Now we complete the service order."

Ah, yes. The order. I thought back to a dinner conversation on the other side of the river.

"One day, word spread across town that they were going to do phones over here. Before that, the phone lines never crossed the river. We went down to the office and got our orders done. And once a week or so, we'd go back to the office with the paper, and were told 'not yet.' Then, one day, trucks just rolled into town to collect orders and do installations. Problem was all the humidity and back and forth had destroyed everyone's orders. So the trucks left, and we had to go back and get our orders redone. And then the waiting resumed," our host said.

"OK, I will now look at the yard," Minor said, carrying his service order pad with him.

"Why does he have to look at the yard?" Laura asked.

"Maybe just to figure out what they need to bring for the installation," I said.

Minor came back almost immediately. "OK, Mr. Glen. You need a 150-feet cable installed from the road to the house. This is no problem," he said with sincere assurance.

"Great!" I said.

"So just call us when it is finished, and we come to do the installation."

"Now you said you were interested in properties?" He scribbled his phone number on the back of the order and tore it off his pad.

"How the heck are we going to find someone to install that line?" Laura asked me.

I watched him head toward his truck after the real estate presentation, and something clicked in my brain. "Laura, let's sit and talk for a second." She was nervous. Lately, our serious conversations seemed to end in discomfort or hostility. "Why did we try to get residency?"

"What do you mean?" She was surprised by the topic.

"Exactly what I asked. You'll see I'm guilty of this too, so I'm not picking on you." Laura had done all the legwork on our failed residency attempt before we arrived. "OK, let me rephrase. What benefit is it really to us to have residency?"

"Well, we don't have to leave every three months if we have residency. And they were going to double the amount of money we were required to send shortly after we got here." She paused. "Oh, I see." I saw the same light bulb go off.

"It was very forward-thinking. Sure. We had to send the biggest check either of us had ever written in our lives to a Costa Rican Bank. We had to fill out tons of forms and make phone calls and faxes and get marriage certificates, birth certificates, certifications from our bank, and wire transfers. But then somehow, the rules had already changed before we got here, and we got squat," I said.

"Right. All that to save nine days of our life not having to leave the country. But I was thinking we could go somewhere and see something new," she said.

"I know, but we could have gone to see nice places anyway. We knew before we arrived that people found ways to get fake passport stamps all the time not to have to leave," I said. "Everyone did it. Why did we have to be different?"

"Well, because we wanted to do it right." She paused. "I guess what was right for us," she said.

"Yeah, see, that was *my* justification. But what we think we *should* do is killing us. We *should* have our own phone. We *should* have constant running water," which we finally now had, *gracias a dios,* "we—wait, I—*should* have two cars to simulate real life."

"We're should-ing all over ourselves!" Laura said, proclaiming her favorite quote from *Sex and the City.*

"Aaaarrrr," I grunted like Chewbacca and thumped on my chest. "I am North American. I come with phone. I must have residency . . . ."

"I must have toilet-paper holder." I doubled over laughing. Ever since our first night in the village, Laura had been afraid that a scorpion would be hiding in the center of the toilet paper. We needed a holder that stood on the floor to not make holes in the walls of a house we didn't own. Every trip back from San José, she threw her hands up in the air and said, "What am I going to have to do to get a toilet-paper holder?" We didn't even find one in Panama City.

The self-defeating cycle of trying to get the things we thought we *should* have but *couldn't* ended that day. And looking back, I realized that when lumping the trucks into the equation, the majority of my own personal struggles stemmed from this very dynamic.

We were just humans—*Homo sapiens*—in a beautiful and spiritually rewarding place. The only thing beneath us was the ground on which we stood. It was time to get over ourselves and live the way we could manage to live, not the way we thought we *should* be living.

CHAPTER 33
Dunlop in the Rough

Creativity is just connecting things. When you ask creative people how they did something, they feel a little guilty because they didn't really do it, they just saw something. It seemed obvious to them after a while. That's because they were able to connect experiences they've had and synthesize new things.

Steve Jobs

March 19, 2007

"You know one of the things I've been thinking?" Laura asked at our usual seaside lunch place. "This is so embarrassing," she said, not able to look me in the eye.

"What? Tell me. You can tell me anything," I said.

"Yeah, well, there's actually more than one thing bugging me . . . ." She stopped, and we stared at one another in silence.

"You don't have to tell me now. Whenever you're ready." I looked down at my food, signaling that it was fine to change the subject.

"I was never a negative person!"

"OK, I agree that since we've got here, you've become less optimistic, but I wouldn't call you negative."

"Well obviously other people would," she said.

Three

"Who?"

"Brenda?"

"Well, OK. If it's smiley Brenda, then she's the one person who can call you that," I said.

"See? That's where you're wrong. She's been coming to me in the Internet café over the past few months just beside herself. She's been an anxious mess with no windows and Paul pacing the property staring at the unfinished house. It hasn't been good."

"Why didn't you tell me?" I asked.

"Well, with all our action-packed adventures, it just wasn't top of mind. Anyway, the other day, she came up to me, and I asked her how she was doing. She said she was really good, but she seemed hesitant to tell me, and I pointed that out. She said she didn't want me to feel bad. I asked her why on Earth I would feel bad, and she said it was because I was doing so badly. She didn't want me to be jealous! I asked her why I would be jealous, and get this. She said a bunch of stuff, but she also mentioned that you were always the positive one and I was always the negative one."

"OK. And that's so odd?" I asked.

"Come on, Glen." I thought about it, and Laura's surprise at Brenda's comment did make some sense. Regardless of where I picked it up, I'd create doomsday future scenarios in my mind to motivate myself to do a lot of the things in life I didn't want to.

"OK, I don't care. But no, I wouldn't have ever considered you a negative person, and it's only been a small sliver of your life. It's impossible that you've changed forever," I said.

"And here's another thing that just blew me away. I asked her what changed. She said she found meds. She's on antianxiety and antidepressant pills. Can you believe that? People come to this tranquil place with peace, quiet, the breeze, and gorgeous nature everywhere, and instead of Pura Vida, they find oneness with pharmaceuticals!"

I started laughing. Laura's tense face gradually started to loosen up until she was laughing, too.

"Look. It's just one person's opinion, and if the jungle is prone to turn us inside out, comparing ourselves to other people is not going to help. Relax. You're the same person, but you're going through a big change. I'm going to go in and get some coffee. You want some?" I turned to go inside momentarily.

"I was never a jealous person!"

"And now you are?" I asked.

"Yeah, she called me jealous, and I've noticed it a bit recently."

"When?"

"Since Indira and Hal finished their house and invited us over, I've been wondering what the hell is wrong with us. I mean they have a kid to raise, they are acting as their own foreman on the construction, and they have a casita and an amazing house built!" she said. They did have an awesome house that was basically finished and that they were living in. It was three bedrooms, and the entire back section was a big covered terrace balcony—infinity style, exploiting every ounce of their view.

In truth, I had the very same thoughts when we entered their house the first time. I was surely happy for them. Yet these two had just built a dream house and were still energetic and optimistic—with a kid to feed and watch. And they were just across the valley from where our struggle seemed to be worsening. It did make me wonder what exactly was wrong with us. But as always, I'd try to fake it to make it.

"Laura, this is the whole should-ing thing again. They've been living outside the ready-made life for a long time. We haven't. I mean they met in Egypt for God's sake and backpacked all over Europe and Africa, eating out of cans and sleeping in ditches. They had already built a cabin in Japan—"

"Oh, yeah. They've built one more house. That helps. Anyway, I go over there, and they're so nice. They'd do anything for us. And I look at their view, and I'm afraid my hatred for myself is splattering all over them and getting in the way of our friendship. I'm even a bit resentful. And it's not their fault that all I'm good at is watching my hair fall out." I went to say something consoling that would likely have just created trouble. Luckily, she interrupted.

"But I guess the lesson is that my crap is my crap, and I can't project it on others. But it's hard."

That night, we went to Hal and Indira's, and I intended to launch an investigation of how their coping mechanisms might differ from ours. Not having seen them for several days, and with my questions pointed toward the information I was seeking, Hal launched into a telling story.

He blew a tire on his truck a few days prior, which again, in Costa Rica was like running out of milk. It was completely shredded, but he was prepared with a stack of matching tires in his *bodega*. Someone would drive him down the hill to have it switched on the rim. It was at the very back of the *bodega*, down a narrow passageway bordered by piles of scrap lumber—prime habitat for terciopelos and scorpions. He threw on snake boots, grabbed his machete, and got his replacement tire.

Needing a free hand for his machete, he just rolled the tire out of the *bodega* through the narrow passage.

As soon as it saw daylight, the tire made a right turn out of sight and down the wicked slope that was their backyard. "I heard nothing, then a crashing noise, some faded crashing then nothing again—just a bad feeling," he said.

Hal did what any male in Costa Rica would do when his tire, which easily costs twice its price in the States, gets swallowed by the jungle. He dropped a few atomic F-bombs, picked up his machete, and went after it.

The remaining hour of daylight yielded nothing. After all, some physics equation surely existed that placed the tire all the way on the *Costanera* five hundred vertical feet below. But the story went on.

At the end of the next day, Hal returned to the rainforest to mill about after the tire. Then he did what any male in Costa Rica would do after hours of searching in torrential rain, covered in mud, desperate not to have to tell his wife what happened. He sat in his favorite chair and drank a few Pilsens, awaiting greater inspiration to strike.

Another day passed, and determined and stubborn, he pondered and procrastinated once again until the afternoon rains reappeared, as wet season was returning. But he resumed the search, unfortunately with the same yield. He faced the stark prospect of never seeing the tire again and having to face Indira. This guided him up the hill again toward his chair—once representing hope and inspiration, now symbolizing despair and possible mourning. There, he drained a couple more beers.

A friend stopped by as his predicament was eating him alive. "This is bothering me so much! Where could it be?" he asked her. "I'm down there every day looking for fallen wood to turn into furniture. I know every inch of that terrain."

In jest, she said, "I know what you can do! I used to be in the jewelry business. When we lost a precious stone, we'd drop a cheap one of the same size and weight, retracing the path of the original. The second leads to the first."

"The second leads to the first." He lay awake that night weighing the prospect of sacrificing another tire for the sake of its sibling and losing sight that his friend's solution was intended as a joke.

The next day, a family of visitors arrived for lunch. Much to Indira's despair, Hal fessed up about his potential loss and huddled the unsuspecting guests together to dole out assignments. Everyone was skeptical and feared for his mental state. While Indira questioned the virtue of having married him, Hal went down the steep slope to the spot where he estimated the rogue rubber ring had entered the rainforest.

He had assigned Indira the untoward job of tire launcher at the back of the serpentarium *bodega*.

Once confident everyone was precisely stationed at their posts, Hal yelled "Launch!" Nako screamed, the dog barked at the tire, and the visiting family peppered along the ridge as spotters—or bowling pins, depending on your point of view—spotted nothing.

"Hold the dog and try again!" Hal yelled up.

Cursing, Indira rolled the sacrificial twin back into the *bodega* as the snakes and scorpions parlayed their bets on Hal's project. Irritated and impatient, she once again heard, "Launch!" The problem was Hal never said it.

Hal recounted the second attempt as, "I was still stationing everyone at their posts, and this tire comes barreling down along the fence. It approached me and the sound barrier at about twenty feet per bounce and plopped right into the jungle."

Not being a toucan, Hal was instantly resigned to having lost a second brand-new tire. Then, it shot horizontally across the rainforest fifty feet below, took a hard right turn, crashed through a barbed-wire fence, and continued sideways to disappear once again. It all seemed to defy physics completely.

The rain picking up again, Hal did what any male who lost two tires in the jungle would have done in Costa Rica. He dropped a few atomic F-bombs, contemplated the other tires in the *bodega* he could launch if need be, and went into the jungle after it—again.

"I decided to just walk around and see what happened," he said. "The rain really started to come down again as I wandered, thinking about wasted time and another possible Pilsen in my mourning chair. Then I saw something big and black to the right. It was a tire! I picked it up to roll it back to civilization and saw another black blob to my left. And I'll be damned if it wasn't another one!"

The day after hearing the story, Laura and I again sat at our ocean-side lunch place. "Hal's story about the tires just blew me away," she said.

"I know. That was some funny stuff, huh?" I said.

"No, not because it was funny. These things people do that sound so absurd to us—I think they're just people changing to cope and survive," Laura said.

"Who takes a chuckling joke from a jeweler friend and turns it into a solution like that?" I asked. We concluded that with self-building a house in the jungle with a three-year-old, the bounds of problem-solving probably broadened significantly.

"I mean look at the ticos," I said. "They're always fixing their issues with what seems to us like nothing available to them! I wonder how many solutions are staring us in the face, but we're not looking wide enough to see them."

"But if we were to adapt like that, we'd have to evolve in more ways than just problem-solving. There's a bigger transformation in how we deal with people and what we expect from our lives day-to-day. People in Chicago wouldn't even recognize us! How could we go back?" I asked.

We were starting to see why, when people went back to the States from the jungle, all they wanted to do was come back. They reacted to the over-stimulation of the commerce and traffic and everyone's emphasis on what toy they could buy next and their careers. It was because their minds changed completely.

"I don't think we have to worry about that right now. We're here trying this out for a year," Laura said. "There's always that thought about whether we are right for this place, and if we're not, then we go home when the year's up. With that psychology, I don't think we're changing that drastically because this is not permanent for us."

This triggered my unspoken concerns. Laura had told me the Berger Family was now calling me Indiana Jones and had expressed wonder at how I had changed so fast. I was no Hal, but was I adapting that fast? In this place where rolling three-hundred-dollar tires into the jungle was just another day at the office, I couldn't measure how much I was changing. Laura and I wrote and talked about it, but she admitted she had no perspective, being engulfed in all of it herself.

Whatever was happening to me, would the new me be compatible with my old friends? What about my wife? If I didn't even recognize my changes, how could I protect my marriage while trying to make Pair-o-Dice Village work?

I realized I just might be on autopilot. If I ran out of fuel, where would we land?

Four

CHAPTER 34
Malice in Blunderland

It is not a lack of love, but a lack of friendship
that makes unhappy marriages.
Frederick Nietszche

March 25, 2007

Through her outgoingness and power-networking, Laura had continued to spread the word that the Car-Cinomas were for sale, but to no avail. The juggling act was pervasive every day: (1) Don't put a penny into them unless we need to, (2) but make sure they'll run for the prospective buyer, and (3) make sure we don't get stuck. Trying to manage this was like an Orkin man going into the jungle to exterminate.

Unfortunately, a grinding noise developed in the Monterror's gearbox that I felt anyone test-driving it would detect. "Seriously, I'm finished with this whole mechanic thing. It's running, for once," said Laura.

"We're not going to be able to sell this to anyone after the whole transmission falls out and it spends a month in San José getting fixed!" I said.

"Look, if you're going to bring it in, you're doing it on your own," Laura said. "I said I'm done."

The heck if I was going to have a coastal mechanic service a transmission, so I brought the Monterror to San José and flew back home. By now, we knew how costly waiting in a hotel could be.

The day after my return to the village, Daniél, the new mechanic called. "You need your transmission repaired, but your car is too modern. I am too afraid to work on it." I had heard this before. While to me it was likely to have first graced the Earth some time after the Pyramids, the country's inhabitants generally considered the Monterror a modern marvel. These thoughts made me feel elitist and somewhat culturally repulsive. But I was irritated with Daniél. He had worked on the car before, and I had told him I was bringing it for the transmission.

"OK, please don't do anything else," I told him. "I'll call you in an hour to let you know when I'll be there to pick it up." I headed to the intermittent-net to look up flight schedules. "OK, Daniél. I'll be there tomorrow around lunch."

"No, you don't need to come," he said.

"Why?" I asked.

"I did it!" he said. *Oh, no, no, no!*

"Did what?" I said, knowing.

"I took it apart, and I know exactly what the problem is!" he said.

"Well, put it back together!" My irritation was evident.

"Oh, no. That would not be good."

"Why?"

"I had to break bolts to get it open. We'd need to find new ones to put it back together," he said. *This is it. This will be monumental.* "OK, so when can we have the parts?"

"This is a Mitsubishi, Don Glen. It will be very difficult. A few days, at least."

I hung up the phone. Then it dawned on me. I had OCD—Obsessive Car Disorder. I remembered the dashboard rattling as my dad took me to school. "Damned rattle!" Dad would say frantically, tapping and punching various perceived points of origin until he took the car into the dealer. "There's a rattle in the glove box," he'd say to the service guy.

"Is there anything else wrong with it?" I'd remember the odd stare on the mechanic's face.

"No, just that rattle," my dad would say.

While obviously hereditary, this OCD was sort of OK when ASC-certified mechanics sprouted around you like papaya trees, and your car was built after the discovery of hydrogen. Here, cars drove by sounding like they were delivering shipments of maracas. The village people had already arrived at a place to which I was certainly destined—surrender.

Here, it was completely ruinous. It had to stop. But had I just pushed it too far? Would this truck now be a total loss?

The next day, Daniél called back. "Don Glen, I'm sorry. I checked everywhere. Please ship the parts from the States," he pled.

I called Jeremy, our next-door neighbor in Chicago who worked on cars as a hobby. He said he'd try to help us and threw in "Mitsubishis are pieces of shit" and "sell that son of a bitch."

"Well, that would be sons of bitches, with two s's," I said.

"What? And they're over fifteen years old? Are you out of your mind?"

"At this point, probably," I admitted.

And then it happened—a hate-filled rapturous malarkey storm of marital venom that rivaled the implosion of an entire galaxy.

"You created this irreversible situation. It was driving fine!" Laura said.

"That gear box was grinding! No one would buy that car like that!" I said.

"No, *you* wouldn't. Others would!" she said. "You're sick! You create drama! That's all you do! We're knee-deep in shit, and every day you back up a dump truck with more! I can take your quirks in dribs, but now you are completely out of control! It's typical. Any time anything is going well for you, you put on the brakes and sabotage it. Everything we invested here! Everything that's happened! Everything we've overcome! We unraveled our entire lives to come here! And you commit to twelve hours of driving and two flights because you don't like the way the car shifts?! We are going home immediately! *And* we're getting divorced! And it's all your fault!"

Whoa, whoa. Wait! Divorce? I started to quietly panic. But in the heat of the moment, I had my ego. That was unfortunate.

"Are you fucking kidding me?" I yelled. "I contaminate the water! I make

tarantulas fall from the sky! I cause seizures and power outages and allergies! Who am I, fucking Zeus?!"

"Oh, stop it! We got through all that. All we have left is your two crap
trucks, and they're killing us! I warned you. But you're never forward-thinking. You're completely illogical—the king of impulse! What would it take to
think something through, even for a second?"

"Look, I like it here! The only time I don't is when you're all wound up,
which incidentally has now become most of the time. So why would I bother
going home to get divorced? You go. Then I can choke on all my own drama
and free you from this cage of chaos that I've put you in. Go!" I said.

"Do you realize what you're saying?" she said.

"Go, God dammit! Just go!!!" I slung a few items around the living room.

"You're right. It's the best thing. I'll go pack." Her shoulders slumped. She
cried as she headed upstairs to the bedroom, and the moment I saw that, I
was eviscerated. It suddenly truly felt like in five short months, we had become permanently incompatible.

I went out to sleep on the hammock, bugs be damned. I couldn't sleep.
*What have I done? But what had she done all this time leading to this? She was
the one who had to get sick on day two and let these thoughts about her reputation in the jungle—as if something like that really existed—consume her all
night, undoubtedly bringing on the allergies and the hair loss. She gave up her
independence, not me. Anyway, she said the "D" word first—not me. Listen to
yourself. You sound like a preschooler in a spat at recess.*

And yet I had been the one to initiate the idea of separating immediately.
Where the hell did that come from? In my mind, I had always been committed to my wife over the jungle, but my actions said otherwise. I had taken
complete charge of all situations, leaving the queen of logic and problem-
solving powerless. Most of my tenderness toward Laura had vanished while
in Costa Rica, like she was some obstacle to the goal. Although I had been
near panicky about Laura's sickness, in that moment, I had clarity about it.
I felt compassion for sure, but it was drowned out by the need to deal with
yet another barrier. Like back at my job, I had taken on more than I could

handle. I had an ambition to live in Pair-o-Dice Village, I was in the weeds, and no one was going to tell me I had failed.

You may have left your physical world behind, but your demons stowed away in those suitcases.

And why did I tell her to go home? *Of course! Because she had become an impediment. What the Hell am I turning into?* In that moment, the most useless natural creation on Earth seemed to be a man's ego—double-so when in the presence of the woman of whom he is most fond.

I wondered what friends and family back home who were so cautious for our move could have seen that we didn't. Whatever it was, we were right in the middle of it and thrashing about to keep from drowning.

Then after a couple hours of thinking, I realized I was on the verge of losing everything. My wife was leaving. I had no relationship with my family. I had no profession. My life savings were evaporating quickly. I felt like I was in the middle of Amityville, where forces were at work completely beyond my control. I looked up toward the ceiling of the outdoor terrace wondering what I might have done to the country or the FlawedShack to bring all this on.

CHAPTER 35
No Hay Can't Take This Anymore!

"I knew a guy had a car like that once.
Fuckin' bastard killed himself in it."
Character of Will Darnell in motion picture "Christine."

March 26, 2007

We now basically couldn't stand the sight of each other. I was hopeful that things would work out between us, but any interaction or look into each other's eyes was a reminder of everything we had gone through. The wounds were fresh.

Nonetheless, with only one car, we had to drive together to the intermittentnet café to position ourselves at opposite ends of the establishment and glare at one another. Maybe foolishly, but mostly because I was a guy, I didn't want to talk about my feelings, not revealing to anyone in the village or at home what was happening. I just sat and surfed the intermittentnet aimlessly all day, trying occasionally to call to find parts for the idle Monterror.

Meanwhile, Laura was frantically on Skype with her best friends back home, working a solution to her greatest obstacle. "I can't buy this stupid ticket," she said after a couple days when I walked over to ask her a question. I looked at her screen, and her pointer was over the purchase button on the Sansa Airlines website. "I'm not separating the cats, and I can only bring one in the cabin at a time. Everyone at home is busy with family commitments and work and can't come to fly out with me. And heck if I'm going to drag my family into this." She was desperate. I actually felt bad for her because I could tell that she really wanted nothing more than to leave. Yet I just shrugged my shoulders and walked away, realizing how this two-cat dilemma could work in my favor. I yearned for this cat obstacle to persist longer than her anger and resentment so that we could reconcile.

Yet every time we made eye contact, I could tell the time wasn't yet right, and I wasn't yet ready to beg. I felt like a complete tool with the mistakes that had been made, and my pride was gagging my better senses. We waited over a week more for parts. We even drove to the Panamanian border to hear *no hay*—despite a prior assurance over the phone that the shop there had them. Thankfully, Daniél was eventually able to procure innards in San José.

It took him another two days to assemble everything, and I flew to San José—a welcome escape. First, Daniél told me that this repair was completely unnecessary and that if I wanted to live in Costa Rica, I would need to be less of a perfectionist toward my vehicles. Even the mechanics who were taking our money were administering therapy for my OCD. I then got an odd lesson from his brother and him on how to drive stick.

"It's bad for your gear box to shift the way you do. You must return to neutral and pump the clutch once before you go into any other gear," he said. Five minutes outside San José I figured out that now the Monterror would not shift gears unless I did just that. But alas, bringing it back would just mess it up more.

What would I tell Laura? What could I tell her but the truth? This was going to be quite obvious.

"They completely ruined the gear box," I said humbly as I entered the FlawedShack. "I have no idea how bad, but it's bad."

Surprisingly, she took it like a champ. *Absence makes the heart grow fonder?* I could tell her level of repulsion hadn't subsided much, but she just might have seen in my eyes that this was my Obsessive Car Disorder knockout punch.

The next day, I hacked a coconut off one of our trees and made coconut milk pancakes. We drank coffee as the mist rolled over the hills. It had
rained a ton the night before, and the air was crisp and cleaner than usual.
We sat and had a meal without talking. This was a plus since at least we
weren't fighting, a situation that now was always triggered by a maximum
of three spoken sentences.

"It's garbage day. I'll take the trash to the road," I said when breakfast was
over.

Taking out the trash was always a completely disgusting process because of
a couple of factors. First, things tended to decompose strikingly quickly in the
jungle heat. People had encouraged us to take up the art of composting, but
we had yet to adopt it fully into our routine. Laura had become increasingly
inspired to do so occasionally but had her own style. Most gringos designated
a place on the property far from the house to start a compost pile. Averse to
the bugs and other jungle eventualities, Laura had no desire to walk anywhere
to re-feed the Earth its by-products. Instead, she would stand at our front
door and shot-put the rind or carcass *du jour* over the property's edge. Actually, she'd hurl it toward the edge, not over because she rarely made it. After a
nice dinner event, our yard looked like a tropical buffet during nuclear winter.

Our driveway was too long to carry the trash on foot, so I'd drive it in a
Car-Cinoma, always smelling like I had thrown three bodies in the trunk for
several days.

That morning, I drove out onto the road, made a U-turn, and began heading up the driveway. I stopped the truck, opened the tailgate and left the two
odoriferous bags at the side of the road. I was always rather astonished that
a town with marginal water and electricity had garbage service.

I got back into the truck and pressed the gas to continue up the steep
incline. Before I knew it, I was sliding backwards. I stopped and checked that
it was in four-wheel. It was.

I let the clutch out again. Mud flew upwards from one side of the truck. I
was going nowhere. I floored it. The Monterror fishtailed sideways in place.
As I examined the spray of the mud, I realized only one wheel was turning!

Four

I punched it again. It slid further sideways. As its engine was the heaviest part, the Monterror was making a natural U-turn to point it downhill. The problem was I knew the driveway wasn't wide enough to fit the truck crossways. I looked over the side of the driveway. *I'm going to slide right off an eight-foot drop.* I tried one last time, figuring I could only be a couple inches from the driveway's edge. I pulled the emergency brake. *Game over.*

I nearly had a heart attack when I opened the door to get out. All the workers coming up and down the driveway in two-wheel drive for our construction projects had dug two deep tire channels along it. The truck, almost perpendicular to those tracks, was teetering on two wheels. It rocked toward the driver's side—my side—wanting to roll down the driveway.

I carefully exited as the Monterror wobbled teasingly. My heart raced as both my feet touched earth. My weight left the truck's interior, and the Monterror swayed abruptly. I saw the passenger's side back tire was no more than an inch away from the edge of the driveway.

Turning up toward the house, I realized I had exited the wrong side! *I'm right in its downhill path!* The Monterror completely blocked the driveway with nowhere for me to pass. I crawled under it. As I squirmed in the mud, my back touched its frame. Chills traveled my spine as I felt it rock over me.

I slithered like lightening out the other side and darted up the driveway as if the Monterror gave chase, arriving at the house completely winded.

Laura sat on the couch on our patio. "What happened to you?" Seeing my eyes as wide as drink coasters and my front covered in mud, this was already the most empathic interaction we had had in over a week. I said nothing. I instinctively went to her and put my head in her lap. My tear ducts turned to warm springs as I uttered doomsday phrases like a machine gun. "Everything's going wrong. Everything! I'm so scared. What'll happen next? We banked our lives on this completely losing bet! When are we going to stop ruining ourselves? What did we do to deserve this? What were we thinking?"

The casualties of the past five months flashed before my eyes. I had sometimes been the creator of tragedy but always carried the torch of our dreams.

But in this moment, I wanted nothing to do with any of it. In this moment I was abruptly done.

I lay there for five minutes, writhing and letting it all out with her hand on my head. Laura said nothing until she finally uttered the magical words, "We'll get through it. We have each other."

A massive relief came over me. And then I heard a toucan in the distance and bolted upright, scanning the valley as I always did when hearing that sound. A green iridescent hummingbird crossed my sight, targeting an orange flower on our bushes. And then, there was the toucan. I waited for the second one to follow as always. *There it is!*

And then all the tragedies in my mind turned to virtues. I remembered the strength I had found in the jungle to carry our torch that I never before knew existed. I remembered that I had a knack for language and an affinity for new cultures. I remembered that at any given moment, we could go hiking, fishing, zip-lining, or jump off a rock into a gorge. Knowing we would see this out together once again renewed me with amazing power.

Just maybe, the taking out of two garbage bags was the moment to bring the two of us into true alignment—such an apparently trashy couple we were.

The next day, we called Hal and Indira and revealed to them why we had vanished from the face of the Earth for ten days.

"You're too maternal," Hal told me as we scoped the next good wave to bodysurf.

"You keep saying it. Mark said it after only a week here from Arizona. But that instinct is deeply engrained, man," I said. "How am I going to change my core when everything else is in a swirl?"

"Your choice, man, but it's one life—not two—and if you didn't take care of everything, Laura's got a really tough center you'd see. I can tell. She'd figure things out," he said.

"We're not taking care of squat, really," I said.

"You're delusional, man. You handle everything, and you're not letting her. She's disappointed in herself."

Four

"We've talked about it," I said. "I told her she should take a truck and experience the place for better or worse. That made her even angrier at herself. She realized she's afraid to go anywhere without me. She said she bought a condo at twenty-six in a pioneering area of Chicago, and now she can't go buy eggs. But what you're saying is that I'm destroying her by trying to save her?" I asked Hal.

"Look, everyone is responsible for their own actions. Like everything else, the more she does it, the better she'll be at it. Refuse to go buy the eggs. She'll get pissed. But she'll come back with eggs and then someday she'll come back with the chicken," he said sagely.

We resumed 10/10 over the coming days. That was when we realized how valuable that simple communication technique really had been. We already knew exactly what each of us was experiencing. Had we had to explain ourselves after two weeks that were so contentious, we likely would have come off the rails again.

Instead, we immediately launched into problem-solving mode, and using 10/10 got us to solutions so much more quickly than otherwise. I realized we were indeed in a perpetual cycle. The worse things got, the more I felt compelled to fix things. The more I fixed things, the worse Laura felt about herself and the more helpless she got, and the worse she felt about herself. The worse she felt about herself, the more she lashed out because she resented me for handling things, feeling she could handle nothing. The more she lashed out, the more I resented her for jeopardizing our dream in which we had invested so much.

And so I realized that the harder I pushed to make everything right, the more wrong it all got. Only by letting go would we be able to quell the vicious cycle. So we did just that.

Laura and Glen's Beach 10/10 from April 5, 2007
What just happened to us, and how do we stop it from happening again? How does my answer make me feel?

Glen's Answer

Dear Laura,

Well, I am glad that this question is phrased in the past tense. It shows that mentally, we've decided we're done with the nonsense we created.

What did it feel like to be where we were? It felt dark, eerie, and dangerous. It felt like a haunted house, where every time you turn around, something jumps out at you unexpectedly. But it was different in that it felt very real. This was no joke. And the more energy I put into trying to make things right, the worse they got. That's a complete tailspin. In fact, it felt like I was sitting at the cockpit of my life, and every instrument and control did the exact opposite of what I had learned it would.

We came here with very high hopes. Two of the big things that resonate with me that people told us when we arrived were (1) you have to lower your expectations of yourself and others to survive here, and (2) that we should buy only one truck and that they should be Toyotas or Nissans. We completely ignored #1, and I disregarded #2. It was like we felt like we knew better. On what basis did we know better other than we were completely elitist? I'm not sure of this, but I suspect we came from a land of sophistication and thought that we could master this simpler land. I think it's mastered us. We need to find a way to stop the spin.

I think we've had a complete role reversal too, for better or worse. The better part is there is probably no better way for us to get to know each other than to see each other in that context. I'm taking care of all the confrontations and negotiations, which you always used to do. You're taking care of all the heady emotional thinking, which I used to always do. We're both amateurs at this stuff, and it's showing.

Again, we need to stop the spin. How do we do that? We have to remove all the causes out of our lives, to start. I think we need to get out of this house some way, somehow. We also need to just get rid of these trucks at all costs and rent one, no matter what it costs. We can fix our finances later. Right now, we're risking our marriage. And who knows, maybe we just need to pull out of the spin and go home for a while like you said.

Four

*I am so disappointed to have just said that, but I need to call a spade a
spade.*

I love you!

Glen

Laura's Answer

*I am angry with myself for being so weak and frail and so dependent on
you. When you said to me "since when did I marry a crier?" it really hurt my
feelings because it made me feel even weaker. I am not a crier and I do not know
exactly what is happening to us or me. It's a feeling that is the color fiery red. It
is rage and anger. I feel like a piece of paper that has just gone through a shred-
der. Can I put the pieces back together?*

*I am a little more comfortable—believe it or not—with our future here and
us. I feel hopeful. I believe that we are working through our issues and beginning to recognize how our fears and disappointments are controlling us and
significantly impacting our personal well-being. When I understand you, I can
be more compassionate toward you and can also encourage you to redirect your
behavior and vise versa. It is not as challenging to redirect behaviors when we
both have discussed why we are who we are and why we behave the way we
behave.*

*I think that is how we ultimately stop this from happening again. Increase
our understanding of the metamorphoses that we are experiencing by sharing
our growing edges, supporting one another in conquering our doubts, and in-
fusing our lives with laughter and joy.*

Love,

Laura

CHAPTER 36
Finding Pura Vida

And this, our life, exempt from public haunt,
finds tongues in trees, books in the running brooks,
sermons in stones, and good in everything.
William Shakespeare

April 10, 2007

We quickly began taking actions to rid our life in the village of all of its detriments.

We first drove the Monterror straight to San José to sell. Don't pass go. Don't collect two hundred dollars. Of course, had I passed go, there certainly would not have been a sign informing me of such. We left the truck on consignment with a mechanic. Depending on the outcome, we'd try the same approach with the Montalloper.

We drove back to the village in a rental car. This allowed us to park the Montalloper.

And then we made a commitment to return to Chicago from May to October to regroup, maybe get some contract work, and execute a do-over. "We are much wiser of what the country has in store for us now," Laura said in a 10/10. "We just need to regroup and fly in for another approach and a fresh start." The rains were also pounding the roof once again, and the eventual restart of good weather at Thanksgiving would mark the beginning of the Chicago chill. As soon as the decision was made, we went straight to the intermittentnet café and bought return travel for May 27 to solidify our commitment. We would also, unfortunately, have to break our lease with the Richardsons.

Although these were rather drastic changes to our plans, once implemented, the country began opening up to us once again. For one, we realized just how much time and toil the trucks had given us when we suddenly had heaps of free time. We even picked up a real estate client who actually wanted to see property, taking his elderly mother and him to an amazing property someone had turned us onto in Lagos del Fuego. It jutted out bluntly off the side of a mountain in Lagos del Fuego and could only be accessed on a dirt road I was surprised anyone had the guts to build. Case in point, our new client's mother could do nothing while on the property but say, "There's no way we're getting back up that road. We're stuck here!" She nearly had a nervous breakdown, and he was none too happy that we had put him in such a position. We became acquainted with and said good-bye to client number one in the span of ninety minutes.

Oddly, despite our difficulties getting business going, we didn't feel this threatened the viability of our selling real estate on the Ballena Coast. All our struggles were chalked up to a rough start. The past months were now a mulligan. We'd soon return refreshed and ready for business.

We still did manage every day, however, to take time to either sit on our property in Lagos del Fuego or relax on the beach, resuming our daily 10/10s. I must have been detoxing from all the chaos because in the past, I could never sit still as if someone were a millisecond away from setting me on fire.

One day as I was standing in the surf, a tico approached. "¡Buenos días señor!" He grinned ear-to-ear and didn't speak a lick of English. For me, that was just fine—even a preference. One positive of our having had to navigate a previously overcomplicated life in Costa Rica was that I had picked up more language skills like a high-powered magnet.

We exchanged "how's the weathers," and I relayed our experience in the country, leaving out the *Bonfire of the Insanities* parts. I told him we hoped we could live here permanently.

He smiled in approval of my wise wishes. "Costa Rica is in my heart," he said. "I have never even left the country. Why should I? It is the land of peace. It is the land of God. I was so lucky to be born here. My heart connects with the water, the air, the sky, the animals, the Earth. I feel its energy all the time. And I don't think that would be true if I lived anywhere else. This beach has taught me so much," he said.

"How is that?" I asked.

"My son drowned over there," he said without the slightest pause. He pointed to the open ocean.

I tried to cloak my shock about his matter-of-factness. "I'm so sorry. What happened?"

"I don't know. We were grilling here for *Semana Santa*." Holy Week had just passed. Ticos reunited their entire extended families for the occasion and flocked to the beach. They would camp in tents and grill along the shore for several days.

My new friend on the beach continued. "The meat was ready, and I went to call my son from the water. I didn't see him. We ran up and down the beach calling him. Two days later, we found him on those rocks." He pointed to a bluff of volcanic rock to the north.

"You must have been completely crushed! My heart goes out to you. *Que Dios le bendiga a su hijo*," I said, meaning, "May God bless your son." Over time, my confusions about God as I had been raised to know him had increased, but I knew this guy believed. Like so many ticos, it was written all over his spirit. If it made him feel better, I was a believer that day.

"Why would I be crushed?" he asked. Luckily, he kept talking, and I didn't have to answer. "And then my best friend—he was surfing a few years ago. He got smashed against those same rocks and died instantly."

He never stopped smiling. I couldn't believe his delivery, listing his greatest tragedies in a tone befitting a sermon called "That for which I'm Most Thankful."

"Was he surfing too close to the rocks?" I asked.

"*¿Quién sabe?*" he said—who knows. "But I'm sure of one thing. He must have taken the power of the Earth for granted. We grew up constantly together. He was the kindest soul I knew. He had an enormous heart. No person had so much wisdom and compassion—not even my wife. And yet, he took the Earth for granted. The Earth is much like our wives. We love them. They bring us happiness. But that happiness does not come for free. Love is powerful. We must respect that power. We must respect the Earth."

"You must miss them so much," I said.

"I did for a long time. These events destroyed me," he said. "But luckily I saw, with no help from anyone, that if I was to enjoy the beauty and kindness of Costa Rica, I had to respect God because this is God's land. God needs capital to produce this beauty—this paradise. He will take it from those who, even for a moment, do not respect the power of what he has created.

"Life is an experience and a negotiation," he said. "I live in paradise. I live where my heart belongs. I live with all creatures, and I have to respect my environment. Of course, I didn't want my son to be lost to the Earth, but that surf," he pointed to the rough ocean once more, "and all of nature gives us happiness, survival, and beauty. I cannot choose what parts of it I want to experience. To a man, the Earth is the perfect woman. And even the perfect woman will have imperfect moments."

I wasn't particularly versed in compassionate Spanish. All I could say was, "You are an amazing person. I would like to speak more with you."

"*Señor*, I am so sorry, but I have no phone and no car. I only have a home. We would not be able to stay in touch," he said. "But remember, if you stand here now and walk over there," he pointed to a spot about ten feet away, "or you get in your car and drive for miles, you are in Costa Rica. You are in the right place. This is the place where those who find their souls live the perfect life. I must go now, but you remember that. And remember that in this moment you and I were completely connected. You were my best friend."

"Thank you for saying that," I said, wondering how this could really be.

As if reading my mind, he answered, "I was completely present with you in this moment. Because of that, I was completely open to you, and our connection was genuine. Well, good-bye. *Poora viiida, mae.*" And then, out of nowhere, he gave me a hug which I instinctively returned as if he truly were a best friend.

"*Que dios le bendiga,*" he said as he walked away happily.

"Who was that?" Laura asked as we walked back toward the car.

I told her everything on the way home. "I so wish I spoke the language," she said. "What a powerful moment!" She was deeply moved just by my second-hand account.

"I know. And do you know what I learned out there?" I asked.

"What," she said.

"Nothing comes for free," I said.

"OK, people have said that before," Laura said with a smile.

"Yeah, but with nature, you give what you get. There's a tax. We're in the middle of paradise, and you have contracted sicknesses and healed somewhat. But they're still with you. I've gotten crush-bone flu. We've endured snakes, spiders, and bats. I've had a scorpion marching toward my ear on a piece of wood I was carrying on my shoulder. And in the end, if we fully experience the beauty of what's around us and are one with every moment, that tax will never be too high. We'll have found what we came here for, whether we know what it is or not."

The encounter on the beach immediately made me contemplate the raw realities we had experienced that juxtaposed the natural beauty that surrounded us.

A few weeks before, the gas station outside the village was unexpectedly closed. A friend of the owners' family was there, something clearly troubling him.

"Why are you closed?" I asked. "Herman died. His motorcycle was hit head-on by a truck on the *Costanera.*"

Herman had pumped our gas since our arrival. "*Lleno con diesel,*" I would say, asking him to fill it up. "*Con mucho gusto, señor!*" he would say, meaning "my pleasure," his face alight with joy for every moment.

Four

Two weeks before, an amazingly kind gringo, who was in his fifties, apparently in perfect health, and who lived two houses down from us, died in his sleep. Days later, an older gringo on Indira and Hal's road who we knew from Friday night pizza—a weekly gringo congregation ritual—had a heart attack. He awoke with pain in his chest one night. Unfortunately, his body chose a week when his wife was visiting the States. With no one in the house and an ambulance forty-five minutes away, he decided to drive himself to the hospital. They found his truck impaled against a tree on the side of the road—he was dead. He never made it out of the village.

Another veteran of the village was a bit luckier years ago. He was doing some yard work on the edge of his property, slipped, and did numerous cartwheels before hitting a tree on the way down a slope. Somehow, he came to, walked himself back to his house to call for help, but collapsed on his floor.

Even more remarkably, he managed to once again regain consciousness in a pool of his own blood. He walked out to his truck, started it, and leaned against his steering wheel, coasting down the hill into the middle of town. One of the village people and his wife brought him to the same hospital Little Laura had visited after her seizure. After his airlift to San José and subsequent surgeries, the doctors told him it was an absolute miracle he was alive. Of all the stories we had heard, he was by far the luckiest.

People obviously died everywhere. But in such a small community, chances were you knew or at least had seen them. And yet the hospital was far and safeguards like warning signs, guardrails, and pavement were rare. The environment was sometimes as ominous as it was beautiful.

What's more, as I conversed with them more and more, it seemed ticos accepted death as more of a common reality than North Americans.

This attitude was evident just when going to buy fresh fish in Cedro. A big white tico house on one of the town's main roads was where most everyone bought their fresh fish. In the back, several workers would pull a pristinely fresh catch out of refrigerators to fillet, weigh, and sell on the spot. Meanwhile, crocodiles waited, mouths agape, in the lake behind the filet tables, wrestling for and gobbling up the stripped carcasses thrown to them.

One day, we happened to get there just after school had let out. I stood frozen in my tracks watching children hop about along a rickety narrow bridge, watching the crocs no more than ten feet below. None of the grown-up witnesses said a thing.

I asked one of the fishermen if someone should maybe tell them to get down. His silent look showed he had no idea why anyone would propose such a thing.

We were silent and contemplative the rest of the way home from the beach as I looked at the jungle with the same new eye of wonder as the day we arrived.

CHAPTER 37
Darth

*Economy is the basis of society. When the economy is stable,
society develops. The ideal economy combines the spiritual and the
material, and the best commodities to trade in are sincerity and love.*
Morihei Eushiba, founder of Aikido

April 12, 2007

It was a day of great blessings. A friend had set up a lunch appointment with someone who wanted to buy our truck.

"Hi, I'm Ricky! It is such a pleasure to meet you!" he said at the realty office in Cordial. Like many others we encountered, I recognized him. He had stood out because he drove a very interesting eight-wheeled vehicle with no roof that he steered with two handles. He would yell to the store owners to bring him fruits and vegetables. I had never seen him out of the car. Now I knew why. Today, he sat in a wheelchair, a paraplegic.

"Hey! I've seen you here before! You drive that eight-wheeled toboggan-looking thing, and you shop at that fruit stand," I said, pointing to the stand just twenty yards away.

"Yeah, that's why I'm here! The toboggan, as you call it, is the only way I can get around. But its days are over. It keeps breaking down, and I can't get parts," he said. *And you want to buy our truck?*

We helped him amble his wheelchair over the rough road toward our beachside lunch place around the block. *How does he get around this place?* It took us a long time to get there since everyone stopped to enthusiastically say hi to Ricky.

"Oh, look at this joyous face," Ricky said as the waitress reached our table.

"Hi, Ricky," the waitress said. She turned to Laura and me, "How did you get the honor to have lunch with the happiest guy in Cordial?" Our table was like a revolving door of visitors, one more excited than the next to talk to him, the only fame preceding him evidently being the quality of his spirit.

"I was in Baltimore driving an ice cream truck in my twenties," he said, launching, unprompted, into the story about the misfortune that would change his life forever. "A couple guys held me up. I gave them money, but they just decided to shoot me in the throat anyway." I counted my blessings as I picked at my food.

"My toboggan, as you call it, is at the house, real sick. I'm stuck up there all day long. I get all my energy from people, and I don't see anybody anymore. It's killing me. I've looked for a real car but haven't been able to find an automatic anywhere. That's all I can drive. Yours is automatic, right?" he asked.

"Absolutely," Laura said.

"That's great! I'd like Bob to see your car, and if he approves, you've got a deal." He explained that Bob was his close friend who traveled with him.

"I'm sorry to ask, but—" He politely, but knowingly, cut me off.

"I have levers that I can use to maneuver the pedals while I drive with one hand," he said.

We confirmed the price, and I explained to him the truck's most recent oddity. I had been getting up every morning at about three because the engine had to be run at least five minutes every six hours. If I didn't, it would take about twenty minutes to start it.

"OK, that's fine. Look, if it's an automatic, it'll frankly be hard for me to turn it down," he said.

We had prior commitments for the afternoon and agreed to bring the truck by the house for Bob to inspect before lunch the next day.

Four

The next day, Bob greeted us and checked out the car. "OK, you have a deal," he said after thirty seconds.

Laura and I looked at one another as if a perfect image of the Virgin Mary on the face of a cheese Danish revealed a set of winning lottery numbers.

We picked Ricky up the next day to go do the deal. Ricky hoisted himself up and into the passenger seat of the tall SUV with amazing ease, and we were off to San Isidro. "If you don't mind, can we take it to my mechanic for a once-over? He's on the way."

We agreed, having disclosed the truck's one true remaining defect. The mechanic, like everyone else, was clearly excited to see Ricky.

"You can speak to him in Spanish," Ricky said. "I don't speak it."

The mechanic walked over to my side of the car. "Is there anything wrong with the car?" he asked. I told him about the same one remaining flaw we had conveyed to Ricky.

"OK," he said, appearing quite happy and satisfied. He then gave Ricky an enthusiastic thumbs-up. *Just like that?*

Maintaining his jovial look, he then looked me dead in the eye and said, "Don Ricky is my friend. If you screw him, I will be very upset. I will find you. You can just tell him I know the car."

"That's all?" I asked.

"Yes, but remember what I said. I know this car," he repeated, still smiling as if I was his new favorite person. I sped away with the mechanic waving behind me.

"What did he say?" Ricky asked.

"He said he knows the car," I said.

"Oh, good," Ricky said. "Then it must be fine."

We were at least thirty miles from Pair-o-Dice Village. I contemplated how the Montalloper had developed such a reputation and for what. Although it was certainly old enough, eight years of Sunday school helped me rule out the momentary suspicion that Jesus was driven to the crucifixion in it.

Ricky waxed excitedly about the beautiful countryside, his wonderful friends, and his happy marriage as we made our way into San Isidro. We went to an attorney for title transfer and then to the bank.

"I'm going to have to give you half in cash and half a check," he said. "There it is, sir. The pleasure is all mine. Thank you. You have really saved me."

I grabbed a wad of *colones* with a check wrapped around it. I looked at the check. *Oh, no.* I looked back toward Laura who was clearly happy beyond description at the transaction. Her smile disappeared immediately as our eyes met.

"Uh, Ricky. Did you think our asking price was in dollars or colones?" I asked.

"Colones." His look immediately showed his concern. "It was in colones, right?"

A sudden blanket of despair came over me. *He's about to experience an 80 percent inflation rate in ten seconds.* Our realtor friend had obviously given him the dollar asking price with the zeroes taken off and hadn't specified the currency, nor had we when we met with him.

"Dollars," I said. "Now I know why it took you thirty seconds to buy it."

"Well," Ricky said disappointedly, "I obviously can't do *that*."

I regretfully handed currency and check back to him.

"Hey! I legally own your car!" he said, laughing. We all chuckled, alleviating the weight of the circumstance. We went back to the very surprised lawyer, who reversed the transaction.

The ride home was tragic for Laura and me. We had finally succeeded in getting the Montalloper into decent shape. Despite its newfound health, we didn't want it anywhere near us. And Ricky could really have used it. He was stuck again, and now there was clear despair on his face making its way through his continued praises of Costa Rica and all the people around him.

The next day, Laura and I assumed our perch on the beach for a 10/10. Our conversation led back to the Montalloper.

"Ricky needs that truck a heck of a lot more than we do," I said. "It's been a complete mess. We should make *something* good come out of it. Let's just do the deal at his price."

Four

Laura couldn't believe it. "I guess I'm fine with it, but are you sure? You're Mr. Finances. I don't want you to wake up the next day regretting selling it to him for half what it's worth," Laura said.

"Well, I'm not positive," I said.

"What does your gut tell you?" she asked. Laura had an admiration for my gut, not because of its hereditary Italian fuzziness, but rather because it seemed to have powerful spiritual acumen at times.

I took a deep breath. "Should we sell this car to Ricky at his price?" I asked myself and waited. *No butterflies.* "Gut says yes."

We drove straight to Ricky's house and delivered the news.

Bob immediately started sobbing. "You two are angels," he said.

"Well, let's not get carried away," I said.

"Really, it's our pleasure," Laura reinforced.

Ricky was ecstatic. "Bless you two. I don't know what to say."

It was an amazing feeling to have been able to do something great for a kind soul.

Ricky stared admiringly at the menacing black hunk of machinery. "I'll name it Darth," he said. There was no name more befitting its ominous look and mysterious legacy of evil.

No matter what its saga, however, we were lucky to know that we had altered it by ensuring Darth landed with the one person on Earth who needed and deserved it the most.

CHAPTER 38
You Wannacaste?

"When the facts change, I change my mind. What do you do, sir?"
John Maynard Keynes

April 14, 2007

While Laura had arrived committed to selling real estate, my choice of a profession was wide open. I knew my talents in the stock market weren't so great that I could sustain the types of gains we had been seeing for a long time. Luckily, experiencing the joy of going into the jungle to show and investigate magnificent properties led me to want to sell real estate too. That decision put all our eggs in one basket. We now needed to embrace real estate as a single source of income.

"Before we go back to the States where all the buyers are, I want to go up to Guanacaste to see what the competition looks like," Laura said.

Guanacaste was *the* region for booming gringo activity and where the big retiree migration had all started. Bordering Nicaragua to the north, its main attraction was the Liberia International Airport with direct flights to North America during high season. While still significantly more affordable than North American property, it was a mature market. We had heard how much more lush the Ballena Coast was than Guanacaste and the much greater value proposition Ballena's land presented to likely buyers. "I want to be able to hold pictures side by side while I tell people up north what view A costs versus view B," Laura said.

Always remarkably forward-thinking, Laura's idea was a good one. We grabbed a couple of plane tickets and were greeted by a real estate explosion. Every major North American hotel chain seemed to have planted their flag in Guanacaste already. In fact, a Bill Gates consortium of investors reportedly owned an entire island housing the Four Seasons and beachside lots going for six million dollars each. And if the Ballena Coast was a jungle of realtors, Guanacaste was an entire ecosystem—with roadside Remax and Century 21 offices every two minutes.

Coming out of dry season, this region was quite arid, reminding me of the landscape from Steinbeck novels. In fact, there were quite a few active fires burning in some open areas.

The coast was a series of small bays lined with concentrated developments. Commerce and the density of people seemed surprisingly equivalent to a Key West or Naples, FL.

The properties were sometimes one-fourth the size of what we were accustomed to and cost four times more—exactly the evidence we had journeyed to Guanacaste to collect. And the concentration of development was such that the edge of a lot was only several yards away from someone else's rooftop below it. The developments were cut in what they called terracing, like a giant's staircase up the hills.

There were rumors of a new reservoir being dug miles away, but water was clearly scarce. In this case, it wasn't a question of bad roadside plumbing like in the village. Rather, too many people had arrived too fast for the supply. Making matters worse, when a water shortage was detected, the municipality reportedly diverted the supply to the revenue-generating tourist resorts. We even encountered a prominent highway billboard advertising a large residential development with a marina, golf course, and other amenities galore. Across it, the graffiti read, *"No hay agua"*—there's no water.

Regardless, a mysterious dynamic befell us on day two of our week-long exploratory trip. "You know, there are so many more people here. There are big grocery stores and an airport nearby. There's actually a real variety of restaurants, and there are a lot more gringos," I said to Laura over dinner. "Could it be that this might be the place for us?"

And just like that, without much of a thought, we started investigating places to rent upon our return in October. This possible detour notwithstanding, the potential for an even more significant off-ramp came on our third night. Rather out of character for me, I somehow was motivated to contact some hoteliers we had met through other hotelier friends in San José. Jerry and Joan invited us to the beachside bed-and-breakfast they had owned for over a decade on Playa Tamarindo. It was a truly elegant, service-oriented establishment with extremely well-appointed rooms and clearly a place where the well-to-do would stay.

Over dinner at a restaurant later that night, we were posed a very unexpected proposition. "I remember in San José you said you spoke Spanish," Jerry said to me.

"Yep!" I replied. "Knowing Italian as a toddler and growing up in Miami will do that to you."

"You said you know a bit of French too?"

"I can get by," I replied.

"And you love to cook?"

"Right." I immediately assumed they wanted to sell their B&B. They were entering their later years, and it would make sense that they were tired of the hotel business. *Umm, well, unfortunately, I left the seven million dollars in my other wallet.*

Joan now jumped in. "And Laura, you seem like such a social person and so energetic and engaging."

"Thank you," Laura answered proudly.

"And you both originally were thinking of coming to Costa Rica to open a bed-and-breakfast, right?" Jerry asked. *Yeah, they want to sell it to us.*

"We've been shackled to the hotel for years, and frankly, we're a bit tired," Joan continued. *Bingo.* "We want to get away during the off season this year, but we need someone to stay and manage it. We still have enough business where keeping it open is worthwhile. We were wondering if you guys wanted to manage it for three months. We've been looking for someone for a while, and it's a bit late in the game. We'd need to know over the next couple weeks."

I immediately became interested. "What period are you looking at?" Laura asked. *She is too.*

"June through September," Jerry said.

And just like that, the million-piece puzzle of life was thrown on the floor. We left the restaurant in a haze of possibility and confusion. "What just happened?" I asked Laura.

"Let's go over there and talk about it." She pointed to a bar across the street. "Well, two people are letting us test-drive a dream we left for dead while living on a beach and getting paid," Laura said at the bar.

"And we'd be able to see what it's like to live out here," I said.

We looked at each other in silence for a few seconds and then, as if on cue, both buried our heads in our hands. "Could this get any more difficult?" I asked. "I mean we have tickets to go to Chicago. We're about to sign a lease on a new house on the Ballena Coast for October. Now this!"

"I don't know if this is an opportunity or a curse, really. It seems like a once-in-a-lifetime shot."

We visited Jerry and Joan's hotel/B&B several times over our remaining three days in Guanacaste, asking questions about the way of life and what would be required of us. Most of it was appealing. "Oh, you just have to be here in the morning for breakfast and midafternoon to receive people when they come back from the beach and excursions. Other than that, we have housekeepers here, so you're free to roam as you please," Joan said.

Some of it was not so appealing, "You will have to be up cooking breakfast by 4:30 every morning, and you'd be required to be on call 24/7," Jerry said.

We were intensely excited about the free test-drive of the bed-and-breakfast idea. Nonetheless, we were overwhelmed and told them we'd go back to the village to quickly consider it. "So what's your take?" Laura asked on the little jet prop plane home.

"I need a lobotomy," I said.

This was confirmed by the reactions from those at home to our announcement that we were now likely going to run a B&B for three months. We did this ten days after declaring our intent to return to the States for a rest.

Of course, Laura and I spent a great deal of time on the beach discussing the proposition.

"Life's training wheels are off, and we're hurtling down a hill, barely even able to steer," I said. "What happened to us?"

"Don't you think you're being a bit dramatic?" Laura asked.

"No, I'm not. Think about a similar proposal in Chicago. 'We'd like to see if you're interested in running our bed-and-breakfast,' which is to say, 'Hi. Just throwing this out there, but why don't you drop everything, pack up all your stuff, and move your lives for three months to start working at something that you have never done before?' And then what's after that? We have no clue!"

"Yeah, I guess I see that. They *did* put it out there like, 'How about we catch a movie after dinner,' and that's how we reacted to it," she said.

"Right. Back home, we'd have wondered if they got a hold of the cigarettes with the curls on the ends," I said. "But here, it's 'Yeah, a movie sounds pretty good right about now.'"

"You're scaring me, but you're right. I guess my only mental boundary now is the Boys' wellbeing," she said with tinge of excitement.

"And it's great, but we have to realize how blasé we're becoming about huge steps. What's next if the B&B thing doesn't work out? 'Hey, guys, I've got a sardine farm in Phuket that needs tending while I'm gone. If you can get over the stench, you'll be naturals!' You left corporate to work in animal shelters, but if that didn't work out, you had a huge business network. When I quit my job, sure I took on more risk as an entrepreneur, but what really changed? I still went to a building and did the same thing I always knew and was good at. Here, we are off the radar completely!"

"That training wheels comment you made is interesting," Laura said. "Here, in the middle of complete freedom, you realize we had training wheels on our lives in North America every moment of every day. There are really a handful of pre-programmed choices you can make in life up there compared to here, unless you really go out of your way to stretch. It's really exciting when you think about it. Our minds are so open now. We don't really flinch at much."

"Yeah, it's cool, but we don't know how to navigate this type of stuff. The best we can do is learn as we go, I guess. I just wish I could hit that button to activate the bumpers over the gutters on the bowling lane."

"Weird analogy, but I get it," Laura said.

"And what really worries me is you've always been a lot more rational than me. You're logical. You see five steps forward in every decision. But now you're getting excited about the same stuff I am," I said. "If we both turn into dreamers, and you're not reminding me that sardines stink, we'll end up on that farm!"

"Hey, wait! I still know that this is going to be no picnic," Laura objected. "I mean they told us what we'll be required to do. We're going to have to provide these guests high-class service, and we've never worked a minute in a hotel! So, yeah. It's strange that I'm considering this, but I'm not nuts!"

"Good. I think we need to realize that just because prospects might be exciting, that doesn't make them right for us. Wait a minute. Feel my forehead. I'm being logical."

Laura giggled. "Sounds like you want the sense of adventure without the adventure," Laura said sarcastically.

The next day, a big-shot realtor on the Ballena Coast told Laura that he could line up a job for her at the Remax office near the B&B in Guanacaste. The table was being set. We stopped looking for a place to rent in Chicago— our home was rented out. Meanwhile, we told our new prospective landlord in Costa Rica that we didn't know if we were going to be back on the Ballena Coast come October.

But then, after a week of inquiries and stipulations with Jerry and Joan, we learned their dogs fancied cats as snack food—actually having eaten one or two in the past. The Boys wouldn't be permitted in the main house, so Laura would have to live in one of the *casitas* on the property with them while I stayed in the main house. Then came the realization that—although we didn't expect much—our compensation was to be only room and board. This might have seemed appealing six months prior, but at this stage we were at the half-year mark and needed to start thinking about our livelihood.

Playa Tamarindo now off the table, we now reannounced to our baffled spectators at home that we once again intended to return.

The training wheels were off. On the one hand, this seemed like a magical development fraught with possibility. Then again, there was still that small North American voice in our heads occasionally reminding us that training wheels were invented to avoid crashes and fractures.

Regardless, for the first time, we saw how our life leap was finally having spontaneous effects on both our personas. And we had come back from Guanacaste knowing a lot more about the hospitality industry than real estate.

CHAPTER 39
The Magnificent Monkey Massage

*That pleasure which is at once the most pure, the most
elevating and the most intense, is derived, I maintain, from
the contemplation of the beautiful.*
Edgar Allan Poe

April 30, 2007

Fancying life in Guanacaste had left us distracted and completely flat-footed, with a little less than a month to arrange logistics for our return to Chicago. On top of that, I had arranged a one-week birthday trip for Laura, and we were leaving in ten days to a place with no access to intermittentnet or phone.

"I can't believe we let this happen!" I said to Laura at the intermittentnet café looking at listings. "We spent three weeks completely focused on this B&B opportunity and completely dropped everything else. I need a set of training wheels!"

There were so many logistics to address. Where would we store our belongings while we were gone? And the new house in which we were to live was completely furnished. What would we do with all the furniture, electronics, and house wares we had bought so begrudgingly and so recently but no longer needed? We also needed a place in San José that would accept pets to stay the night before our early-morning flight. Then, out of nowhere, a schedule of planned blackouts appeared in the *Tico Times* newspaper. The pervasive political news since our arrival had been about the Central American Free Trade Agreement (CAFTA) to be signed shortly. It would allow foreign competitors into the market to compete with the government's electric and phone company. Pay cuts and layoffs were feared as ICE's monopoly status fizzled.

The *Times'* report of a malfunctioning hydraulic generator at a local dam causing the blackouts was met with wide skepticism. Rather, the common thought was that these outages were ICE showing the masses what life would be like once the layoffs and cuts hit. Regardless, we were under the gun and needed "constant intermittentnet" to pull off any semblance of an orderly departure.

May was quickly becoming a nail-biter, with intermittentnet available a half hour at a time. We also found the schedule to be loose guidance, which made it difficult to plan ahead. "It's out. You got the *Times*?" I'd ask Laura. And then we'd race down the *Costanera* to any locations that weren't scheduled for blackout at that moment. Of course cafés were packed with everyone having the same idea. This would bring everything to a standstill regardless. We tried calling a realtor, but logically, none wanted to get involved in a four-month rental.

We often became frantic, asking friends back home to view suitable apartments—precious few since we were, in effect, attempting a vacation rental during Chicago's high season. The stress became overwhelming as we bickered continuously over monthly rates and blackout schedules. But there was an added layer. Having spent so much time indoors at the intermittentnet café, removed from our tranquil natural settings and 10/10s, seemed to add a very thick additional layer of torment.

"I just can't take this anymore!" I said after intermittent intermittentnet surfing morning, noon, and night for six days. Laura insightfully recommended we take morning seven for ourselves. "Things were so much better when we were present to ourselves and the universe and really talking things out. Now we're just indoors, fighting technology, and wrecking our last few weeks here!"

We had befriended the owners of a prestigious five-star resort. Despite having only been open for several months, it had already been featured in *Conde Nast Traveler* as one of the "100 Sexiest Hotels in the World."

They had invited us up repeatedly to have dinner or get a massage. Yet, it was at the top of a very steep and brutal forty-five minute mountain road. Accordingly, they had a fleet of SUVs to bring guests who had reserved rooms to their Utopia from the base of the mountain, but we lacked said reservations. Rumors of its high-profile guest list persisted as we resisted the trek up the mountain. Then, Sheryl Crow was spotted riding horseback along the coast. Our curiosity became piqued.

We booked two massages and headed up the road, which had the pitch and contour of a wedge of Swiss cheese. Our little Suzuki Jimmy 4x4 rental braved the incline like a champ. We, on the other hand, felt like two cans in a paint shaker, my spinal discs about to burst like fish roe.

Upon arrival, we were escorted to a free-standing couples massage room with louvered wooden doors. It opened toward the ocean, where we had a direct view of the Whale's Tail formation resting in the Pacific. Effectively a huge natural sandbar, the Whale's Tail was *the* iconic fixture of the Ballena Coast, the exact shape that its name indicated. It extended far and wide out into the blue water off the beach—seeming much longer and wider than an American football field. The prospect of being face-down for ninety minutes instead of enjoying the view made me reluctant to disrobe.

The masseuses reentered, turning on the customary relaxation CD. "Could you please turn that off?" Laura asked after five minutes. The masseuses obliged, and all that remained was nature's soundtrack.

The sounds were the same as at the FlawedShack, but we had never given ourselves permission to lie eyes-closed to consume it in a manner distilled from any distraction. We heard the howler monkeys, kiskadees, crested caracaras, chachalacas, toucans, and peccari, small white wild hogs. Notoriously one of the loudest mammals on Earth, they sounded like the suction of water swirling down a drain but amplified a thousand times. Even *they* had an oddly relaxing effect in this setting.

Since when do I know animal sounds? In that moment, I realized how absolutely aware I had been of the natural beings around me during our life leap. When people came to visit, I was the one who told them about the nature, often more than Hal or Indira or others who had been there much longer than we had.

And through the ups and downs these curiosities about nature and language and culture proved that my love for Costa Rica endured. Despite intermittentnet, phones, logistics, sickness, and sometimes each other, I couldn't help but take it all in.

Our time was up too quickly. I turned my attention to Laura. Throughout the massage, I strangely could feel her relaxing from across the room. She ran across the room and gave me the tightest hug.

"I am so glad we came here," she said.

"Me, too. It's such a nice resort," I said.

"No, I mean Costa Rica," she said.

I hoped like hell that this was an emotion that could endure for both of us.

"Where are the showers?" I asked. We looked around the room and saw nothing.

Our eyes then simultaneously met. "Do you think?" Laura asked. She put her robe on and walked to the vast opening facing the Whale's Tail. "Yep, they're here." I examined the showers, an open façade to the ocean for the entire world to see. Laura immediately dropped her robe and started to shower. I walked out to a metal grate hanging over the edge of the steep mountain face—the rainforest down below—and turned on the water. I immediately heard a truck down below and to my right and froze. *I look like an albino human tongue depressor.* I quickly realized that, in truth, anyone hiking the jungle or with binoculars on the *Costanera* could probably see us. Even still, this was a once in a lifetime experience. Voyeurs be damned, we took our showers, occasionally glancing at the postcard of the Whale's Tail and the rainforest hundreds of feet below.

Four

We reluctantly dried off and went to the pool area. We sipped club soda over the Whale's Tail for hours, making it a point not to mention anything about our pressing Chicago logistics.

We reentered the paint shaker and bounced down the hill to grudgingly fire up our laptops and resume our agonizing search.

That afternoon, out of nowhere, the universe rewarded us for taking the time to remember its beauty. We confirmed a place to live in Chicago. Our greatest pressure was off.

CHAPTER 40
Berger Melt

*God gave us the gift of life; it is up to us to give ourselves
the gift of living well.*
Voltaire

May 9, 2007

"We're going to Paraiso del Cielo!" Laura exclaimed as we turned off to Monteverde.

"I can't think of anything better! I get to spend seven days really knowing myself! It's perfect!" She teared up upon learning of her birthday present. I should have hired a dump truck to carry all the brownie points just scored.

Paraiso del Cielo was the B&B in northwest central Costa Rica where I had sat on the magic rock and hatched the idea to come to Costa Rica. It was a seven-acre mountain grassland with three cabins built by the owners themselves exclusively of materials from the very land upon which they sat. We knew it as a place for total relaxation and introspection. Hanna, its owner, was an undeclared spiritual guru. Moreover, Paraiso del Cielo was outright mystical, seeming to awaken spiritual awareness with a mere step onto its grounds. I could think of no better way to end this sabbatical than on the very land on which the idea originated.

Four

Hanna greeted us with her usual warm spirit. When we first met, I called her Helga the Hugger because of the engulfing embraces she gave like the one that day. From the moment of her first hug two years prior, a benevolent invisible teacher united with our soul and began its work.

We chatted with her briefly and took dinner to our cabin to recover from a ride over bridges barely standing and every surface known to man. The cabin and its furniture had looks and smells constantly reminding us they came from the Earth—hardened sap still hanging onto the side of the logs like organic glue.

The B&B was just close enough to make out the ocean behind the rolling green hills, still quite green despite the relative aridness to the Ballena Coast. The next morning, we awoke to the magnificent view that had started the experience that changed our lives forever.

"This is perfect!" Laura said. "Hardly anyone's here now. We'll be able to talk to Hanna, to each other, 10/10, reminisce about the last few months, and really embrace our return to Costa Rica."

We walked to the main house where bowls of chopped local fruits, baskets of fresh artisan bread, jars of homemade jellies, and piping hot mugs of coffee awaited.

"During ziss time of year viss no tourists, my vissitorss are old friends of Paraiso del Cielo," Hanna said. "Zey come here to ssink and talk and just be."

"Well, this is the best place for that. Where is Hector?" I asked. We had yet to see Hector, her Spanish husband.

"Oh, well, he left," she continued in her German accent.

"Left to go to town?" Laura asked.

"No, he has left Paraiso del Cielo. He left Roberto and me."

We were thunderstruck. Hanna, Hector, and Roberto, their young son, ran the B&B like a cell's nucleus. Hector did the cooking and handy work. Roberto entertained with wit and good nature way beyond his teenage years, imparting his profound knowledge of nature on his famous horseback rides.

It was sad to hear their relationship had ended, but I couldn't help thinking that Hanna's uniqueness might make her difficult to live with in the marital sense.

"Yes, apparently he was not happy here. Now, the voices have told me that it is time to be ready to move. Now I leave my clothes hanging over an open suitcase by my bed. When the angels tell me to leave, I will be ready," she said. Hanna tended to hear things in her sleep—coming to breakfast with premonitions and visions that the "voices" had communicated about her guests and their lives. It would have been easy to dismiss them as gimmicks if not for the information often being extremely relevant to aspects of the guests' lives never before revealed.

"The family has not been too well. I worry about Roberto. Hector has not been nice to him," Hanna said. "But this is how life happens. I accept it for all it is. The worst way to control life is to try to control it. Unfortunately, Roberto finds everything harder to accept than I do."

I had lain awake all night for reasons unknown. Upon finishing breakfast, I returned to our cabin to possibly catch up on sleep. Unfortunately, I was disturbed by the sound of what I could tell was a large insect stirring behind a painting above the bed. I caught a glimpse of a claw peeking from the edge of the picture. This resulted in no sleep for me, more out of curiosity than fear.

Laura had gone to the outdoor pool that faced the ocean view. She came back after almost an hour, clearly melancholy.

"You asleep?" she asked.

"Nope." I wasn't about to tell her why. "How was the pool?"

"Nice, I guess," she said.

"What do you mean you guess?"

"Well, I was lying there in the sun, quite content with the clean breeze and beautiful blue sky. Hanna and two guests came to the pool, and they were already in deep conversation. I was disappointed to not have her to myself, but I understood that everyone takes their turn with her," she said.

"We're here for a while," I said.

Four

"I know. But then Hanna just stripped naked and dove in right in front of them," she said.

"Really?" I asked.

"I lay there thinking it would be awesome to be able to feel so free like that. But my logical side got a bit weirded with those guys there. So I left," Laura said.

"Sorry to hear that," I sympathized. *Scratch, scratch, rustle rustle.*

"What was that?" Laura asked. *Crap!*

"We have a little friend behind that painting."

"That doesn't sound little," Laura said."

"I'll talk to Hanna about it." I would have taken a few whacks in its general direction, but I was afraid of damaging the painting, which was quite nice but not framed or protected in any way.

We went back to the main house for lunch with the other two guests. We were used to being completely alive at Paraiso del Cielo. Instead, the air at the table seemed heavy.

After lunch, Roberto came to visit. "You've grown so much! With your intelligence, outgoingness, and good looks, you must be quite a catch with the ladies," Laura said.

"You'd be surprised," Roberto said. He was being modest. He was maybe the most delightful teenager we had ever been around. Despite Hanna's prior warnings, he seemed to be his usual surprisingly composed self, mature beyond his years.

Until then withdrawn from the conversations—tuning a guitar all the while—a long-haired fellow with a sex symbol air about him introduced himself with a soft, relaxed smile. He was Simon de Leon, a singer-songwriter of modern Costa Rican folk pop. I come to Paraiso del Cielo to get inspiration for my music. Paraiso del Cielo brings me back to Earth and opens my guitar and me like no other place on Earth," he said.

We listened as he sang for hours. Hanna knew the words to every song. I was a sucker for a talented musician, and this he was.

Unfortunately, it seemed the beer was flowing a lot more than we had remembered, clearly not helping our hopes for introspection and philosophical conversation. What's more, this was a tranquil setting, which to me usually equaled boredom. Without the spiritual outlet to resolve that tranquility, I found myself wanting to resolve it with beer, but I exercised restraint in honor of the potential these days had for us.

Simon took a break from his guitar. Hanna fetched another round of Imperials and turned on Harry Belafonte. Everyone stood up and started dancing. Dancing was one of Laura's favorite things. Her face ignited as she hopped up and began her rhythmic and attractive shake.

My gaze wandered as I danced, and there he was. *Darryl! Wow!*

Darryl was *the* person who pointed out I had had my revelation on the Magic Rock to live in Costa Rica. On that life-changing day two years earlier, he ran across the river, stood in front of me with a maniacal look, and said, "Looks like the Pura Vida of Costa Rica just got ya!" Then he cackled almost insanely, sprinted back across the river, and left me by myself to ruminate. Had he not done that, who knows? The revelation might not have stuck. But now in this moment, I remembered it like it had just happened the minute before.

The only thing that kept Darryl working as an architect in New Hampshire was to spend the rare time he could get away at Paraiso del Cielo and with the Boruca Indians. It seemed he hated his work so much that he would have otherwise quit, even at the risk of financial ruin. Darryl was a lover of the Boruca people. We hadn't met anyone else who would spend weeks on the reservation laboring with them and assisting them financially. They, in return, would give him food, shelter, and a great feeling of satisfaction.

"What the hell are you doing here?" I asked.

"Eh, I heard you were here so figured I'd drop by," he said.

"Drop by? You don't just drop by from New Hampshire or Boruca," I said. He just shrugged his shoulders as if it was a completely natural thing.

The group talked and caroused for hours. Beer continued to flow freely until it was time to get ready for dinner.

"She ripped the painting off the wall!" I said back at the cabin as we changed clothes. I had told Hanna about the creature behind the painting, which now lay in the trash can, torn into thirds. Now that I saw she had dealt with it, my newfound curiosity about nature was killing me. I still didn't know what it was, but trusted Hanna did now that she had dealt with it.

"Why do you think she tore it up?" Laura said.

"I don't know. I just get the feeling someone near to her painted it," I said. "I really hope that's not the case. How about Darryl? You know he's here to invest in Paraiso del Cielo. He wants a place of his own where he can come and go as he pleases."

"I think that's great!" Laura said. "Hanna is his guru. I just hope he's in control of his thoughts."

"Why do you say that?" I asked.

"Because whatever is in you will explode out of the box here. The question is will you like what you see?"

"Is that happening to you?" I asked.

"A bit, yeah. I can feel emotions trying to fly out of me right now—not good ones," she said.

I also could feel my essence wanting to burst forth for discussion and introspection with Hanna as it had the last time we visited Paraiso del Cielo. Yet, the activities of the day had stifled it. But Laura's remark presented an issue. Could it be that the Paraiso del Cielo had indeed ignited the internal discovery we so craved, but in a negative way?

"Well, tomorrow we'll make it a point to get time with Hanna," I said. "My worry is that inasmuch as she's a healer, she's going through quite a bit. She might need some help herself right now."

"Maybe we can be the ones to help her," Laura said.

I shook my head. "That would be like John Wayne Gacy teaching parenting," I said. "Wish we could though."

"Yeah, you're right," Laura said. "The fact that a woman so wise and with so much clarity is having issues is really sad. I guess no one gets a pass. Let's go to dinner."

The scents coming from the kitchen in the main house were amazing, as usual. "Hanna," I said, "thank you for taking care of the critter."

"Oh, don't worry," she said. "It was a whip spider. They are harmless, but they look terrifying."

"You didn't have to tear up that painting. I hope it wasn't dear to you," I said.

"Oh, it was one of my favorite ones I painted," she said. "But the energy was right for change today."

We had dinner with Darryl, Roberto, Hanna, Simon, and two other guests. The beer consumption continued to be impressive. Simon played more guitar after our meal, and we retired and thankfully got some much-needed sleep.

After an early rise the next day, it wasn't long before we got an after-breakfast conversation with Hanna. "You are in Costa Rica now with no industrial distractions or all the craziness of home. You have an opportunity to truly understand yourselves. I see your blog where you tell your friends, 'look what we are doing' and 'this is so hard.' And then I see quickly after that, you are having the best time and signs are going well. Like now it seems like things are quite good. It is OK for you to want to share these things, but this is not the way to resolve your problems."

I had been writing a blog on and off since we arrived. It was a promise to those at home to keep them informed of our goings-on, and it happened to be quite therapeutic for me when things got difficult. "I'm not trying to solve problems by blogging," I said.

"Yes you are," she said. "Did you write a blog at home when you were working and running errands on the weekends?"

"No," I said.

"Then why now?" she asked.

"Because I want to keep everyone informed of what is happening," I asked.

"And why now and not before?" she asked.

"I'd have to think about it," I said.

"It's because you are in a different place that is causing discomfort and fear. And you feel like if you release it all, it will be outside you and you won't feel it. Costa Rica was always here. It has never changed. What changed is you came to a new place, and you refuse to change. And releasing everything to your friends and family, you won't really examine and learn from everything you have experienced. Where there is pain there is learning, but you write it, release it to the world, and to your mind it is gone. And then you make the same mistakes again. You need to keep it inside. You need to let it take you over and really feel it, almost to the point you can't take it anymore. Only then will you get to know it. Only then will you know how to deal with it," she said.

"You mean just sit an hour a day and meditate?" I asked.

"Not a day. A week, a month, however long it takes. You only stop to eat and drink. Your problems become your full focus—but not to fix them. To watch your reactions to them. You are the only person you need to talk to. Not Laura, not your friends. Only you can free yourself. And if you do it, you will see how quickly you adapt to all this," she said.

"Of course, the same applies to Laura," she said, turning to Laura.

"I don't know, Hanna," Laura said. "I've swung in a hammock for hours and days, and writing and talking to each other have seemed to help. So has trying to live in Costa Rica as tourists."

"Yes, of course. You release the problems to one another and this is good to a point. But unless you process the problems for yourself first, what you are releasing is not accurate about what you are really feeling. And living like tourists is just avoiding reality. I can feel your energy. I see a damaged spirit. Whatever you think you resolved is going to resurface very soon. It will continue; you will have to reconcile with yourself," she said.

"You're in Costa Rica. No one will say you missed work or an appointment. And you're in the quiet with nature around you. You can sit and understand. The healing is faster—more permanent—but the experience is more intense. And your subconscious knows it. So instead of sitting to watch your misery or whatever it is you feel, you go to Guanacaste and visit the cell phone store and go to see your property every day. And you write blogs thinking that if you get it off your chest, it will be therapy. Sit. Be. Suffer. Come out the other side a better person. Understand."

"You know, what you're saying happened to me," I said. "During Laura's and my most difficult moments, I'd sit on the pool deck by myself in the pitch black. I'd stare at the night sky with the eyes of a million different creatures staring at me and the orchestra of jungle sounds. This was really when I felt the most healing.

"When I got into a car accident in my teens, they injected dye in me to find the internal bleeding on the x-ray. I remember that the warmth of the dye going through my body started in my hand, went up my arm, and spread throughout my body, as if I could feel my circulatory system. I felt that same type of inner warmth when I was on that deck. I was alone staring at the stars for hours. My only alternative was to go inside to a woman who I knew—whether I was right or not—wanted nothing to do with me. There was healing there, and processing what had happened each day helped me make the next day just a little bit better. If I hadn't had that time to myself to experience and analyze intense misery, Laura and I might not be sitting here talking to you now."

"I am glad you mentioned the nature. Every time we feel lost and out of balance, the Earth is where we should go to realign. It is the ultimate energy source. So when you are doing your work and going deep into your issues, you must be in contact with the Earth as much as possible, so part of your therapy is also alignment of energy. Lie on the bare Earth. Walk in the jungle, look at the ocean and the trees and the running water, and when it is giving you a good feeling, tell that to the nature out loud or in your head. I hate the saying kill two birds with one rock, but this is what you are doing."

"Oh, there are the other heavenly guests of Paraiso!" The others arrived at the main house for their breakfast, diverting Hanna's attention and ending our conversation.

I slept late the next morning. Laura was already outside on the cabin's back porch hammock when I woke.

"Happy thirty-fifth birthday, hon!" I said.

"Thank you," she replied in a low tone, staring out at the view with a notebook in her lap. *Something's wrong.*

"So, are you enjoying the view?" I asked.

"Quite the opposite," she said, "but it's nobody's fault but mine."

"What do you mean?" I asked.

"Here. Read this," she said, handing me her dialogue book. I skimmed the most recent entry. Laura, a writer of few words, had already managed to compose several pages.

My heart wrung and writhed as I read.

Laura's Journal—Thirty-fifth birthday morning

Happy birthday to me. I am lying in a hammock at Paraiso del Cielo as I turn thirty-five. This was a surprise from Glen and although its purpose was to rejuvenate me and center my energy, the trip really benefited Glen more than me, which is good for him.

I could have used some cleansing of Costa Rica myself—a spa/kick-ass workout to get my body back to health. It has been beaten up. It shows in my face and my lack of toning.

The stress of self-evaluation and change are very taxing on me. The headaches, allergies, hair thinning, and lack of desire to exercise have taken over a bit, at least from my perspective. But who knows? When we return to Chicago people may think I look the same. I highly doubt it.

At thirty-five what do I know about myself? I know that I can survive extreme change and our relationship can as well. I do not manage change very well, and it attacks my body because I internalize emotions and fear. I know I am anxious and worry about shit that never actually happens. I need some core stability and structure in life. Without friends around me, I feel like a leaf falling off a tree as it enters winter. I feel like that one leaf that held on for so long and is now resigned to falling only to be buried until winter passes. Maybe come spring it will be whole or maybe it will have disintegrated.

When I mention structure and support, I am referring to support and stability from friends, community, and finances—support from people that is real and heartfelt. These last seven months have lacked those support structures. I need community. I never thought it was that important until it was gone. I had my little community back in Chicago—wonderful people whom I could trust and rely upon in times of need. I had my community of close friends to share my innermost issues. Here, I don't feel connected to people, and I guess for me it is all about connection.

So let's see. I have learned that I want community, intimate (trustworthy) friendships, and family close by (not six-hour flights plus five-hour drives). Wow! These are all things I knew before. Now I feel even stronger about them, but what have I learned from my move to Costa Rica? I didn't learn how to cope with massive change. I managed my changes poorly, and it is reflected in my feelings about my body and myself. My self-esteem has been stomped on, and although I will get it back, I feel a little depressed and hopeless. Who would have thought I'd be writing this on my thirty-fifth birthday?

I guess I should be proud that I took the plunge, but I feel like I sank more than swam and now am just bobbing up and down for air. On days when I get air, I feel a little better about myself, but mostly I am underwater—down on myself and my inability to adapt. It makes me cry just thinking about it.

Maybe I am being too hard on myself and when I return to Chicago I will experience positive change and see ways in which I was successful here, but in this moment I think that I am too deep in the water to see the sun glistening on the waves above me.

I wish I could stop worrying so much about the unknown entities in my life—like where we will live, where this is taking us, and whether I am making the right decision. That's a big one—even the little things like how will Skippy and Rugby do on the flight home and will we get stuck in Charlotte? If I should have learned one thing down here, it is not to worry and to just let things happen and come as they come, but worry gets the best of me and affects my health.

I have had wonderful experiences down here, but they have been little events: deep-sea fishing, waterfall rappelling, zip-lining, and spending time at the beach with Glen, but I haven't fully embraced the joy that these activities have to offer because I am not well mentally, and through all of this I feel unstable and alone in many ways. I do not have reliable friends down

Four

here, friends to enjoy meals with and entertain, good deep conversations, and long days sipping tea with the family. Even camping with my family, I believe, was more enjoyable than any of the above activities that I have done because I was surrounded by people I loved. Here I am not and will not be. I was saddened by my family's visit because it could have been so wonderful, but the stresses and difficulties of Costa Rica stole the show. As beautiful as it is here, its wonder was not strong enough to overtake the challenges that we experienced during their visit. Maybe this is all in my head, and they remember the wonderful time that they had here, but I don't think so. I think that the illnesses that they experienced, the seizure, the lack of infrastructure and the hostile environment had more of an impact on them than the beauty. That truly saddens me, and I only wish we could have had a more beautiful experience together.

What do I think that I will miss about Costa Rica when we return to Chicago? I think I will miss the quietness in the mornings—waking up hearing the birds and the ocean—the open air and blue skies surrounding me and the views on the *Costanera*. I'll miss having tea in the hammock and reading a book, swimming naked, the zero concept of time and day or even week, the nature and smells of flowers and other scents, taking showers during the day and seeing the mountains in the background, people's ability to not be hurried, the warm weather all the time, Skippy and Rugby enjoying a stroll on the roof and looking out the screens at the action in the jungle, and working on my laptop over a good lunch overlooking the breaking waves.

The truth is you know when you know and I will only know what life will be like back in Chicago and what I will miss in Costa Rica when I cross that bridge.

I put the book down. *"Whatever you have going on in your life will jump out of the box when you arrive at Paraiso del Cielo."*

"I'm sorry you feel this way," I said.

"How did it come to this?" she asked. "I am in the middle of all this beautiful nature. A tourist would go home and tell everyone she had found paradise. I should be experiencing an enormous awakening, and I feel like I'm going to sleep—dying inside. All I can do is think of how I miss my friends and my family, and I keep persecuting myself for being sick and an anxious mess and screwing up your dream."

"You're not screwing up my dream," I said.

"Oh, yes I am," she retorted quickly. "You told me on the beach when we decided to go back to Chicago for the four months that we were doing it because of me," she said.

"I said I was fine staying, and you were not," I said.

"OK, suppose you did. Doesn't that still mean we're going home because of me?" she asked. "Stop being so passive-aggressive."

"Laura, I can tell where this discussion's headed. We're going to end your thirty-fifth birthday on nonspeaking terms," I said. "Why are you doing this?"

"I don't feel like talking anyway," she said. "I just want to swing here and be by myself. I've never felt so horrible. I really feel like my life as I knew it could be over. How am I going to recover from this?"

"What the hell happened? We've been having a pretty good time. We did all those things you listed in that journal and made great friends with Indira and Hal," I replied.

"I don't know. I don't know anything anymore," she said. "Just go to breakfast."

"When you don't eat, you implode. You'll just feel worse. Come on. Then maybe we can come back here and 10/10 because talking is dangerous right now. I guess my dynamo birthday present was a dud," I said.

"This is not about you, dammit!" she said. "The world doesn't revolve around you! You are not the cause of everything! If someone looks depressed at dinner, it's not your fault! You always think my mood has something to do with you! I never asked you to fix me, and you're always trying! The more I break, the more you try, the more you fail, and then you resent me! Stop it!"

"We know all that's true, but who said anything about resenting you?" I asked.

"You didn't need to. You do," she said.

"OK, as I said, bad road. I'm stopping now. At least humor me into thinking that maybe you could salvage your birthday by coming to breakfast for

Four

God's sake!"

Laura poured her heart out to Hanna at breakfast. Her knowing look made it seem that this was the first step in a program she had set in motion the day before. The food was exactly the same as the day before, but everything tasted different. There was a pitch-black cloud over us now.

Laura abruptly left breakfast as soon as she finished eating. I followed her back to the cabin. We 10/10ed on a few questions, our conversation deteriorating with every one.

"I need to go back to Pair-o-Dice Village," Laura said. "Do you mind?" This was the first civil exchange in two hours.

"Not really," I said. "Clearly, train's left the station on the perfect birthday."

She grabbed my hand. "I couldn't have thought of a better present. But it's like *The Shining* right now. We need to get out of here," she said.

We asked Hanna for forgiveness and told her we had to leave. "This is best. Sometimes the teachings of Paraiso are not pleasant, but the important thing is that you started to really see what is inside. Please keep spending time on your own going deep. Then, and only then, you can be strong enough to come back together and resolve the issues as a couple," she said. She comped us all our food, a delightful and touching surprise, and handed me one of Simon's autographed CDs.

"Thank you, Hanna." In that moment, I realized she hugged as tightly as Laura's brother.

"I know a person in the capital. He can help you. And I think you would like him. You should pass through on the way home," she said.

"What is he like?" I asked.

"Well, he's not really a shaman . . . ," she said.

Close enough.

"Thanks, Hanna, but we've seen a few people. You're right. Our terrors are inside us. We brought them here from the States, and if we don't work on ourselves, we'll take them to the next place and the next and the next," I said.

"Sounds like you're on the right road," she said.

She hugged us long and hard, and we left.

"Great! I can tell everyone on my thirty-fifth birthday . . ."

". . . that someone told you to see a shaman." I finished Laura's sentence as we drove off the grounds. "Sha-man you, Laura!" We laughed for the first time in two days. "That place will always be special to me," Laura said.

I agreed.

"Bad timing," Laura said.

"Yep. You should have moved your birthday. What the hell? Nobody keeps an appointment here anyway!" I said.

We barely spoke on the long ride home. With no radio stations accessible, we listened to my new CD. We already knew all the songs. I broke the silence as our tires hit the beautiful pavement of the *Costanera,* nearly home.

"I'm staring out the window at the landscape, watching the people in their cars and families walk along the side of the road. Costa Rica still feels like home," I said to Laura. "This is my spirit's resting place. I know it."

"I do feel I could maybe see that someday for myself," Laura said. "That's why I want to come back. And I did learn from Hanna. There's nothing in this country that is tying me in knots. My reactions are. We called this paradise, but experiencing paradise is not about putting ourselves in a setting. If paradise isn't inside us, it won't matter *where* we are."

"We didn't know just how much we'd put ourselves to the test here. We're in spiritual boot camp and the drill sergeant in our head is screaming at us with a big-ass megaphone day and night. And now there's another dilemma."

"Another?" Laura asked sarcastically.

"Aside from the blackouts, things were getting better for us. Was Paraiso del Cielo just some kind of blip? Seems like time's up to figure that out. We have only two weeks left here. And life in the village is just going to be packing and logistics for here on out. I guess we'll go back to Chicago with a wild card in our pocket and pick up again in November. See where life takes us."

"Well, the good thing is that we'll try it all again," Laura said. She paused in silence for a number of minutes. "Poor Hanna. Having to deal with us the last few days. She always says she can feel the angels around us. I hope she includes herself in that company."

CHAPTER 41
Karmakaze

Gliders, sail planes, they're wonderful flying machines.
It's the closest you can come to being a bird.
Neil Armstrong

May 17, 2007

Laura was trying desperately between departure activities to internalize what Hanna had said while still in the village's environment. However, finding the time and ambition to "just go wandering off into the jungle by myself" proved a challenge. We also resolved that, while in the States, I would reconcile my family situation. I had mailed a few letters to my father, but my mom said he just set them aside and didn't read them. I understood why. I knew the situation was killing him, and the old-school Italian in him made it difficult to process feelings. For that same reason, I knew a live conversation was out of the question. Nonetheless, the situation had cast a huge weight on my ability to navigate thoughtfully in this new land. I was sure we would have otherwise fared better free of such momentous circumstances.

Finally, we hoped we wouldn't have a replay of Laura's allergies and headaches—which were better but of which we still didn't know the origin. A friend at the intermittentnet café had just been cured of a major skin allergy he had had for over a year. He referred us to the mastermind behind his healing. This was curious as we thought Dr. Nando was the only practicing physician on the coast.

We drove up to a house in the center of the village. Paco was a dark-skinned tico late in years, his hair disheveled and crooked teeth poking out of his joyous grin. Two words immediately shot through my mind—*medicine man.*

The floor of his house was soiled and the walls barely painted. The openings in the walls had screens over them but no windows, and the entire house seemed to be lit naturally by the sunlight. We were reminded of how stiflingly hot it could get in the valley, even sometimes during the wet season.

I sat on a loveseat, Laura on a couch, and Paco on a metal chair from a dining set. All were covered in thick, clear plastic.

Paco asked no questions. Rather, he peered analytically into Laura's eyes from across the room as I explained her circumstances and symptoms in Spanish. He then launched into his diagnosis and cure—a shockingly direct mirror of Hanna's. Laura's energy was now outrageously out of balance with the Earth's. The only way for her to physically and mentally heal was to sit in nature and sort through her issues—long, hard, and by herself.

He asked us to return the next day to fetch two medicines he would prepare. The next day at Paco's house, his grandson handed us a plastic grocery bag house containing two large soda bottles filled with potions. One fluid looked like a sludgy green tea and the other like milk. *She's not going to take this.*

"I'm not taking this," Laura said on the way home. "So now what? And, hello! I ended up at a damn shaman again! You can call him whatever you want, but that's a shaman. I didn't even know what one was six months ago! Brenda came to Costa Rica to find Lexapro, and I found bat claw martinis!"

"Actually, when I put my nose up to the white one, I smelled lizard tits," I said.

"Very funny. And I am to lie in the grass to meditate with a million stinging ants just waiting for the first gringo to be that stupid?!" she said.

"Look, three people have recommended these shamans. Seems to me it might be what you need. These guys exist for a reason, don't you think?" I asked.

"I guess, but if that's the case, now we're going back to Chicago. I can't just go lay on the sidewalk," she said.

"Not necessarily. People lay on the sidewalk all the time."

"Glen, I know you're trying to be funny . . . ."

"Sorry."

"I don't want to come back here for a do-over of what we just did. And I supposedly need to become one with the Earth, and fast. How the hell am I going to do that?"

That night at Catharsis, she decided to jump off a mountain.

We ran into Jean-Pierre, the co-owner of Adèle's B&B, who mentioned a paragliding business they had just started. "You joomp of ze montáin, and zen all of a sudáin, zer eez nussing undér your feet but emptiness," he said.

"Awesome! When can we go?" Laura asked. It did sound amazing.

"Tomorrow morning," Jean-Pierre said.

"Laura, I'm so glad you aren't afraid of heights anymore, but I have to ask if you realize you might be starting to place a little less value on life than you used to," I asked after Jean-Pierre walked away.

"What are you talking about? It'll be fun!"

"Oh, I agree it will be fun, but I just wonder if you took the whole 'be one with the ground' advice a bit literally," I said.

She laughed. "You're serious, aren't you?"

"I'm gonna blush when I say this, but kinda," I said.

The next morning, Jean-Pierre loaded two large backpacks and some electronic gear into our car at the B&B, and we stole down the *Costanera*.

"Well, Paco said to be one with nature. If that chute doesn't open, I will have taken his advice," Laura said.

Jean-Pierre laughed. "Funny to a point," I said.

Laura's potential aerial hari-kari site was an empty residential lot two thousand feet over Cordial Bay where Fisherman Matt's boat was anchored. The view distracted me from all my concerns. It was so high off the ocean, but close at the same time, it felt like we were hanging over the front of a cruise ship.

Jean-Pierre, a chute trailing on the ground from his backpack, hooked himself to Laura and gave her the rundown. "Joost keeeep rooníng, even aftáir we are in ze air." He made the motion of two legs running over his open palm with the fingers of his other hand.

They took a few practice runs, stopping at the edge of the empty lot each time.

"OK, now we go real zeess time," he said. "Your only job is keep rooning."

Jean-Pierre regulated Laura's forward progress as he examined the chute's readiness for flight amidst "Joost keep rooníng" shouts. Laura looked like Fred Flintstone scurrying his feet to get the car moving. "Stop. No, no, we go back," he said several times, and they retreated as he shook his head.

He has only five seconds to make that call!

On the fourth try, "Yeaaaaaaaahhhhh!" Just like that, my wife launched off the edge of a cliff like a cannonball. This was a bad time for my next thought. Why were we placing our lives in the hands of some nylon string with all the equipment malfunctions we had experienced to date?

Racing down the rugged mountain road to the landing beach below while taking pictures of Laura, I almost hit a friend's SUV head-on traveling the opposite direction. Admittedly, my excitement was fueling a voyage at ludicrous speed on loose gravel, possibly lethal to myself and others.

My speed proved unnecessary, however, as Laura stayed in the skies for over forty-five minutes, appearing to completely defy gravity. If Jean-Pierre wanted to kidnap her, he could have just stayed up there and phoned in his demands. Of course, Laura could have called his bluff. "Don't pay him! There are no snakes, bats, spiders, cultural adaptations, or Car-Cinomas up here!"

They finally made their way toward the ocean and oscillated over the beach like a feather with a graceful landing.

"Oh, my God!" Laura said. "That was one of the most amazing experiences of my life! You're gonna love it!" *Maybe Paco needs to make a potion out of toucan toes and adrenaline.*

Back up the mountain, I went through the same routine, but with more failed attempts. "Sheet!" Jean-Pierre said. He was not pleased with the wind. "I don't know eef we weel be able to go."

By the sixth try, I was completely deflated at the prospect of missing an experience my wife had so celebrated. I ran halfheartedly, assuming another mission aborted. "Go, go, go!" Jean-Pierre said as we neared the edge.

Wait! What? He pushed me, and I ignited the afterburners for the two steps of running space I had left. Jean-Pierre grunted behind me like someone had put his foot in a vice. "Go, go, go!" I flung our collective mass off the mountainside.

Unlike Laura's magnificent start, we immediately dipped to the point I could confidently disprove the common notion that one's life flashes before his eyes upon imminent death. Only after the second time I kicked a branch atop a tree below did our ascent begin.

"Hey, Jean-Pierre," I said.

"Yes?" He was breathing heavily.

"How do you say diaper in French?" I asked.

"Oh, eh *couche*."

"Avez vouz une couche?" I asked.

"Yes, zat was not so good," he said, forcing a calm voice. *Beep, beep, beep.* His altimeter board assessed the vitals of our progress.

I could see south all the way to Panama and past Manuel Antonio to the north. It was the closest I would ever become to knowing what it's like to be an astronaut, floating through the air, forgetting the concept of gravity altogether. I saw all the colors you would from outer space, but on a much closer scale. The varied greens of the rainforest, the diverse shades of blue in the ocean, the red earth from the building sites and mudslides, and the foamy water lapping up against the shore were a spectacular collage. What's more, the parachute shielded me from the hot sun. It was the perfect vehicle for taking in the perspective of the ocean-side jungle.

And then I understood how Laura had stayed elevated for so long. Every time we needed a bit more altitude, Jean-Pierre would just steer toward the mountain into a powerful and hot vertical updraft.

A vulture hovered no more than twenty feet above us for ten minutes. We then oscillated over the beach and had the same graceful landing as Laura's. She was there waiting.

"You were right. That was one of the most magnificent experiences of my life," I said. All three of us high-fived on the beach and took pictures of an already unforgettable moment.

With adrenaline still coursing through our veins, we passed by to pick up the lease for the new house we'd be renting, which was nearby.

"You were right above Movies in the Jungle," our landlord-to-be said.

"What's that?" Laura asked.

"It's hard to explain, really," she said. "But it's not far off from what I said. Here." She handed us a flyer that had a weekly schedule of "Movies in the Jungle."

"There's one tonight. I'll be there. You really should go. No experience like it on Earth," she said.

"I don't know. We just had a once-in-a-lifetime experience," I said.

"Trust me," she said reassuringly.

That night, we turned off the same road up to the paraglide site into a residential driveway packed chockablock with SUVs. There, a retired Hollywood movie couple had built a fully functional outdoor movie theater atop their house overlooking Cordial. Per the movie flyer's instructions, we had made lasagna for a pot luck dinner before the movie.

The theater occupied the entire courtyard built on the roof of part of the main home with a large thatch canopy atop. It had a projection room with an old-time back-lit theatre sign over its glass doors, a large screen, and a real theater-style popcorn machine. A few short features were shown and then bugs the size of cigarette lighters graced the screen as it lit up. Impressive thunderstorms passed in the Pacific distance to our left and jungle fauna screamed in glee as we watched *House of Flying Daggers,* the subtitled Chinese main feature.

The juxtaposition of modern technology with the bare organic essence of the jungle assured us we were having an experience like nowhere else on Earth—twice in one day.

Four

"Here we are, struggling to get all the things we've been so used to," Laura said on the way home, "and then we have access to a private outdoor world-class movie theater. The irony is killing me. I'm not sure I have had a day this fulfilling in my life."

"I know. It would take a serious case of amnesia to ever make me forget this," I said.

"Well, one thing is for sure," Laura said, "living like tourists suits us just fine."

"Well, not so fast," I said. "That place was all gringo locals."

"Yeah, you're right!" Laura said.

"Kind of makes you hopeful that there's a lot more of that social, inter-personal undiscovered treasure out there," I said.

As we drove the rest of the way down the *Costanera*, I realized that after having lived in the village for seven months, we really did know more about what the village had to offer. Ironically, what we didn't know any more than we did on October 26 was whether we could live in Costa Rica long-term, something I had been wondering for almost three years.

I was sick of wondering, but what other choice did I have? No matter what, I was thankful that we had these experiences and that we had made it through them—together.

I grabbed Laura's hand as we entered the village. She showed me an excited smile.

CHAPTER 42
Parting with Pair-o-Dice

If you want a happy ending, that depends, of course, on
where you stop your story.
Orson Welles

May 20, 2007

All the major repairs we desired of the FlawedShack were finally complete. A provincial ruling would have been required to fix the town's water problems, but our own hydraulic defects were no more. And, not that we cared, but the exterior had been replastered and repainted. The hole to the bat cave had been plugged, and the midnight reconnaissance missions had ceased. Regardless, the house was still as practical as a coal-fired wristwatch, and we found the prospect of leaving it quite exciting.

Our new house leased for our return would be farther north, closer to Cordial and immediately off the *Costanera*. It had no view to speak of, but our priorities had shifted. The house was an old yoga retreat facility with six beds and a partially detached bathroom—its only downfall. It belonged to a delightful female yoga instructor and spiritual teacher who lived in San Isidro.

Given it was fully furnished, we engaged in the mandatory but idiotic exercise of getting rid of most of the things we had bought since our arrival.

Four

The Beatles could have written a song about our last week called "While My Bank Card Gently Weeps." Anything we were keeping would go in a small storage facility next to Dr. Nando's office in Cordial. Within a year's time, we had put our Chicago home into storage, brought the balance of our items to Costa Rica in eleven suitcases, bought and sold a house full of furniture and house wares, and were now moving belongings into another storage unit. We were making Christopher Columbus look like a homebody.

After a good rummaging from friends and a liquidation sale, there was still a not-so-small contingent of smaller items that remained. Everything from food to vases to bungee cords lay in a big pile on the back porch. We invited Los Desemparados, our gardeners, to take whatever they wanted. They arranged a friend and his pickup truck.

"Doña Laura and Don Glen, you have always been so good to us. We are sorry to see you go to Cordial. May God bless you," one of the brothers said when he saw the items.

To our excitement, they took absolutely everything. As they were loading the truck, one brother came to me holding an eight-pack of canned black beans we had bought in San José and never opened.

"*¿Qué son?*" he asked.

"*Frijoles negros.*" I waited for a punch line, as black beans are part of almost every Costa Rican meal.

"*¿Frijoles negros?*" He looked at the can as if it may contain plutonium. "What do I do with them?" he asked.

I just stood there—silent—not knowing what to say.

His brother now came over. "How do you open it?" he asked. Forgetting how to say it in Spanish, I went inside to grab a can opener.

"Here," I said. "Take it."

That moment gave me a new appreciation for just how distant the traditional tico outside the capital was from our own circumstance.

Things were going quite smoothly until four days to departure. That day, our Chicago landlord informed us that the current tenant of our new apartment in Chicago had refused to vacate. The scheduled power blackouts were still in effect, so a new search was hopeless. We rerouted our plane tickets to Laura's family's house in Pittsburgh and called it a day, turning our sights to saying good-bye to our new close friends.

"Well, you've got four months to go back there and fix the American economy," Hal said. "You know, it's started to collapse while you were down here. I still don't understand a lick of what it was you two did, but whatever it was, go do it again."

"Do me a favor," I said.

"What's that?"

"Since I'll be gone for my birthday, launch a tire into the jungle in my honor. I'll help you look for it when I get back. That search will be my present," I said.

"Don't worry. You'll still be here," Indira said as we all hugged good-bye. "You guys basically furnished our guest apartment. When it's done, we're going to call it the Glen and Laura wing."

We gave big hugs to all the jovial tico waiters at our coastal lunch spot. The good healing and happiness they wished us already shown in their eyes but were even more empathetic in their words. They knew of our roller coaster as we often couldn't contain our emotions during our lunches. But they also knew we had a true love for the country.

"We hope you had a wonderful time in our country," the eldest waiter said, "even though I know you had a hard time. Many gringos do. But you'll go home and know how to always be happy with Pura Vida when you return. You are a light on this restaurant whenever you come. May God bless you."

At Paul and Brenda's house, we celebrated their joy at having windows, Internet, and a running pool. "So how are you going to maintain your cover?" Paul asked.

"What cover?" Laura asked.

"Well, you're the witnesses," Brenda said. "Are you sure it's OK to go back up there?"

"As in 'Costa Rica is the land of the wanted and unwanted?'" I asked.

"Bingo," Paul said.

"Glen's a CPA. You guys are too young to be out here 'just because.'" Brenda made quote signs in the air. "You're the Witnesses—as in the protection program," Brenda said. "You have to be on the run from *something*!"

"Yeah, Glen. I dropped a bunch of cash in the mud today. You can help me clean it, can't you?" Paul said with a smile.

"You guys are only half-joking, aren't you?" Laura asked.

"Wait, you didn't know? It's not only us, you know," Brenda said.

"Who else?" I asked.

"It's your nickname on the coast now," Paul said, laughing. "Seriously, put yourself in everyone's shoes. If you saw a couple like you come in here, you'd wonder why. And if that couple got taken back to the airport in steel bracelets, would you be surprised?"

He was right, and I found it all fascinating. Me—a criminal.

As a kid, the cops actually encouraged me to practice running faster. They knew I only watched the action and would always get caught when my friends ran away from the scene of the crime. In six months, I had progressed from the guy who overpaid his taxes just to be safe to Don Indiana Jones, CPA, and *capo* of the Mango Mafia.

Once all our items were placed in storage, our last good-bye would be at Catharsis. As we walked out of the FlawedShack that night, the sun dunked into the Pacific. It was by far its greatest show yet. Oranges, reds, purples, blues, and white streaked across the sky all the way to the east over the valley, meeting the mountains behind us like a splash painting.

"Do you get this weird feeling that's for us?" I asked Laura, knowing well I might be reaching.

"Who knows?" Laura answered, staring at the sunset. "All I know is it's stunning and the perfect image to remember while we're gone."

We walked to the edge of the pool deck, and I took a picture of her. I hugged her from behind, and we both started to cry quite dramatically.

"I don't know why I'm crying," Laura said. "I mean it's only four months."

"I know it's not because we're going home. I still like it better here. Maybe it's just a release," I said.

"Yeah, I guess with everything we've been through, it's just a release. No more, no less," Laura said.

I could have clearly articulated what I was thinking. Nonetheless, this was a tender moment to be left alone. There would be plenty of time to ponder the questions. How did we end up deciding to go home? It all happened so fast. Had the train left the station forever on leading a "normal" life? Was that a good or bad thing? I was deeply sad to be leaving and felt my entire being anchored to the village, but I had to admit it had been like a dysfunctional marriage. And then there was the fear—ironic in many ways. People at home said I should be terrified to leave their land I knew so well. I never was. Rather, I was now profoundly scared of going back to that very place they said I should fear leaving. In ways I couldn't yet articulate, Costa Rica had changed me profoundly. What would my relationship with myself and others be like back in the land I knew so well?

At Catharsis, Françoise had our usual meal ready for us when we got there. For months, Louis had refused to put his delicious mustard sauce on the same plate with shrimp. This was apparently like wearing overalls to the opera in French culinary circles. On my dish lay a filet mignon and six beautiful shrimp almost drowning in the stuff.

Despite our brutally early wake-up the next morning, we stayed long after closing and talked with Françoise and Louis past midnight.

"When we first saw you, I could tell Laura was ready to come here. I could see it in her eyes," Françoise said. "And while you were here, I could see that you, Glen, became tico. Your heart belongs here. I am so glad you came to live. You are like my little treasures," she pinched Laura's cheeks adoringly. She must have said good-bye and hugged us five times before we managed to leave.

We don't even remember our heads hitting the pillow that night. All I remember was a dream of my father coming to me and saying, "Stay on the path."

The problem was he never said which one.

We loaded the tiny rental car before sunrise the next morning. Already brutally exhausted, we were thrilled to experience the rousing of the jungle once more as an orange glow revealed our paradise the last time for a while.

Four

The trip back was borderline almost mission im-paws-ible. Having learned our lesson, we weren't going to put the Boys through the coma-inducing drive as on the way in. We needed to fly them, and the baggage limit on the aircraft back to San-José—the size of a large no-see-um—was about one-twentieth what we were bringing. She would fly while I got lost in San José yet again in a rental car not much bigger than a Yoplait cup.

The snag was the airline's limit of one animal per person, a flawed formula for us. So Laura put both cats in one bag and became a smuggler. Luckily, they seemed to comfort one another, preferring to be in the same bag when they flew.

We left with so many emotions alive inside us. We regretted having to part with these glorious mornings. We were thankful that we had the guts to give it a second try. We were thrilled to bid good riddance to the Flawed-Shack. And we were scared of the way we were now living life. We drove to the local airport with every sense ablaze, taking in the last dose of the Ballena Coast for a while. I waited for the plane's takeoff. If they turned Laura away, we'd be forced to return to the village to wait for another day to attempt the voyage. Laura took off without a hitch. I put Simon's CD on repeat and was off to San José.

My sensory factory remained fully engaged, keeping the windows down all the way. I made sure to take in some of the typical treats on the way back. I stood over the twelve-foot crocs on the Tárcoles bridge and stopped for a *casado* of garlic snapper, rice and beans, and hearts of palm salad. I also bought a roadside *pipa fria* (cold coconut with the top hacked off and a straw) for the first time. Also for the first time, I made it through San José without one wrong turn.

"That was rough," Laura said. "Those propellers really terrorized them."

"Where are they," I asked.

"Under the bed." I moved the bed skirt to see four glowing eyes peering at me from against the wall—as far from me as they could be. "At least it was only forty minutes," Laura said.

Ricardo, our San José cab driver, came by to pick up his niece's cell phone.

Seeing that he had referred us to Carlos, who had told us that our Car-Cinomas were *buen carros*, we had been through a lot together. In fact, he was the only tico who ever saw the fullness of Glen 2.0—more than once. And I felt bad now because he was truly a kind and well-meaning soul and had always done the best he could to make us happy under the circumstances.

Regardless of our saga, he gave me a warm smile and firm handshake. "You, my friend, put too much in your life. When you come back, live simple. Costa Rica is not a country for the complicated. When I saw you buy those two cars in three days, I went home and told my wife I had met the craziest person I had ever seen. But you will always be a good friend. *Pooora Viiida, you crazy, crazy mae.*" We both laughed, hugged, and parted.

I returned the car and went back to the room. The cats had finally come out.

"We've got a big day tomorrow. Let's just hang on the balcony," Laura said.

It was a small terrace facing the wall of another building. The sound of large air conditioning units from neighboring structures made it difficult to relax, especially as we were used to the jungle's own paradoxically calming blare. I closed my eyes and calmed my spiritual center. *Hey! I've surely gotten better at this!*

After ten minutes of meditation, my eyes drifted to a copy of *La Republica,* one of the national newspapers, sitting on a small table on the balcony. There, emblazoned on the cover was the lead headline, *"ICE Apresura Compra de Celulares* (ICE Quickens the Purchase of Cellular Phones)."

My blood pressure spiked. I picked up the newspaper and read the article. "What?" Laura asked.

I translated a sentence from the article. "The Costa Rican government acknowledges falling behind in cellular service and will flood the market with new cellular phone lines in the next two weeks."

We laughed so hard we could barely catch our breath. Then it dawned on me. "We're in the capital! We could get a cell phone line today! It's perfect!"

I stood and headed abruptly into the room to put on shoes. Laura grabbed my hand.

Four

She silently looked into my eyes. *It's time to let go.*

I turned and sat back down moving my chair toward hers. She put her head on my shoulder.

We sat there quietly. After barely a wink of sleep, Costa Freaka redeemed, Don Indiana Jones CPA, Skippy, and Rugby were wheels-up toward their homeland. After we figured out how to get back to Chicago, we'd be comfortable for a while. Everything would be exactly the same as it was before.

It was on the outside. On the inside, nothing was. *We* were different. Everyone is after a radical sabbatical.

And that made it all worth it.

Afterword

I left the ending ambiguous, because that is the way life is.
Bernardo Bertolucci

November 10, 2009

We rocked back and forth as Dumaka, our driver, tried to free his Toyota Land Rover from the muddy grips of the terrain along the Mara River in Tanzania's northern Serengeti. He threw up his hands and jumped out of the topless vehicle. Over the prior three days, tourists in every vehicle—all of them with a proper roof—looked at us as if we were completely crazy. Little did these terrified onlookers know that we had requested it. Laura's parents had taken a topless vehicle on safari over twenty years prior. "There's nothing like it," they said.

Laura and I, happy to give our achy safari vehicle butts a break, gladly followed suit and got out of the truck. The three of us migrated to the rear driver-side tire, which was buried in the earth like an oversized seed. Dumaka shook his head, an extremely troubled look on his face. I thought back to the brief Swahili vocabulary self-study I had engaged in on the flight from Egypt for a colorful way to tell him we were fine.

"*Hamna shida,*" I said, meaning "no problem."

He continued staring at the tire and sighed. "No, no. This," he said, waving his finger, "This is *shida!*" He very deliberately radioed our camp for help.

Of course it's shida! Over three days of touring, we had already witnessed countless furry and feathered carcasses laying out in the open—many of the kills fresh. The dividing line between hunters and hunted—eaters and snacks—was clear to us just on the fifteen-minute ride from the airstrip to camp. The circle of life was palpable. Sitting out here with no way to go anywhere, in a vehicle with no roof ... *we just became snacks.*

Seemingly oblivious to the danger, Laura wandered along the imaginary border ten feet from the vehicle that Dumaka declared before ever allowing us in the truck. She was taking pictures—happy as a clam to be able to stretch her legs.

She's so calm. So am I! Why?!

In that moment—two years after we'd returned from Costa Rica—I realized the effect that Pair-o-Dice Village had had on us. A satisfied grin migrated across my face. I realized how profoundly all the learnings from our radical sabbatical had influenced our life. In this case, we were spontaneously living the teaching not to fear that which cannot be controlled. And fear had become our friend.

After our return from Costa Rica, Laura and I spent three months in distinctly different modes. Laura committed lengthy daily blocks of time evaluating her reactions to our experience and the circumstances of Pair-o-Dice Village, in solitude and discussing with friends.

I spent that same time wanting nothing more than to go back to the village. Yet my hopes were becoming increasingly polluted by despair. Continuing our research of Costa Rica real estate from afar, blog postings from realtors said that the rainy season—typically slow—was the slowest they had ever seen. The market was already falling apart, and more quickly than in the States. In the meantime, I became ironically disappointed that my predictions of the stock market falling apart came true. Although I could never have fathomed how bad the banking crisis became, I knew that Wall Street would not be a source of income for quite some time.

In October, with only a month left before our planned return, it was time to buy our plane tickets. Yet something held us back. And thankfully so, given that the speculative real estate market contracted by as much as sixty percent over the next three years on the Ballena Coast. Given that we would never have been able to make a living there, the radical sabbatical, redux, was called off.

I was plunged into dismay. For once in my life, I had done something amazingly bold outside a corporate office and risked everything—my ego, our marriage and relationships, and our finances. I had risked it to be in a place where, from the moment I sat on the magic rock, I felt my heart rooting into the earth through the bottoms of my feet. I lost all perspective. In my eyes, it was a complete and utter failure.

All the signs. All the preparation. All the enthusiasm. And for what? We had nothing to show for it but some hiking pictures, an extension cord that melted as soon as it saw a US plug socket, and a machete.

As I despaired, Laura continued her upward trajectory, and she quickly got a point of pride for having gone to Pair-o-Dice Village.

"Yeah, but we *did* it! And think of everything we learned!" she'd say. "Who else can say that?"

And in that moment on the Serengeti in 2009, it dawned on me the wonderful impact Pair-o-Dice Village had had on our lives. We tell everyone, "It was the greatest and most dreadful part of our lives." And we recovered, which empowered us to constantly seek everything we wanted from life at almost any cost. We had made fear our friend.

By that time, we had already declared that were going to have purely mobile lives, a risky proposition given our goals for the lifestyle we wanted. I quickly revived my contracting business—lucrative, stable, and entirely done from home. I could work anywhere, which allowed us to start spending winters in Fort Lauderdale and taking vacations that would otherwise have not been possible. Costa Rica still didn't have reliable enough telecom for me to conduct business there. Nonetheless, Fort Lauderdale was warm, and we truly grew to love it.

In 2008, Laura started The Berdéo Group, a business coaching corporate executives and leaders. In 2009, in a hot tub in Fort Lauderdale, I gave in to writing this book with her. I had gotten over the failure aspect of the radical sabbatical. I wasn't yet at the point where I could tangibly understand what we had learned from it. That's what changed in the Serengeti.

In the months and years that followed, Laura and I both started hearing from friends that they "always want to hear the crazy and fun thing you're up to next."

Then, in 2011, Laura told me one day, "I want to see if we really have a story here," she said. I had no idea what she meant at the time. Since that day, one or both of us have appeared on countless venues including radio programs, local news shows, CNBC.com, *The Miami Herald*, *Redbook*, *Self* magazine, and *The Dr. Oz Show* to promote our story.

We also published our first book, *Fall in Love Again, Every Day: 3 Steps to True Connection for Any Couple*, which documents our 10/10 communication technique and how to do it. What's more, recently, in addition to coaching executives and leaders, Laura speaks as a keynote to Fortune 500 companies about "Life and Leadership Lessons from the Jungle."

People wonder how we keep it all going. Sometimes, so do we. In the end, the magic lies in one fundamental truth—fear is our friend.

Most of us live life within our comfort zones. Our training wheels are on. Do you remember riding around with those pesky little wheels? You'd have to stay on the beaten path. You'd look at your friends and see them having a blast, riding faster to places you couldn't go. They had more guts than you. They were having more fun than you. But you couldn't get yourself to take the wheels off until one day. All you had to do was get the guts to do it, and then off you went—completely free.

If you'll take at least three months to go on a radical sabbatical to a place where your geography and daily life are drastically different, you'll see the training wheels that were on your life. The great thing is, once you stretch, you'll never want to ride with them on again. In that moment, you'll wake up every morning, like we do, immediately thinking of how you can take life to a place where you never have. Don't worry. You don't have to jettison to bats, scorpions, and reverse high-speed drives down mountains. But you will want to pick something that creates a good dose of healthy discomfort, preferably in a setting where you've always wanted to live.

"But where will I end up in five years?" you ask. To that we answer, "Exactly." You'll end up exactly where you end up. After a radical sabbatical, it becomes all about the journey, not the destination. And you know what? You'll automatically have the courage to live this way because you'll have seen that no matter what you go through, whether it's life after Pair-o-Dice Village or the unexpected vehicle that came along to pull us out of the mud in the Serengeti after fifteen minutes, everything always works out if you'll have the courage to let it. Fear becomes your friend.

The training wheels are off, and it's an awesome, thrilling ride. There's magic in it. It's a life without boundaries. It's a life that's all yours.

LEARN MORE ABOUT YOURSELF AND
HOW YOU CAN TAKE A RADICAL SABBATICAL

*Are you the type of person who is ready to get out
of your rut and take a bold life leap?*

Take the comprehensive, free online assessment at

www.lifeleapsprogram.com/radicalsurvey

---

*Interested in regular updates on the keys and tricks
to planning and making a big life change?*

Subscribe to our free, informative, and outlandish newsletter at

www.lifeleapsprogram.com/email-newsletter.

Get the companion book to Radical Sabbatical!

Discover how to move your relationship from "remember when" to "joy is now" in just a couple hours!

Use the amazingly simple 10/10 technique to:

- Awaken your power to create a deeply satisfying, passionate, joy-filled relationship.
- Create the intimacy and connection you've been seeking.
- Easily share your deepest unmet needs and get the response you've been waiting for.

Whether you're in a relationship on the brink or just want to bring more happiness to your lives together, you too, can *Fall in Love Again, Every Day!*

Now available at Amazon in paperback and on Kindle.

Acknowledgements

"The world is my country, all mankind are my brethren,
and to do good is my religion."
Thomas Paine

A WONDERFUL LIFE is lived through unity, not as units. Being in the position to fondly thank these blessed people is a power source like no other.

We thank our families for their support and patience. Thanks to my mother, late father, and sister for watching us turn our lives upside down without having a stroke. Our precious nephew put smiles on our faces on weekends and over FaceTime. Laura's mom and dad celebrated every step of our journey, big and small. Laura's brother kept us laughing out loud. Her sister and husband let us crash at their place in Manhattan countless times for media segments and publicity opportunities. Our niece publicized Pair-o-Dice Village with everyone as her favorite place in the whole wide world. Through thick and thin, they have always cared and loved deeply.

And then in sometimes alphabetical, but otherwise no particular order, I begin by thanking Pauley Whitney, English teacher at Gulliver Preparatory School in Miami. This book never would have been written had she not told me, "You're an excellent writer!" in November 1988. Those simple words changed my life forever.

We thank our close friends Amir and Kari, Clarence and Kathryn, Claudio and Marie, Darek and Laura, Dave and Lindsey, David and Amy, Jenni and Bill, Mike and Paula, Rich and Megan, Rohan and Masha, Stephen and Andréa, Bucho, Carolann, Carolyn, Jim Gibson, Jimmy, and Tammy for all their support in our radical sabbatical and book writing and their very likely thinking us complete lunatics while treating us as emblems of sanity. Our gratitude goes out to all our great friends in Pair-o-Dice Village—left anonymous for privacy reasons—who watched the sabbatical unfold and backed us at every step.

A warm embrace goes to Linda Bollinger, our most wonderful cheerleader.

Thank you Doua Moua for being the first Hollywood figure to celebrate our story.

Laura's girls' night crew—Evelyn D'An, Lauren Smith, Marilu Kernan, Michelle Dunaj, Nancy Hullihen, Paula Black, Shannon McKee—and coffee crew—Alan Roth, Christina Akers, Gail Stage, Pam Hickson, Rose Bogan, Vicki Pestrichelli—get a warm embrace for all their empowerment and willingness to listen. Her fellow Tiaras—Alison, Andrea, Beth, Betsy, Ellen, Franciska, and Peg—have been deeply inspiring every step of the way. Cynthia and Rita on our dog walking route kept Laura's brain from igniting by their patient listening skills.

Christine Pride's meticulous editing skills are showcased in this manuscript. Likewise, Hobie Hobart and Kathi Dunn of Dunn and Associates' creativity shout from its cover design. We thank them for their seasoned direction and patience.

Rhonda Kokot and her team at Simple Truth are in our debt for donating their time to our publicity page.

Paula Halfman's amazing graphic design skills are pivotal in getting us publicity appearances and exposure.

Thank you to our legion of volunteer book readers and accountability team: Amy Riley, Jaime Wolf, Lindsey Levy, and Dr. Mark Cochran. A huge shout-out goes to Vicky Townshend of Inspiration University for coordinating our focus group. All our Facebook friends deserve a medal for voting on potential titles and book cover designs for two years. We are blessed to have these friends in our lives who care so much about our success, they are *de facto* consultants: Laurie Woodward Garcia, Lea Fruchter, Barbara Geller, Melissa Giovagnoli, and Vickie Hyman.

Many thanks to Laura's Saint Mary's College Alumnae—Adriana Trigiani, Karen Fink, and Stephanie Capparell—for their expertise and supportive networking in making this book a success.

My life took a quantum leap when I met Dave, Rick, and Sherwin, my life-long Tae Kwon Do buddies who showed me the joy of a life spent being funny.

Thank you to the Second City Training Center for their brilliant comedic training, model students, and professionals. My comedic idols of yesterday and today constantly feed me with passion and wisdom: Bill Bryson, Bill Cosby, Christopher Guest, Colin Mochrie, Dave Barry, David Sedaris, Dennis Miller, Eddie Murphy, Eugene Levy, Frank Caliendo, Garry Meier, George Carlin, Howie Mandel, Jeff Dunham, Jim Gaffigan, Jimmy Fallon, John Stewart, John Pinette, Kevin Pollak, Larry Miller, Paul Castronovo, Robin Williams, Rodney Dangerfield, Roe Conn, Russell Peters, Ryan Stiles, Steven Wright, Tina Fey, Wayne Brady, and Young Ron Brewer.

In *Long Way Down* and *Long Way Round*, Charley Boorman and Ewan McGregor showed us that people really cared to follow two people out wandering the landscape turning over every rock to learn about the world without getting killed—as did Anthony Bourdain, but we thought he'd die by the fork instead. In *Eat, Pray, Love* Elizabeth Gilbert gave us a wonderful and inspirational read about personal exploration through travel. Andrew McCarthy's *The Longest Way Home* and Scott Wallace's *The Unconquered* have inspired us by showing that no matter how far you explore, you can always go a little further.

This book is very likely in your hand through the precious publicity coaching of Steve and Bill Harrison, their Quantum Leap program, team, and associates—Aviva Goldfarb, Brian Edmondson, Danette Kubanda, Eric Kampmann, Dr. Gaby Cora, Geoffrey Berwind, Kevin White, Mary Ann

Block, Martha Bullen, Michael John McCann, Peter Miller, Raia King, Rob Hartley, and Stacy Rollins. A thank you also for the Bestseller Blueprint Program, put on by Steve and Bill Harrison with Jack Canfield.

We greatly appreciate all our media outlets' faith in granting us appearances and their associates: Bonnie D Graham, Cindy Krischer Goodman, Dr. Hemmut Oz, Kaja Perina, The Mary Jones Show, Nicole Yorio Jurick, Sasha Andrade, Veria Living TV, *Redbook*, and *Self* magazines.

"So the last will be first and the first will be last."
Matthew 20:16.

Frankie, Puck, Rugby, Skippy, and all the animals we pass each day have brought constant smiles and therapy to our lives like no other Earthly creation or being ever could.

Printed in Poland
by Amazon Fulfillment
Poland Sp. z o.o., Wrocław

55139207R00201